A CUP OF COLD WATER

AN AUTOBIOGRAPHY BY

ED HEIL

Other books by Ed Heil:

The Double Portion
…But I Must Decrease

MORIAH GROUP **Published by The Moriah Group**
Chattanooga, Tennessee

ISBN 1-887033-03-3

Printed in the United States of America

Published by The Moriah Group
Chattanooga, Tennessee

Printed by Williams Company
6129 Airways Boulevard
Chattanooga, Tennessee 37421

Design: Joe McCullough

TABLE OF CONTENTS

TABLE OF CONTENTS

FOREWORD

I met Ed Heil in 1994, shortly after I had accepted a new position as Chairman of Primerica Financial Services. In my new role, I conducted a series of regional meetings and invited members of the P.F.S. Field Cabinet, the company's elite leadership group, to attend. It was at the Atlanta meeting that I met Ed Heil. Shortly afterward, I invited Ed and his partner, Letha, to my office for a personal meeting. At that first meeting, I knew that Ed and Letha were special people.

In a way, Ed is a typical P.F.S. Personal Financial Analyst. He shares an excitement and enthusiasm common among the entire organization. Yet in other ways, he is atypical. Ed was past 52 years of age when he affiliated with P.F.S. When this book goes to press, he and Letha will be seventy years old. Although they are older than the average P.F.S. leaders, they exhibit all the intensity and excitement of the newest team members. Through all their years with P.F.S., that youthful exuberance has remained one of their most appealing characteristics.

As former missionaries, the Heils made a difference in the lives of many people. That same missionary zeal carried over to P.F.S., in their commitment to the families that they could help through P.F.S.' programs and services. Their honesty and integrity was evident. Although they have many career accomplishments to their credit, it is their 'heart' that immediately makes an impression.

During his years with P.F.S., Ed has been a pioneer. He moved from Tennessee to Hawaii to open our first office there. From Hawaii, he moved more than three thousand miles further to spearhead P.F.S.' operations in Guam. Then, on to Saipan for further growth and expansion.

But that is a geographic sketch. Personally, the role of pioneer fits Ed well. After becoming involved with P.F.S., he quickly rose to the position of Regional Vice President. Just a year later, Ed made Senior Vice President; then National Sales Director. In 1989, before a convention crowd of 38,000 in the New Orleans Superdome, Ed was inducted into the P.F.S. Wall of Fame, the most prestigious honor in the company. His Wall of Fame portrait hangs at the P.F.S. headquarters in Atlanta.

Ed has been the recipient of a number of honors. He is a charter member of the Golden Eagles Club, signifying a $100,000 income; a charter member of the Millionaire's Club, signifying more than a million dollars in potential deferred earnings, and a charter member of the P.F.S. Field Cabinet. For the past several years, Ed has earned an income of more than half a million dollars annually. I say 'earned' because P.F.S. income is commissions only: no salary or guarantees. Every dollar Ed has been paid represents tremendous effort and activity.

Recently, Ed and Letha retired but they did not quit. You will sense, as you read this biography, that they are simply going forward to another new phase in their lives. The enthusiasm that they bring to this new period is typical of the enthusiasm they bring to whatever endeavor they undertake.

Ed's story is the story of a life well lived. There have been tragedies and triumphs: valleys and peaks. But never, ever have he and Letha faltered in their determination to overcome, their desire to take on new challenges, and their total commitment to excel in every area of their lives.

Joe Plumeri
Chairman and Chief Executive Officer
Primerica Financial Services

DEDICATION

As the chapters of this book have unfolded, I have been made conscious of the fact that anything significant I have ever done, and anything good I might become is attributable to a special group of people who have impacted me from the day of my birth, continuing until the last day of my life. This book is about giving, but it would never have included me as one who delights in giving, except for this select group. For that reason, this book is affectionately dedicated to the ladies I love.

In many books brief mention is made on a dedication page of some person whom the author loves, admires or respects for some special reason. This dedication will be quite a departure from that typical pattern. This book is dedicated to the ladies I love, which group includes seven special ladies in seven distinct specific categories. They are my mother, my sister, my wife, my mother-in-law, my daughter, my daughter-in-law and my grand-daughter. Interestingly, in each of these seven categories, there is just one person.

Thelma Heil is my mother. Of course, it is only possible to have one mother. I had no choice in the matter. But if I had been given a choice, I could not have selected a better mom. Proverbs, chapter 31 is a brief depiction of a king's mother. I could have borrowed the loving attitude and glowing complimentary comments of that writer and inserted my mother's name and it would have been completely appropriate. That she is a magnetic person is apparent in the fact that literally hundreds call her "Mom" and they love her as a mom. She is my Mom too, but she is also my Mother.

Wanda Statum is my only sister. She is a beauty! She was cast in the mold of the beauty queen the king wrote about in Solomon's Song 1:15. "Behold, thou art fair, my love; behold, thou art fair; thou hast doves eyes." Maybe the sincere compassion visible in her teary, dark eyes has evolved through her many difficulties. She has been on the surgical table 33 times, and yet, she always has a refreshing smile and a sincerely warm greeting for everyone. When I was sixteen years old, I left home to go to school in another state and then married less than two years later. Because of my leaving home when Wanda was not yet eight years old, we were not close in our early years. Wanda is a very talented person and I admire her special artistic skills in music, both at the keyboard and as a vocalist. Artists usually excel in one field, but Wanda is multi-talented. She creates beauty with a brush. Even though this work on a canvas is done as a hobby, many of her oil paintings compare very favorably with the art of professionals. Her hands that are outwardly scarred still create beauty in sight and sound for the enjoyment of others. She is a special sister!

Of the seven special ladies in my life, six were God's gift to me, but one was mine by choice. At times when I cannot verbalize my deepest feelings, I like to borrow from the writings of Solomon. We think so much alike: but what I can only feel, he articulated so perfectly. "There are threescore queens, and fourscore concubines, and virgins without number. My dove, my undefiled is but one." When I was not yet eighteen years old, I stood awestruck at the altar as Letha, dressed appropriately in white lace, walked down the aisle into my life to become my beautiful bride. We have had fifty-two wonderful years, and we anticipate many more happy years together. You will meet her later in the book.

Mrs. Ruth Petty became my mother-in-law the same day her daughter, Letha became my wife. In sharp contrast to the mother-in-law cliches that are often offered as sarcasm thinly veiled in humor, my mother-in-law was a terrific lady. Of the seven special ladies in my life, she is the only one who has already gone on to her eternal reward. Based on the exemplary Christian testimony she maintained throughout her life, it is very fitting that she was the first of the seven to be welcomed to heaven. The Bible teaches us that none of us deserve the pure bliss our Lord has prepared for his children, but she came close.

The next beautiful lady in my life was born into my home almost forty-seven years ago. I have no idea how I qualified to have such an extraordinary child as my daughter, Janice. From the time of her birth, continuing until today, she would be bad news for the other contestants in a beauty pageant. She is talented, she is creative, she is intelligent, she is caring, she is beautiful and she is mine! No daughter ever made a dad more proud. Like the others, I did not choose her: she was God's selection for me. But if I had been choosing from a million, there is no question, she would have been the obvious choice. I love her.

One of the greatest favors my son ever did for me was when he picked a wife. Diane is my daughter-in-law, only because she captured the heart and love of my son. "Daughter-in-law" is the technical appellation, but it would be difficult to find a more caring daughter. So much of her time is spent helping the needy. She makes an effort to learn who is sick, who is in need or who has a problem, and then she quietly appears to lend a hand of help. She fits appropriately into the select group of the seven ladies I love. Worthy of mention also is the fact that Diane has a special involvement with the last lady in this group. Not only did she give birth to my only granddaughter, but being such a caring parent, she has had a telling influence for good in her children.

I am from a family of nine boys and only one girl. I have four grandsons and one granddaughter. Hopefully, the grandsons will be understanding of my foolish affection for my only granddaughter. Ginger Heather Heil is my special little lady. The first nineteen days of her life were spent in a hospital bed, which makes her extra special. When I first saw her in the intensive care unit, I could not expect that she would live, but the grace of a great God and the love of two caring parents nurtured her to health. Today she is a healthy, happy, vivacious college coed.

From my totally unbiased perspective, Heather is "pleasant and pretty." All of her other special qualities are just icing on the cake. My life has been made meaningful by these seven beautiful ladies to whom this book is affectionately dedicated.

INTRODUCTION

There is no heaven or eternal life.

Hell is the figment of a frustrated imagination.

There is no God. Life after death is a fable.

Because there is no heaven, no God and no life after death, there can be no reward for living right and doing good.

Because there is no hell, it is ridiculous to be concerned about punishment for sin.

Assume all of the above statements are absolutely accurate and true (which they are not), and even so, it is still better to live according to the precepts and principles of the Galilean teacher than to lead a self-centered existence of indulgence.

Make all of the above fallacious assumptions, but you will never feel more fulfilled and gratified than when you live life for others. Jesus taught, "Greater love hath no man than this, that he lay down his life for his friends."

You say, but that is so extreme. That is too idealistic, let's be real. Alright, I agree it is certainly extreme and possibly idealistic. Check with Jesus again as He spoke to an audience eager to ascertain the real meaning of life. "Whosoever shall give to drink unto one of these little ones a cup of cold water only in the name of a disciple, verily I say unto you, he shall in no way lose his reward."

It is rewarding, not only in the life to come, but also in this life to concentrate on giving rather than getting. Jesus spoke of giving a cup of cold water. The emphasis seems to be that this is such an insignificant act of kindness. However, to the man delirious with fever, or the weary traveler with a parched throat, few things could be of greater value.

It is a small kindness to give a thirsty person a cup of cold water. It is his thirst that establishes the value of the water. This writing is not so much concerned with the greater or lesser value of the water received. Rather, it is a look at the one who gives the cold water. The only person who is more enriched than the desperate recipient of the water is the person who gives it!

This book is about giving small gifts and being greatly rewarded in return. It is the life story of an inconspicuous man who experienced total fulfillment in finding needs and meeting them. I understand the limitless gratification and undiluted pleasure that accompanies giving. This book is the story of life as I have lived it.

To me, it seems presumptuous to write an autobiography. It presumes someone will want to know about me. It also presumes that what I have done deserves to be put in permanent record form. Thirdly, it presumes that I can write about myself in such an interesting manner that some stranger will actually be inclined to want to read about me. For these reasons, and many others, I have resisted the suggestions of a number of friends that I should put my life story in print.

Another reason I have been extremely reluctant to follow the suggestions of my well-meaning friends is that I know myself too well to want to put a record of my life in permanent printed form. A biography should be an accurate record about the person who is the subject of the book. That is graphically illustrated in the Bible as attention is given to the achievements, as well as weaknesses, of some of history's most prominent personalities. The Biblical record is similar to the statement of British Prime Minister Gladstone when having his portrait painted. To the artist he gave instructions that the portrait should be a perfect portrayal, "warts and all." He demanded reality in preference to flattery.

The Bible record does not limit the biographical vignettes of kings and dignitaries to their Godliness and exemplary conduct. It tells the entire story.

The information presented about Adam and Eve in Eden would have been story-book-perfect if it had not recorded the temptation and the fall into sin.

Lot was a terrific person. He lived in Sodom, an extremely corrupt city. The Bible records that he was "vexed with the filthy conversation of the wicked." And the record continues — "(for that righteous man dwelling among them, in seeing and hearing, vexed his righteous soul from day to day with their unlawful deeds)." Even though his daily living seemed to epitomize righteousness, after he was delivered from Sodom by angels, he brought shame and humiliation on himself and his family because of his uncontrolled appetite for strong drink, culminating in the ignominious conception of two illegitimate children by his own daughters.

The Bible goes on to display the weakness of Abraham in Egypt when he colored the truth a disappointing gray to save himself from an imagined danger. The accuracy of the biographical record was certainly not kind to Abraham.

Samson judged Israel for twenty years, and his activities as Israel's strong head of state are punctuated powerfully with the recurring phrase, "The spirit of the Lord came mightily upon him." Samson did a masterful job of delivering Israel from the Philistines, but just mention his name in any crowd of people and their immediate response will be "Delilah." Forgetting so many worthy accomplishments of Samson, we recall the darkest blotch in his biography. Biographies are not always beautiful.

Few men have measured even near to the stature of King David, yet when the spirit of God inspired the preservation of the holy record, it included the gory chapter about David's adulterous escapade with Bathsheba and the unconscionable murder of her innocent husband. No, I don't believe David was overly intrigued when his biography took top billing on the best seller list.

11

The list is long of good men whose portraits in Biblical biographical form show them precisely as they are — warts and all.

Yes, I resisted putting permanently in print everything about me. I would prefer that my friends continue to be my friends, and that I could continue to show them my better side. That is only human nature. I don't want to expose my weaknesses and my failures. But in response to the continuing urging of friends who insist that my story should be preserved, I have come to the position that if by knowing about some of my weaknesses and warts, others could receive inspiration to keep pressing forward, possibly I should put personal reservations aside and "write it down and sign it."

More than any other person, my wife, Letha, has suggested on numerous occasions that I should put my life's record in book form. At the time of this writing, more than half a century has passed since the Sunday afternoon she walked down the aisle into my life: and if she feels there is something worth writing after seeing me at such close range for so long, maybe I should take her advice. Since I made that decision, I have devoted a large portion of my time to preparing the chapters that follow, because within a few months I will arrive at that destination spoken of in Scripture as "three score years and ten." Because the years behind me are quite likely many more than those ahead, it seems prudent to make haste so I will have time to tell the whole story, as much as is humanly possible.

Of necessity, the last chapter must be the work of a substitute. Of course, it is highly unlikely that the concluding episode will be recorded by another and still find its place in print in this undignified volume. It may be nothing more than a brief eulogy by a kind minister at my funeral — but there will be a final chapter. I pray it can be positive and good.

I cannot report any sensational accomplishments, but if I have been a worthy water-boy in this life, you may correctly conclude that I have lived a happy, fulfilled life. Further, you may be sure that until the last time I am privileged to emulate my Master in offering to a thirsty person a cup of cold water, I will be blessed more as the giver than he who is the recipient.

CHAPTER ONE

IN THE BEGINNING

It started in a small cubicle no more than ten feet wide and fourteen feet long. Four teenage boys occupied this room in a college dormitory in the small town of Sevierville, Tennessee. Classes were scheduled to begin the next morning at 8:00 a.m., but midnight Sunday found these four naive, young fellows discussing how they were going to change their world.

Sunday evening vespers had been conducted in the college chapel. This was ordinarily about a one hour service, after which there was expected to be a gathering at the college canteen where the fellows could sneak a brief glimpse at the coeds. At best they might exchange a few words or knowing smiles with the girls, who for all practical purposes, lived a world away in their dormitories.

On that Sunday evening in the fall of 1943, the four fellows went directly from the chapel to their dormitory room. The worship service in the chapel had been different. The students really believed they had experienced a heavenly visitation that evening, and they were more than ordinarily sensitive to things spiritual. So much so that as they walked to the dormitory, they continued the praise that had ended the service in the chapel.

Upon entering the small room, without any discussion, one by one the four fell to their knees in worship and adoration of the King of Glory whose presence they had been experiencing all evening.

What started as a private worship attracted the attention of others, and soon the door to that tiny room was opened and the hallway became a chapel as many joined the group.

The assembled group was listening intently as one of the four related to them what he had just experienced. He was not sure of some of the specifics. Whether he had been so engulfed in the atmosphere of worship and had seen a vision, or if he may have prayed until he was exhausted and then fallen asleep and dreamed, he was not certain.

This unassuming, very ordinary novice from a small town in the prairies of South Dakota related that he had just experienced leading a vast group of people. (He was aware that he was in a foreign environment, although to that date, his world had been pretty narrow because the only thing he knew about any foreign place was what he had read in his grammar school geography classes.) As the group continued to follow him, it kept expanding as more people joined. That's it. Who these people represented was not made clear. Neither was there any information about a location. The only thing that was absolutely clear was that many people were eagerly following a stranger, completely trusting themselves to him.

I was the teenager who saw that vision, and so my life was redirected by a brief Sunday evening interlude of prayer. Until that night, I had a different plan for my life. My goal had been to become a civil engineer and build giant bridges across the world's largest rivers and widest chasms. My father had been a building contractor for as long as I could remember and I appreciated his expert ability to create fine homes. My goal had been to do something similar, but bigger! When I was quite young, I had read the biography of Henry J. Kaiser, one of America's foremost bridge builders. My dream was to emulate him. From the U. S. Army Corps of Engineers, I borrowed (without permission) the slogan, "The difficult we do immediately; the impossible takes a little longer."

Possibly my goals were quite ambitious, and my dreams may have been somewhat idealistic. Even so, I was to learn that what I had envisioned as worthy of my best effort was far less than God intended for me. He wanted me to help him in building bridges from a world of sin to an eternity of righteousness. The great God of Heaven had invited me to be a junior partner in the greatest bridge building operation of all times. I was to understand what the missionary statesman, William Carey meant when he stated, "If God calls you to be a missionary, don't stoop to be a king."

There were two more similar experiences later to confirm to me that God definitely had a plan for my life as a foreign missionary. I shared these unique spiritual experiences with only a very limited few. It seemed people were not interested in such weird happenings. Such strange experiences do not fit into the pattern of our modern culture. Visions and dreams with significant meanings just do not occur in the lives of ordinary people.

Joseph in the Bible had some strange dreams that caused him problems for years.

The prophet Isaiah saw a vision and for the rest of his life his writings were uniquely different. He wrote about an inconceivable concept that a virgin would conceive and give birth to a son. As if that were not strange enough, he continued to write that her son would be the Saviour of the whole world. Isaiah's acquaintances may have had reason to imagine his mind had snapped as he spoke of lions grazing with lambs and children playing with vipers. But these writings were the outgrowth of his visions.

Daniel became very prominent because of his reputation for interpreting dreams. But sometimes things seem to get out of control. At the zenith of his political popularity, when Daniel had just been elevated to the third most powerful position in the empire, he explained the king's dream to be a prophetic revelation that the expansive nation of Babylon would cease to exist before the next sunrise.

No, to be a dreamer, or an interpreter of dreams, may not be such a good idea after all.

Dreams and visions do not occupy a prominent place in our sophisticated twentieth century culture, but this vision would not go away, and nine years later, with my young wife and two year old daughter, I learned that what God plans is destined to completion. August 1, 1952 found us on board a ship with Japan our destination.

My first credentials as a licensed minister were issued to me just before my eighteenth birthday. I had completed a course in ministerial studies at a Bible college, had traveled as an evangelist and had served two brief tenures as pastor during the intervening nine years from the time of the vision until departure to the Orient as a fledgling missionary.

I maintained a keen interest in missions through those formative years and there was never a question but that I had received a divine call to be a missionary, and in God's time it would become a reality.

While still a student in college I had submitted an application to the General Missions Department of our church denomination. For a number of reasons I had volunteered to serve in the Middle East. Appropriately, I developed a keen interest in that area of the globe. Reading and researching about the Holy Land consumed me. That was prior to the reestablishing of Israel as a twentieth century nation in its ancient homeland.

We received our appointment from the World Missions Board in February, 1952 and in August of the same year we were crossing the Pacific (not the Atlantic) and in our passport was a seven year visa issued by the government of Japan (not Israel). The few intervening months allowed only a little time to make practical arrangements to move half a world away, and there was no possibility of even a cram course about Japan's history, its culture, religions or language.

When the freighter, which had been our home for nineteen days, docked in Yokohama, the missionary from another denomination who had been scheduled to meet us was not on the pier. We did not know a person in Japan and were totally illiterate in the strange language being used all around us. I was a grown man, but the little boy inside me panicked. I had always prided myself on the fact that I could keep things well under control, but that day, I was completely inadequate for what I faced.

Through the kindness of another church organization, a house had been rented for us to occupy. It was on the west side of Tokyo, no more than about forty miles from where our ship was docked, but it may as well have been in the mountains of Nepal, because there was no way I could locate it.

Somewhere in that vast city of six million population, there was a house waiting for us to move in, but I had no document to establish that house was reserved for our use. I knew it was in Tokyo, but if I had the address written down, I could not have pronounced the words, nor could I have instructed a taxi driver where I wanted to go (if I'd had the money for taxi fare).

PROBLEMS, PROBLEMS!!

Nearly three hours later our contact person arrived on board and inquired about us. Just seeing the "familiar face" of a person we had never met released the tension and as quickly as it started, the panic was gone. Yes, I was a grown man! I was in control again, and the brief interlude of panic could remain my well guarded secret.

CHAPTER TWO

MOBRIDGE

Why would anyone start right in the middle instead of at the beginning? Well that's what I did, so please accept my apology and travel with me way back in time and space to May 23, 1927, in Mobridge, South Dakota.

Mobridge has a unique place in U. S. geography and history. Whereas there are numerous cities and towns throughout the nation with the same names, there is only one Mobridge. When Washington is mentioned, it is not clear if reference is made to the nation's capital or Washington, Pennsylvania or Texas. Cleveland may refer to a place in Ohio, Tennessee, Texas or Mississippi, and the list could go on. But there is only one Mobridge.

Before there was a town, or even a village, in this wilderness spot in the north-central part of South Dakota, enthusiastic pioneers were moving west in covered wagons and commerce was following via the newly contrived technology known then as the iron horse. The coal burning locomotive was opening the west to expanding U. S. Commerce. The Northern Pacific Railroad, as well as U. S. Highway 12, crossed the Missouri River about one hundred miles straight west of Aberdeen, South Dakota. It was very important that the railroad engineers took note of this location, because it was the last place they could load up their steam driven locomotives with water before starting the long mountain climb through the western part of the state and on over to Montana.

On the railroad map was a small mark where the railroad crossed the Missouri River. It was abbreviated to read "Mo. Bridge" Very soon the railroad crewmen stopped referring to that last watering stop as the "Mo" bridge. It became just "Mobridge." Later, when a small group of farmers needed a place to buy supplies, trade horses, etc., a little town emerged from the prairie which was auspiciously referred to as the "City of Mobridge." That's where I entered the picture about seven decades ago.

Like most ordinary people, I was born of ordinary parents. My mother's family always announced with pleasure that their forebears came to the U. S. from England on the Mayflower. I never could reconcile that with the fact that the family name was Fougeron, which somehow suggests "French." Pop's family originated in Germany. Late in the nineteenth century, his parents migrated to the Crimean area of Russia seeking some improvement in their circumstances better than Germany afforded at that time. Not finding what they expected in Russia, they migrated again in 1893 to the United States.

I don't know how he found it, but somehow my grandfather located in South Dakota, which seemed to have some good possibilities for farming. Two years later my father was born. Their version of the American dream was actually more of a transplanted German community in the U. S. Like many of his siblings, my father spoke primarily German until he entered grammar school. His mother lived in the United States the last 50 years of her life, but never did learn even to converse in English. When she lived with us after my grandfather's death, I learned a few very important German words, like dumkopff (dummy) and ruich (be quiet). So you see, I had a little exposure to international culture at an early age.

Not very much of earth-shattering consequence happened in the first decade of my life in the Dakota wilderness. Although I was born in the latter part of the roaring '20s, my earliest recollections were not of the prosperous times prior to the economic crash of 1929, but rather of the great depression in the years just following that fateful event. As a young man, my father served an apprenticeship in carpentry, and except for a brief stint in the United States Army during World War I, he spent his entire life as a builder, proudly considering himself a master craftsman. Some of the finer homes in our town were the evidence of his proficiency and skill. Unfortunately, he was also very proficient in another area. He was a near-genius at the billiard table and at the bowling alley.

With an uncanny ability at his favorite games of skill came the temptation to flaunt his superiority and to challenge anyone who considered himself good enough to compete. His skill was the reason he usually won the games he played. His pride and boasting put him in competition in a different league where he experienced some difficulty. The players were not more skillful, they were just more adept in the art of manipulation. Soon Pop was trapped in the vice of competition mixed with gambling, the addiction which resulted was his ruination. Believing he was unbeatable in these games, he allowed wealthy men to lure him into tournaments where the bets were high, and he lost everything to this addiction.

Even though Pop had been quite successful as a small town builder, those huge losses, coupled with the ravages of the great depression, moved our family from one of the finest homes in Mobridge to a despicable existence of poverty. It did not happen abruptly, but gradually our standard of living spiraled downward until we could go no lower.

Coupled with Pop's insatiable need to win in his games, the international devastation of the great depression put us into an economic situation which no one could envy. When the worst days of the depression struck, and every possibility that a contractor could find work had disappeared, Pop was reduced to the position of a common laborer moving dirt and rock on a government subsidized project. One of President Franklin D. Roosevelt's rehabilitation programs called for damming up small rivers and streams to reclaim some of the land that had been denuded by erosion from the great drought. Our home was in the driest county in the United States at that time.

Apart from Pop's servitude to gambling, one could not have looked for a father who took his responsibilities to his family more seriously. Regardless of his personal physical feelings, and without regard for the most bitter weather conditions, he rarely missed a day's work. The burgeoning young builder who had earned upwards of $100 a day in his heyday in the late '20s was now bringing home $1.20 a day for ten hours of what was only slightly above slave labor.

Shortly before his death, Pop was engrossed in a conversation with my brother, Gebo (his name is Jerome, but most of us have nicknames, which cannot be explained by any reasonable method, and if we were to call him Jerome, he would most likely not even know to respond). Pop apologized to Gebo because he had no estate to leave to his ten children. Gebo replied, "Pop, if you had given each of us a million dollars, that would be less than what you actually gave us. You taught us to be honest and responsible, and you taught us by example how to work. No one could have a better inheritance than you gave us."

Some look back and sigh for "the good old days." When I reflect on those times, I can do nothing else but shudder at the memories and thank God for deliverance. With eight of us around the crude homemade table for meals three times daily, that meager $1.20 income just was not enough even for the simplest fare.

But then there was Mom.

The world has known few women more generous or more help-ful. Literally, she was everybody's friend. In fact, when we later moved to Texas, my parents came to be some of the most widely known lay people in the Church of God, and literally everyone in Texas (in the Church of God) called them Mom and Pop Heil. Although Mom was very generous and totally unselfish, she could be frugal when necessity required it. In those darkest days when she saw her children's future threatened by that monster called gambling, and then saw even her smallest hopes dashed to destruction by an uncontrollable worldwide depression, Mom learned to stretch a dollar bill until the eagle's wingspan was at least ten feet. She taught us to appreciate such filling, but inexpensive, staples as macaroni, potatoes and beans, occasionally made even more tasty with a small piece of fatback pork.

As much as possible, Mom tried to serve us meat on Sundays, which was more often than not a chicken she brought in from the back yard. Somehow she would manage to find a few eggs in the spring which she incubated and then would carefully make certain that even the scrawniest chick lived. After all, the supply of eggs for breakfast and meat for Sunday dinner depended on their continued good health. One of Mom's chickens wouldn't dare to die.

Possibly you will have no difficulty understanding that our chicken dinners were not exceptionally greasy. A chicken did not have a chance to get fat when it had to forage for worms and bugs in our backyard and have its natural diet supplemented only by the meager table scraps that might be left after one of our thrifty meals. Even though the chickens never got fat in our yard, the pieces on the plate looked strangely larger than should be expected. Mom generously floured and battered the chicken before she fried it and it did have the appearance of being adequate. What creativity Mom had!

When Mom fixed the usual Sunday chicken dinner, I don't remember her ever eating anything except the neck or the back. She often stated that the best flavored part of a chicken was the back and neck, and the reason most people did not eat them was because they were too lazy to pick the good meat from the bones. Much later, I learned why Mom "liked" the neck best.

Grocery shopping with Mom those days was fun. Of course it was different. As a carryover from the earlier glory days when money was readily available, there was a car and a pickup truck parked at our house. (Now, don't speculate that I am going to relate to you how Mom drove us to the supermarket for shopping. The actual story does not unfold like that.) Yes, there was a car and a pickup truck parked at our house. They had been parked there for a long time, because when they needed maintenance or repair, there was no money to have the work done. Of course, that didn't matter. It would have been the same if they been shiny and new because the main reason the vehicles did not serve as transportation is that there was no money for gasoline.

When Mom went shopping those days, she usually took along at least two boys. We walked along beside her pulling a small red wagon that had been a Christmas gift from friends who fared better than we. The man of that house had a good job with the railroad and they had a regular income when most others had forgotten what money was. Strangely, Mom didn't take money when she went shopping. Her destination was the local outlet for what we came to know as the government relief store. It was a place where those who could prove their poverty were given a dole of relief goods. The large room was stacked high with surplus food items which our government unceremoniously distributed to the poor. We qualified! Swallowing her pride, Mom took two young sons to this relief center and in total disgrace acknowledged that she was poverty-stricken and needed charity.

Not being privileged to know we were disadvantaged, we children happily pulled the little red wagon home, knowing there was a good supply of food for days to come. A typical shopping spree would net for our family of eight a fifty pound sack of flour, six or eight ten pound sacks of rice, beans, macaroni, or dried fruit. The bags were not always correctly marked, so we impatiently waited until we arrived home to watch Mom open each bag to see what we had been given.

Being quite young, I guess I was not expected to know that it would not always be necessary to sift the flour a number of times before making bread to be sure there were no more weevils in it. I was much older before I was made aware of why beans, rice and macaroni had to be boiled for a little while and then the water drained off before they were boiled again. The first boiling procedure was to kill the bugs, worms, or weevils hiding in our food and Mom had to drain the infested water before starting the final cooking process for her family. I didn't know this food doled to us was hardly fit for human consumption, but Mom knew it. Even so I never heard her complain. She did her job well. She not only fed and clothed us when it was next to impossible, she also taught us never to be ungrateful.

To supplement the wormy beans, the stale and foul-smelling pork lard, and the occasional dried fruit we received from the government, early every spring, just as soon as the last snow melted, Mom plowed the ground and planted as large a garden as our backyard would accommodate. When her garden flourished in spite of the near-desert condition, we ate fresh corn, tomatoes, beans, cucumbers, carrots and more. Knowing the South Dakota winters were long, she carefully allocated her resources, frugally furnishing just enough in the summer (but tolerating no waste) so she could put away the remainder for the inevitable long winter. It was not unusual for Mom to fill 100 Mason jars in a day in anticipation of the future when food was certain to be scarce. In the heat of the summer, she worked relentlessly in a kitchen with no air conditioning and not even a fan.

By the end of summer Mom would go down to the basement and count the jars she had filled with tomatoes, green beans, corn, dill pickles, and the list goes on. I remember yet the broad smile on her face as she would announce to Pop at the supper table after the last day of canning that she had 1,500 quarts of vegetables and fruits plus about 200 pint jars of jellies for the coming winter. Too many years have passed for me to remember precisely how many quarts of vegetables and fruit were in our cellar, but as I recall, the numbers used here are reasonably accurate.

Only a good German family could appreciate the fact that besides filling 1,000 to 1,500 quart jars with vegetables and fruit in a typical year to be reserved for the coming cold winter, my Mom had some huge 20 or 30 gallon crocks which served a unique purpose. By the end of the cabbage season after we had feasted on slaw for as long as we could tolerate, Mom took all of the remaining cabbage and cut it into fine shreds. With this cabbage she filled the crocks and let them ferment to provide the favorite German staple all winter long. We were the envy of all German people who bought their sauerkraut in a can. We had genuine homemade sauerkraut by the crockfuls.

The Bible speaks of a woman similar to my Mom in the last chapter of Proverbs. As I write this, Mom is now nearly ninety-three years old. Pop predeceased her a dozen years ago, but until last year she stubbornly insisted that she wanted to live alone because she did not want to be a bother to anyone. When it became apparent that it was not safe for her to continue living alone and driving her own car until she was past ninety-one, thankfully we were able to build her an efficiency apartment adjacent to the residence of my youngest brother, Dan, so he and his wife can keep a sharp eye on Mom from close range.

It goes without saying that many more visitors now come to Dan's house than before, because they are coming to visit Mom.

CHAPTER THREE

WHAT'S IN A NAME?

My father and mother, Henry and Thelma Heil, were the progenitors of a family of ten children. I was the third son, born May 23, 1927. In the days just prior to my birth, Mom had given a considerable bit of attention to names in anticipation of naming her new baby.

The first two children had been boys. Mom and Pop both were eagerly anticipating the birth of their little girl. In fact, after the first son was born, every time another child was born into our family, it was expected to be that sweet little girl. Finally, child number seven was a girl – my only sister, Wanda. After Wanda became the apple of Pop's eye and the object of Mom's beaming pride, there were three more sons born to bring the total to ten.

When I arrived at the Heil house, my parents were looking for Wanda, so from the beginning, I had a legitimate justification for having a severe psychological imbalance. Just in case the third baby might not be a daughter, Mom had settled on a name for a third son. I was to be christened, Delbert Heil. Seventy years ago in a small town like Mobridge, South Dakota, it was not expected that such insignificant details as reporting a birth and registering the name of the newborn should be done within the confines of a rigid schedule. So two weeks passed and the registration of my birth had still not become priority number one. That is the second reason I have a right to be emotionally disturbed and a social misfit. For two weeks, I was nobody! Sometimes I wonder yet how I ever made the adjustment and turned out to be such an outstanding person in spite of that terrible negative situation when I was too young to express my frustration at being left dangling for the crucial first two weeks of my life!

Just about the time Mom had finalized in her mind that she would contact the proper authorities and have my records forwarded to the bureau of vital statistics in Pierre, South Dakota, the State Capital, she received a letter from my uncle August and Aunt Merle, who lived far away in Minnesota. The letter included an announcement that their fourth child had been born about the same date as I was. They had named him Delbert. Mom decided then and there that my name could not be Delbert because it would be too confusing to have two Delbert Heils when the families may meet together. Never mind that we lived in the north central part of South Dakota and they lived in southwestern Minnesota. Such probable confusion was just not acceptable.

Because I was not a girl, "Wanda" was out. Now because my cousin two hundred miles away had managed to make his debut into the real world a few days before I was born, I couldn't be "Delbert" either. More delay. I was getting severely frustrated. Everybody referred to me in an impersonal way as "the baby." I didn't have personhood, but because I had not yet learned to speak intelligibly, my mother could not be expected to know why I was crying.

A few more uneventful days dragged by and I remained nameless. That may not be exactly an accurate statement. Maybe the days were not completely uneventful, but because whatever happened could not have happened to a baby who did not exist, those events are forever lost. Now you can understand why I have resisted numerous suggestions from well-meaning friends that I write my autobiography. There is no way I can tell the entire story because the first three weeks have been irrevocably committed to oblivion.

One day in June, Pop returned from work to be met by Mom's

exceptionally excited greeting. Waving a current copy of the Mobridge Tribune (our small town's weekly claim to journalistic excellence), she read to him an item of purely local interest about a young man whose name was Luverene Bougner. Why he happened to attract the attention of a news editor that week, I will never understand. But my fate was determined. The damage was done and it was irreversible. Mom actually sent that name to the bureau of vital statistics to be entered into the perpetual records maintained in Pierre, South Dakota. She reasoned that "Laverne" spelled with an "a" was an appropriate name for a girl, but spelling "Luverne" with a "u" made it masculine. Prior to that infamous moment in my brief life, I just thought I was upset. I now had adequate reason to become a completely maladjusted recluse. Would you believe it: when the birth certificate came back from the State Capital, my name was spelled with an "a" instead of a "u." To be frank, I didn't care if it was an "a" or a "u," I just didn't like it!

Another problem developed early in my pre-adolescent life. Wayne was born November 15, 1924. Alton Carrol (another of Mom's choice selections for a boy's name) was born January 29, 1930. A. C. was the fifth child, and the five were all born within the span of six years and a few days. I was right in the middle. There must be an explanation which I have yet to discover as to why the first two sons were almost identical in size when they were small, and the next three were so nearly the same size, we were sometimes mistaken for triplets. We came to be identified in family circles as two groups. There were "the two big boys" and "the three little kids." The two big boys had grown big, so they had no problem. The fourth and fifth were as big as I was, so they were moving up, but me — let me tell you, I can fully appreciate Napoleon's frustrations!!!!

So, I had the wrong name and I was too small. Thankfully, something was done about the first part of my problem, but I was to remain short throughout my life and always feel inferior because of it. To soften the impact of "Laverne" for a name, family members started to call me Buddy. I am not aware why, but thank the Lord for small blessings. That name stuck. Although I have somewhat outgrown what seemed to be an acceptable nickname for a young boy, but not too appropriate for a mature man, family members and a few friends from way back still call me Buddy.

My mother registered me in the first grade in school as Luverne, so like it or not, that was my name throughout grammar school and high school. When I went out of town to college, I registered myself, and I took hold of an opportunity to rid myself of the name I had never wanted. I registered as Edwin Heil. It was so easy. I just wrote my name as Edwin on the various forms when I registered and in a moment of time I was able to rid myself of a trauma that had frustrated me for most of two decades. What a relief! Never again would I hear someone in a large group call out "Laverne," expecting a girl to answer and then observe the strange looks on the faces of everyone nearby when I would respond to the call of that name.

It worked! Whenever I met someone on the campus I simply introduced myself as Edwin Heil. To them it was no big thing. They had just met a guy named Edwin. But it is not possible for me to express my feelings when it dawned on me that I had succeeded in changing my name. With a tiny ballpoint pen I had moved a mountain. Finally, I was a boy and no longer had to be identified with a girl's name. With the shedding of that old name, I was free from the schizophrenic frustration that had irritated me all of my life. That name was forever blotted out of existence. I was free at last!

Or was I?

I am uncertain as to what happened, but I think that when my High School transcript was requested by Lee College, the documentation came in under the name of "Laverne Heil." Almost all of the grades on that sheet were "A"s, but I would have been very happy to have those A's changed to B's or even C's, if only that old name had not been at the top of the page.

There was another glitch in my contrived plan for escape from the humiliation of having a girl's name. There were a few students in the college who knew me before "Edwin" Heil arrived on campus. You guessed it. They called me "Buddy." It seemed I was destined to be referred to as a girl or to be thought of as a little boy. In spite of my gallant effort at escape, I had not succeeded. For the rest of my life I was doomed to be either Laverne or Buddy.

When I left school, I developed a pattern of signing my name as L. E. Heil. My friends continued to call me Buddy (which pleased me so much better than Laverne), and new acquaintances usually called me Mr. Heil. About thirty years later in Chattanooga I took a job in insurance sales and wrote my name on the application forms as usual – "L. E. Heil." In that office, everyone used first names only, so I was called "L. E." That was all right until some of the people there heard my name called, but had not seen it written, so it is understandable they called me "Ellie." **Trapped again.**

After a year I moved to Honolulu where I knew no one from the past, and no one knew me either as Laverne, Buddy, L. E., or Ellie. After all the metamorphoses I had gone through it was surely worth one more try. I signed my name as Ed Heil. I told everyone I met that my name was Ed. By moving to the other side of the world, I had finally succeeded in changing my name. What a long time and a horrific process for such a small accomplishment.

Recently I made a gift to the School of Theology of our church denomination. The capital funds coordinator, Anthony Horn, had been instructed to respond. Fifty years ago, I had attended college with Dr. Cecil Knight, now the president of the School of Theology, so when he spoke about me, he spoke of a gift from Buddy Heil. Others in that town who had known me for a long time spoke of me as L. E. Heil and Anthony had seen my correspondence signed as Ed Heil. Anthony was to visit me about this matter and while making preparations for the trip, by chance he met my son, Ron. He inquired, "Ron, do you know a man named L. E. Heil?"

"That's my Dad," Ron responded.

"Do you know who Buddy Heil is?"

Again Ron gave the same answer, "That's my Dad."

Not just a little confused, Anthony fired the third question, "Then who is Ed Heil?"

With a slight grin, Ron replied very slowly and deliberately, "That's my Dad."

What's in a name anyway? Looking back through all of those insignificant, but complex details, I will have to admit the problem was altogether subjective. Apart from my personal foolish concerns, possibly no one ever noticed. However, against that backdrop, one thing stands out. The wise king Solomon told us in Scripture, "A good name is rather to be chosen than great riches." Proverbs 22:1.

In the Revelation the promise of Christ to the Apostle John was recorded, "To him that overcometh will I give to eat of the hidden manna, and will give him a white stone, and in the stone a new name written" Revelation 2:17. In this life I think I would have preferred a different name, but in the life to come, I will accept with uncontrollable pleasure and gratitude the new name Christ Jesus himself shall give me.

A name is very important in this present life. Further, it is especially important that we maintain the highest integrity so as not to tarnish our name. But in the life to come, my new name will be engraved on a pure white stone. That often causes me to ask myself, "Is my name seen by the people I meet daily as a pure and clean name against a snowy white background?" I have experienced more than a little frustration regarding my given name. Possibly it was all subjective and superficial, but to me it has been real.

In a much more important vein, I made a decision quite a long time ago to give serious attention to living and conducting myself in such a manner as not to embarrass my ancestors, my immediate family or my children and grandchildren.

So, what's in a name?

Everything!

CHAPTER FOUR

EARLY INFLUENCES

From my earliest recollections, church has been an integral part of our schedule. My parents taught us from an early age to believe in God, to respect the church and to cultivate decency and morality. Memories of Sunday school and vacation Bible school at age five and six are still clearly etched in my mind.

Mom was from a family that placed emphasis on church involvement and spiritual values. Being of a Lutheran background, she followed that tradition and had the first five boys baptized into the Lutheran church shortly after birth.

Pop's awareness of spiritual things and his involvement in church activities could best be defined in a single word: nonexistent. These things were not considered important in his home and he grew up in something of a spiritual vacuum. After he and Mom married, to please her he accompanied her to Sunday morning worship, but Mom often said, "He was the first one out the door." They attended the Norwegian Lutheran Church. Our town was largely populated by immigrant families from northern Europe, so the appellation "Norwegian" made that church the choice of many. We were German, but because there was no German Lutheran Church in Mobridge, I suppose Norwegian was next best.

As our family increased in size, Sunday school attendance at the Norwegian Lutheran Church grew in number. Although Pop had little background in spiritual matters, he supported the law established in our home by Mom that every Sunday morning found all of us in Sunday school.

When I was age six, I first attended Vacation Bible School. As I recall, the curriculum consisted of study of the catechism, Scripture memorization, snack time and games, in that order. I still remember learning the Lord's Prayer, the twenty third Psalm and the beatitudes as well as memorizing the books of the Bible. Although I remember little about Lutheran catechism or litany from that first Vacation Bible School, I can look back to that experience as my first actual exposure to the Bible and I have maintained a keen interest in Bible study since that initial exposure. In fact, when I was a third grader, my parents bought for us a copy of "Hurlbut's Bible Story Book," which was essentially the entire Bible in children's language. I read the entire book within a few weeks, even though I am sure Mom tired of the many times I carried that heavy book to her to inquire about the pronunciation or meaning of a word beyond my third grade vocabulary. For that elementary book I will always be grateful because it formulated in my mind a structure of events, chronological sequence, and genealogical connections of the various occurrences and Bible characters I would come to know more intimately later in life.

One other item before I leave the Lutheran Church. I do not remember the pastor as a person, nor do I recall anything of his family. I have no memory of ever hearing him preach a sermon, because at my young age then, my church attendance was limited to Sunday school attendance. One thing I do remember vividly. As the small children filed out of the Sunday school facility each Sunday morning, Reverend Helixson stood at the door and laid his hand on the head of each child and pronounced on us a blessing. What that did for the other children, I have no idea, but it created in my mind an admiration and respect for pastors as representatives of God in a needy world. I have no way of knowing exactly what kind of person that Lutheran pastor was, nor the extent of his commitment and dedication to God, but in my world he seemed to be a saint and I owe him a debt of gratitude for being concerned for the poor, insignificant, nameless children entrusted to his care because I was one of those children.

In an earlier chapter, you were given a glimpse into the drastic change our family experienced as we moved in a downward spiral from a comfortable life style to abject poverty. In the same general time frame, there was another significant and abrupt change taking place. This was in the spiritual atmosphere of our home. Pop had attended church for a number of years, but that was only to please Mom. Like so many people do, when our father saw his world crumble and his hopes for the future disappear, he began to show evidence of some interest in spiritual things. He began to reflect, "Maybe there is a real God somewhere. Possibly he is aware of my difficulties and he cares."

About the time Pop first evidenced any interest in God, an acquaintance invited him to attend a small church near our home. For about six months we attended that church. Although I was very young at the time, I vividly remember those months because we no longer attended Sunday school, but Sabbath school. Sunday and Saturday changed places on our calendars as we attended church on the Sabbath and took Sunday as a vacation day. As I recall, it was about a six months' indoctrination with the primary emphasis on the sanctity of the sabbath day, the ten commandments and the Jewish traditions which our host wanted us to believe constituted the only true Christianity. Much of what was taught seemed credible, but when someone there began to publicize the belief that participating in Sunday worship was tantamount to receiving the Mark of the Beast, Mom insisted that the family would be better served to return to the traditionalism of the Lutheran Church.

Trying to stay warm in the inhospitable environment of a construction sight to dam up the frigid waters of a winter stream in sub-zero temperature, some workmen stood around a small fire talking during their break. Someone mentioned an evangelist who was conducting revival meetings each evening in a vacated retail store building on main street in Mobridge. Pop was one of those men, and the discussion attracted his attention. He went home and told Mom some of what he had heard and suggested they attend the strange meetings. Not very many weeks had passed since the interlude at the Seventh-day Adventist Church, and Mom was not overly ecstatic about the prospects of another spiritual fiasco.

After some persuasion, Mom agreed to go one time to check things out. Upon entering the less than appropriate sanctuary with its nondescript furnishings, they were immediately impressed by the spirited singing, which was quite a departure from the typical quiet hymns performed by the high church choir.

If the music was properly considered impressive, the preaching was shocking. A young man from the desolation of North Dakota was the preacher. His name was Paul H. Walker. His "preaching" incorporated the essence of a divine message, the deliberate delivery of a courtroom attorney, and the persuasive power of logician delivered in the staccato style of an auctioneer. Although this unconventional style of preaching seemed to my parents to border on the bizarre, something in the message and the apparent sincerity of the evangelist attracted my father's attention. When sinners were invited to an altar of repentance, Pop turned to Mom and said, "Let's go."

Mom rejoined, "You can make a fool of yourself if you want to, but I am not going with you." However, Mom later acknowledged that when Pop took one step toward the front of that humble chapel, she was right behind him.

I was not there when my Mom and Pop were miraculously born again. I was a six-year-old asleep in my bed, but that was one of the most important days of my life. Our home was completely changed from that day forward. On a wall in our dining room hung a small plaque which appropriately epitomized the new home we had. This is the verse on that plaque:

Christ is the head of this house,
The unseen guest at every meal,
The silent listener to every conversation.

We still lived in the same dilapidated four-room hovel, but that day it became for us a new home.

Pop had been a chain smoker for years. The day after his conversion, following a habit which had become a part of him, he lit up a cigarette. Inhaling one time almost killed him. He became violently ill from the smoke of one cigarette, even though he had previously smoked many thousands of them. No one told my dad that smoking was wrong. He simply decided that if he gave his life to God one night and the following day a cigarette made him sick, it just could be the Lord was telling him not to contaminate the body he had committed to God. From that day until he died, approximately fifty years later, he never smoked another cigarette.

It has been speculated that when the blood of a German is tested, it will show 75% beer. Pop was a true German, but he never drank another glass of beer. Also put behind him were the billiard table and the bowling alley. I am not necessarily making a statement that these things are wrong; nor that the discontinuation of them constitutes Christian living, but Pop associated them with his former life of sin and determined they were wrong.

Pop had little formal education, but his learning habits as a Christian were above average. He learned as a new-born believer the fundamentals of Christian living and without delay he incorporated them into his mind and his actions. For more than five decades, in good times and bad, he and Mom practiced these five things faithfully:

Bible reading
Prayer
Church attendance
Witnessing
Giving

A dozen years ago, Pop went to his reward, and we have no question as to what his destination was. When he was buried, appropriately the family floral spray on his casket was inscribed, "Welcome to Heaven, Pop." Pop went to heaven and left Mom to live alone for the declining years of her life, but in a way Pop lives on as Mom continues the patterns he established in our home. If you were to walk into her apartment today, you would almost certainly find her with an open Bible in her hands. Sunday will find her in church, and when the offering plate is passed, she will drop in her check as she has always done for these sixty-three years. Yes, they taught us well, because they taught by example.

The events in the life of a young boy growing up in a small town are hardly worthy of publication, and I was no exception. Whether in the quiet atmosphere of a small town or in the tough environment of a big city, boys will have to learn to defend themselves. One day as I walked home at lunch time from the elementary school which was in sight of our little house, one of the school bullies jumped me, started calling me unkind names, and proceeded to work me over severely. As soon as I could free myself, I ran toward home. That day Pop had come in from work just prior to my getting humiliated on the school ball field. He wanted to know why I didn't stand up and fight instead of running away like a coward. My reply to him was that Mom had told all of us that if she caught us fighting, she would whip us. Pop said, "If I ever see this happen again, and you don't fight, I'll whip you."

With that sort of dilemma, I was afraid to fight and I was afraid not to fight, as that same big bully was to learn the next day. As I was going home for lunch, he accosted me with a challenge to fight, as he had done every day for some time. He seemed to enjoy the recognition he received from showing his superiority. That day was a shocker for him. He stood in my path to block me from going home and called me an ugly name. Within a split second, I floored him with a fairly fast fist to his face. If he was shocked, I was stupefied! I had no practice or experience in fighting because of Mom's strict rules against it. But that day I learned fast. It was my last time to be intimidated by that boy. Thankfully, Pop had preceded me home for lunch that day again and he watched what happened from our kitchen door. When I walked in, I was greeted with his comment of congratulations. Then he issued me a severe warning that what I had done to defend myself was right, but I was never to start a fight. That is when it becomes definitely wrong.

It was in that same general time frame that I was fighting another serious battle, although it was not so clearly defined. The fact that my family attended the Lutheran Church, then the Seventh-day Adventist Church, back to the Lutheran Church, and then the small new church on the east side of town was of little significance to me because I was very young and therefore unable to comprehend any difference. But in this new church, the Church of God, I was exposed to a more serious spiritual atmosphere than I had known in the other churches. My Sunday school teacher made me feel uncomfortable as she taught about doing right or wrong, and I began to understand the difference.

At that time our church was pastored by Reverend David Boatwright, a young man in his thirties who might appropriately have been considered a clone of Paul Walker because of the similarity of style and persuasion in his impassioned preaching. It was more than sixty years ago, but I recall distinctly one Sunday morning when Pastor Boatwright did not preach. Instead, his wife preached the sermon using the very unusual, but descriptive text in the Song of Solomon 2:15. As she spoke about the little foxes that dig around the vines and eat the tender roots, thus destroying the vines, it somehow translated to me as the secret sins and disobedience which kept the life of a small boy in chaos. That Sunday morning I had been sitting on the front pew and when the pastor's wife finished her sermon, immediately I was kneeling at the simple altar crying, praying and repenting likc as if I had been a hardened criminal. That day my name was added to the innumerable list of the redeemed in Heaven's record and Jesus became Lord of my life.

Since the onset of the great depression, my parents had been frustrated. They felt trapped in a little town where there was little economic opportunity. Because of the severe drought and unprecedented soil erosion in that area, farming also had become virtually impossible, so living conditions and economic frustrations were worse than in many other parts of the country. They often spoke of moving away, and would have done so but for two problems: where would they go, and how would they find the small amount of money needed to make a move. In 1937, when the worst of the economic disaster had passed, two of Mom's brothers moved to Houston and found work. They wrote back that there seemed to be no depression in Houston and suggested that we move there. From that time we dreamed of living in a story-book place called Texas, but it would be two years before Pop could manage to save enough money for that long distance move.

Near the end of a long inhospitable winter, Pop made a small trailer on which he would transport a few necessities. After an auction sale when everything in our house considered non-essential was sold, he packed the trailer and connected it to the rear bumper of his 1936 Chevrolet. (It is hard to imagine who would have attended an auction to buy what we had, and it is even stranger to try to conceive that the small amount of miscellaneous junk brought enough cash to fund our 1,600 mile move.) That was the early spring of 1939.

Hitching the trailer to the back of that 1936 Chevrolet was the easy part; crowding our ever-increasing family into that small two-door sedan was the miracle. At that time the passenger list in the tired, little Chevy was Pop, Mom, seven boys and Wanda. Pop had made two small stools that were set just behind the front seats in a space so restricted they had to be placed in the car after four boys lined up on the rear cushion. Then the two jump seats were occupied. One child had to sit in the front where the seats divided. That was the least desirable place because of the uncomfortable split seat, and because the gear shift was on the floor and often the passenger in the center was battered with the repetitious gear shifting necessary to keep the heavily loaded car moving. Lastly, Mom got into the passenger side of the front holding on her lap the baby, or another of the smaller children during that entire 1,600 mile trip which took ten days.

Pop drove.

The trip was tiring for a number of reasons, not the least of which is described in the paragraph just above. Many of the U. S. Highways sixty years ago were not paved, so we lumbered along on wide paths covered with river gravel, which tended to form ridges and ruts if it had been some time since the road maintainer had been there to rearrange the gravel. Safe driving practices would dictate the tires on the car should have been replaced prior to starting the long trip, but the overriding budgetary considerations emphasized that the tires "might make it." So we stopped often to repair flat tires and replace an occasional blow-out.

The cash receipts from the auction sale before our departure suggested our menu. We ate cheese and crackers, bologna sandwiches, fresh fruit when it was available at the right price and occasionally whatever kind of cookies may have been the cheapest at the wayside store where Mom carefully selected our food for the day.

The course of the trip was charted so we would stay in the homes of relatives or friends at night because hotels were out of the question (and because they were out of the budget). Also, can you imagine Pop going to a hotel clerk and asking for hotel accommodations for ten for the night?

Our longest day started right after an early breakfast in southwestern Minnesota. The nearest relative after that lived in Lincoln, Nebraska so that determined how far we intended to travel. Because of a number of unplanned stops, we arrived at the home of the next relative at 3:00 a.m. the following morning.

Traveling at a top speed of 35 miles an hour so as not to overtax the tires, stopping occasionally to let ten cramped people out for a brief stretch, or to buy gasoline might explain why the miles were covered so slowly. This is not to mention that it did take a considerable amount of time for everyone to get untangled from where they had been riding and even more time to get back in, given the fact there was always the question of who had to sit on the split front seat, which two had to sit on the hard wooden jump seats which faced the interior of the car and offered no outside view. Nor was it unusual that within an hour or less after loading the little Chevy with ten tired travelers, somebody had to stop to use the bathroom. Of course, no one would even suggest that eight children under the age of 15 would be completely synchronized about something so mundane as toilet timing.

The one thing I would love to have as a memento of that trip would be photographs of the expressions on the faces of service station attendants when we stopped – not to buy gasoline – but just to use their rest rooms.

CHAPTER FIVE

A TEENAGER IN TEXAS

On the eighth day of our trip we crossed the state line from Oklahoma into Texas but nothing happened! I am not sure exactly what we expected, but Texas seemed to be no different from Oklahoma – or the other states we had passed through. We had heard so many wonderful things about Texas that maybe in my young mind, I was actually expecting it to be something like heaven.

But wait – it could be I am just a little ahead of myself. I abruptly jumped from Lincoln, Nebraska to Greenville, Texas. Let me assure you, it did not happen so suddenly as that. There were many tiring days in between that could be characterized by the words, "crowded," "irritable," "exhausted," "cheese and crackers" and "flat tires."

As we advanced farther south, there were no more relatives, so stopping at night constituted another strain on the extremely limited budget. Somewhere in Kansas, for the first time we saw a motel. To us it was a brand new concept. Mobridge had one hotel which was a multi-storied brick building called the Brown Palace. The owner was the town millionaire, Albert H. Brown. His name explained the first word of the hotel's name, but I never could figure how the word "palace" fit into the hotel's name. It just did not have the ostentation to merit being referred to as a palace.

Just like the Brown Palace did not at all look like it should be called a palace, what we saw in Kansas should not have been considered a motel, if we had reasoned correctly that "motel" was derived as a contraction of the two words, motor and hotel. What we found was a cluster of a few small buildings that looked very much like garages, except there was no large door in front to allow for driving a car in, and the buildings were considerably smaller. A typical motel in those days was made up of eight or ten of those small huts, spaced far enough apart to park a car between two buildings. The surface of the parking area was covered with gravel and there was no roof.

Because we had distanced ourselves from all relatives by the fourth night, there was no option but to check out this novelty. Upon inquiring, Pop learned that the rate to stay one night was six dollars. After conferring with Mom about the amount of money remaining in her anemic purse, Pop decided to take one cabin. Inside, the building had a bed, a chest and a couple of straight chairs, which nearly filled the small room. At the rear of the room was a clothes closet and inside plumbing (which was just barely inside). Really, what was in the room made little difference. By the time Mom had ingeniously placed most of us on blankets or towels on the floor, and with her, Pop and one or two of the smaller children on the bed, nothing of the furnishings could be seen anyway.

One item in the motel fascinated me. It was the heater. It was a small unit recessed into the wall. Following instructions, Pop turned a small lever and struck a match. I believe I began to comprehend how Moses felt when he saw flames dancing on a dry bush that was not consumed by the fire. I saw the wall of our cabin burning in one spot, but the fire did not spread to other areas of the wall. This was our introduction to the marvel commonly known in the South as natural gas.

One of the most difficult and disagreeable aspects of the harsh winters in South Dakota had been carrying into the house huge, heavy buckets of coal to be burned in the heater and then carrying out the same buckets, filled with ashes taken from the bottom of the stove. There was one redeeming factor. We scattered the ashes on the driveway and they made an acceptable substitute for gravel to keep the driveway from becoming muddy ruts when the snow melted in the spring.

In the motel room I watched the fire burn and felt its warmth without having carried in any firewood or coal. And there were no ashes to be carried out. This was almost heaven!

On the ninth day of our travels, we were about 100 miles south of Dallas and making good time. The highways in Texas were better than in some states we had passed through. This prompted Mom to look at the map and to look in her purse. The map indicated we were just over 150 miles from Houston. The contents of her purse suggested it would not be prudent to expect the luxury of a motel that night. Thankfully, gasoline was only fifteen cents per gallon in Texas, so Mom figured there was enough money left to buy the necessary gasoline to finish the trip and food for the next day. She and Pop had a conference and decided to push up the speed to about 50 miles per hour on the good paved Texas highway and try to arrive in Houston some time after midnight.

Shortly after sundown things were going as planned until a tire on the rear of the car blew out. The car swerved and corrected, but the trailer did not follow precisely, resulting in the trailer's rolling over spreading our only worldly possessions along the side of the highway. The trailer remained fastened to the car, so after the upper part containing the furnishings separated, the trailer bed skidded upside down behind the car (apparently making quite a noise) until Pop could get it under control and stopped.

In farmhouses nearby, the noise was heard and very soon Pop had enough volunteer help to repair the trailer and reload it in light provided as different ones parked their cars nearby with the headlights directed toward the scattered items. With this delay, and needing a replacement tire, it was not possible to drive further that night, so in spite of the limited budget, Mom found the necessary $5.00 to pay for a motel room where we camped for the remaining hours of the night.

The only item of value Pop had remaining from the good times prior to the great depression was a gold Elgin pocket watch, which he proudly wore in one vest pocket of his Sunday suit, with the gold chain draped across to the vest pocket on the opposite side. As soon as the sleepy Texas town awoke the next morning, Pop was out searching for a pawn shop. He laid his gold watch and chain on the counter and the proprietor offered to lend him $35.00. It was agreed the loan was to be repaid within 30 days. The thirty five dollars was sufficient to buy the needed tire and gasoline for the remaining miles to Houston.

We had driven away from Mobridge, South Dakota with snow piled six feet high on both sides of the road, and ten days later were welcomed to Houston with a view of lush green lawns surrounded by roses in full bloom.

Not only was the spring weather a real treat for us so early in the year, we had a bright future because Pop immediately found work building small homes for a real estate developer. We stayed a few days with Mom's two brothers, with our large family divided between their two residences. They made us very welcome, but five extra persons in each of two small apartments was not exactly an ideal living arrangement, so finding a house to rent was top priority. As soon as Pop could make a draw against his contract, he found a new two-bedroom bungalow not too far from his job site. The rent was $35.00 a month.

It was important that we return to school just as soon as we had situated into a house because we had been out of the classroom for more than three weeks. When I registered, I went to the junior high school to continue in the sixth grade. In South Dakota the sixth grade was the last year of elementary school. Texas at that time had an eleven year system, so sixth grade was a part of the junior high school. The school principal and the sixth grade teacher had a brief conference and decided that it would be better for me to finish the fifth grade in the few weeks remaining in the school year and enter sixth grade again next year. They reasoned that the end result for me would not be a problem as I would finish high school at the same time as if I had completed the course in South Dakota.

I don't know if I should appreciate what they did or resent it. I was always frustrated because of having been arbitrarily set back a year, but the fact that I learned easily in the higher grades may have been attributable to doing the sixth grade twice.

Near the end of the first month living in our new house, Pop announced he did not intend to pay that exorbitant rent for very long. The income from Pop's first contract in Houston had been sufficient to meet the first month's budget, plus redeem the gold watch that had been pawned on the last day of the move and there must have been a little left because Pop went searching for another place to live. He located a little two room building about 16' x 30' situated to one side of two building lots in a sub-division. It seems that somehow he negotiated a deal for an extremely low down payment, because we moved in after having rented just one month.

The house was divided into a kitchen and a combination living room/bedroom. Behind the house was a single car garage and nearby was the typical rural outhouse. Mom found some old army cots and lined up six of them in the garage. That became the bedroom for all of the boys, except Dean who was not yet two years old.

Summer came and I was restless. In May I had turned 12 years old and I decided that I should look for a job. In the employment section of the newspaper classified ads, I found an advertisement of an ice cream company, wanting young men to sell ice cream from a bicycle. I went to the address listed in the newspaper and was hired on the spot. The ice cream company had the unique name "Have-A-Bar." It was owned by Mr. W.L. Barr. Each morning I rode the city bus to downtown Houston. I loaded an insulated box with ice cream snacks packed in dry ice. The box was then fastened to the back of a bicycle. On the handlebars was a set of bells, which notified children that the ice cream "man" was coming up their street. That was my first job.

The ice cream company paid me on a commission basis. I checked out ice cream on consignment every morning. At the end of the day I returned any unsold merchandise and paid my bill. I paid at the rate of 75% and retained 25% of the money taken in. I learned later that some of the fellows were on a different rate. They owned their bicycles so they retained 30% of the money. It didn't take me long to figure that with the additional 5% I could pay for a bicycle and keep it after the summer job was finished.

I talked to Pop and he agreed to go with me to the Western Auto Store between our home and the ice cream plant to buy a bicycle. Before going, he made me understand that if I wanted a bicycle for my work, I would have to pay for it. I don't know what Pop arranged with the store manager, but I rode away on my own new bike and then paid the entire balance before the first payment was due.

When I had my very first income, my parents taught me that Christians should tithe their money to the Lord. My income from that first job was about $1.50 to $2.50 per day, depending on how much I sold. I did not know precisely how the system was to work, but the pastor of the church we attended lived next door to us, so every afternoon when I returned home on my bicycle, I stopped first at Brother Smith's house and gave him seventeen cents, twenty-one cents, or whatever figure was exactly 10% of my income that day. Many years later, Pastor Smith told me he was often amused about that little 12 year old boy who came to the pastor's house every afternoon and placed a few small coins in his hand. But he knew it was very serious business with me and he never made light of my sincerity. That teaching has never left me, and to the best of my knowledge, I have faithfully returned to the Lord a minimum of 10% of every dollar that has ever come to me.

Next in importance to the teaching I received about tithing was Pop's instruction to me about maintaining good credit and standing by my word regardless of the consequences. The day after I rode away from the Western Auto Store on my new bicycle, I stopped at the store and paid one dollar on my bill. The manager's wife took my money and wrote me a receipt showing the balance due. Every morning on my way to work, I stopped at the Western Auto Store and paid one dollar on my account. The total price of that bicycle was $27.95 and subtracting the two dollars I had paid down, within 26 working days, the bicycle was completely paid for (no interest because I had paid within the first month). The manager of that store later told one of my brothers, who bought his new bicycle on the same basis I did, that either of us could buy anything in his store on credit.

When school started in the Fall, I contacted one of the local newspaper companies and asked for a paper route for delivery after school each afternoon. From that time, I sold ice cream each summer and delivered newspapers during the school term. The newspaper route manager often announced a contest to encourage the boys to increase circulation. I won every prize he offered.

The third year I worked for the Houston Press, the largest route in Houston with 230 subscribers became available and it was offered to me. Of course, I accepted it. Within six months I had increased that route by another 105 customers. When I moved on to bigger and better things, my route was divided and given to three boys.

Even as a young teenager, I was an exaggerated optimist. In 1942 and 1943, World War II was putting huge numbers of men to work in defense and war industries. Pop discontinued his building business and took a job at a shipyard that employed 20,000 men, on two ten-hour shifts. I began to try to calculate how many ice cream bars could be sold if I could get them to the entrance gate of the shipyard when the shifts changed.

I was able to secure a permit to set up shop for one hour a day. At 4:30 p.m. when the night shift workers arrived, we had our ice cream ready. But when the day shift came out of the 14 gates like stampeding cattle, we were far from ready. I don't have any idea how much money we lost or how many times we gave too little or too much change in the midst of that industrial pandemonium. We soon learned. Instead of packing each piece separately, we kept all of the Eskimo pies and ice cream sandwiches in cartons of a dozen and would only sell them by the dozen. Very quickly the workmen learned our method and one man would stand in line and buy a box of ice cream for himself and his buddies. Basically, we were wholesaling the product at retail prices. But it was not all easy. Let me go back.

Problem Number One: When this project began to crystallize in my mind I was only 15 years old and a high school sophomore. First, I had to visit the office of the school principal and get a release to attend school only from 8:30 a.m. until 12:30 p.m. That allowed me to take four high school credit hours, and I took no electives and no study hall. The principal approved my plan with the provision that I could continue that limited schedule as long as I maintained good grades.

Problem Number Two: In order to sell the ice cream at the ship-yard entrance, which was approximately 30 miles east of the ice cream company's business location, I would have to have a car. Pop and I went to a used car dealer and found a 1934 Plymouth that appeared to be in very good condition. It was priced at $135. That was more than fifty years ago, and factoring the effects of inflation since that time, the price would have been approximately the equivalent of $1,000 in today's currency.

I paid cash for the car and the dealer prepared the title application and transfer documents. Incidentally, that was one of the few cars I bought without the help of a bank or finance company.

Problem Number Three: I did not have a driver's license and being only fifteen years old, I could not get one for another year. I spoke to my older brother, Tex, who had dropped out of high school a few months earlier to take a job as a truck driver for the Railway Express Company. I told him I would go to the ice cream plant and pack all of the boxes while he was still working at the Railway Express. Then he was to come directly to the ice cream plant at 3:00 p.m. and drive the car to the shipyard. For that, I agreed to make him my partner and we would share the net income 50/50. It was a good arrangement for both of us.

Problem Number Four: The car I bought was a two-door coupe. What we needed was a truck. We solved that problem by removing the trunk lid and building a truck-bed into the large trunk space. It worked! There was enough space to stack about eight ice cream boxes on the floor and another eight on top of them. Everything was falling into place. We had our permit. I was allowed a short schedule at the high school. I had bought the car and converted it to accommodate our need. I had a driver/partner. There was just one more small matter that needed serious attention.

Problem Number Five: There were two of us and the shipyard had 14 gates. Where would we put our ice cream boxes and how would we manage the crowd? I contacted some of the school boys I had met previously at the ice cream plant. They did basically what I did: they sold ice cream in the summer for $2.00 or $2.50 per day and then found some other type of work for after-hours when school was in session. I offered them $2.00 a day to meet after school and help me at the shipyard shift-change for just one hour. They were well pleased with the pay and I had my crew. I am sure it was a hilarious (not to mention dangerous) sight to see our little converted Plymouth with three teenagers in the front seat and about five more teenagers on top of those ice cream boxes.

It was a smashing success from day one.

After a grueling ten-hour shift the workmen were more than pleased to find this refreshing treat made available as they exited the work area and we sold out in just over half an hour. Pop had been a successful builder for thirty years. He was now on the inside working at journeyman's wages of $12.00 for a 10 hour shift. I was a fifteen year old boy with no experience, no credentials, and not even a driver's license. I was working on the outside and my take home pay for the one hour of selling was more than my father was paid for ten hours of skilled work. When top union scale at the shipyard brought the workmen $12.00 a day, I was taking home $15 and sometimes $20 a day. If I had not given away 50% to my brother to drive for me, I could have made twice as much — or maybe, I would not have made anything because I could not get there without him.

It was an appealing situation. I had my own business. I had five employees. The income was well above average. Although I did not even know the word existed, I was on my way to becoming an "entrepreneur." The owner of the ice cream store also liked the way things were working out. My exceptionally large volume of sales positively impacted his business. A few months after I had started this new business, Mr. Barr called me aside one afternoon to show me a brand new Chevrolet truck on which he had put a customized refrigerated storage. It had his company name on it for advertising, but he told me he had that truck custom-fitted for me.

From the next day, I would not be loading boxes on the back of my little converted Plymouth coupe, but I would be using this new refrigerated truck. Mr. Barr had more than fifty men selling ice cream for him on the streets of Houston, and when he bought his first refrigerated truck, he got it for me, a fifteen year old boy! Actually, I had just passed my 16th birthday a few weeks earlier. I was growing up in a man's world and winning!

CHAPTER SIX

GIRL OF MY DREAMS

Growing up in a large family with limited resources meant taking on responsibilities early. When I was not delivering newspapers or selling ice cream bars, I was helping Pop in the building business. In the depression days when money was scarce and the family was getting larger, Pop did virtually nothing but work to try to provide for all of us. After completing the eighth grade, my older brother, Wayne, dropped out of school to help Pop. As the others got older, we joined the family work team on Saturdays and sometimes after school. Because of the work load, there was not time for extra curricular activities.

Possibly the one school-related activity I remember most distinctly is that my regularly assigned job every evening was to prepare the lunches for the next day for Pop and Wayne to take to work and for five or six of us who would take them to school. It was up to me to figure out what to fix and where to find it. For as long as I can remember, Mom baked our bread, so we always had sandwiches. What kind of sandwiches was the question. Lunch meats like we saw in the deli section of a grocery store were not for us. They were much too costly. Occasionally I would find some wieners in the refrigerator and cut them very thin to be divided over enough bread to fill seven lunch sacks. Alternatively a single slice of processed cheese food substituted for lunch meat. When supplies diminished, there was no option but to use sandwich spread, which was little more than a salad dressing with a few chopped pickles. That did not make a very thick sandwich. Mom occasionally found sliced dried beef which was packed tightly in a six ounce glass. I am sure the slices were not more than 1/32nd of an inch thick. Try stretching that small amount of meat in fourteen sandwiches. Sometimes Mom fixed a large beef roast for our evening meal. Depending on how much was left, I cut the slices of meat either thin or thinner so as to have enough to prepare the sandwiches.

When Mom shopped, she always looked for cookies in very large packages with a low price. I would ration these into the seven sacks each evening. If it had been some time since Mom last shopped for groceries, the supply of cookies diminished and we had nothing sweet for the lunches. I learned to make cookies, cakes and pies as a matter of survival — if there had been nothing in those lunch sacks but two sandwiches each, I may not have survived. Later when I married, I found it advantageous that I had learned to cook because the young girl who became my wife attracted me with something other than her reputation as a cook. Her experience in the kitchen was limited to opening and warming Campbell's chicken noodle soup or vegetable soup, and sometimes she mistakenly opened the wrong can.

At school, I sometimes noticed a girl who was cute, and occasionally one I thought was pretty. However, I never had a girlfriend. Being short and shy, I was at a disadvantage. Because I was so short, I always considered myself unattractive and being shy, I was afraid to approach a girl. Social life for me as a young teenager consisted of meeting friends at the small church we attended and going as a group after church service to an ice cream parlor for refreshments.

Then one night while I slept, all of that changed. It could hardly have happened while I was awake as I was too bashful. I dreamed I was with a group at school and somehow noticed in the crowd a girl I had not seen before. I remember little of what she looked like except for the dress she wore. Everyone else was in ordinary school clothes, but she wore a royal blue crepe dress with the skirt pleated all around. The upper part of the dress was trimmed tastefully with black velvet. Wonder of wonders — she came to where I was and talked to me.

Shortly after that dream, Will Petty visited our church, which was so small that when a new person attended, everyone was aware of it. Mr. Petty mentioned that he had moved to Houston to accept employment in one of the shipyards and he hoped to bring his family just as soon as he could locate a house for them. One young fellow remarked to me, "He has two very pretty daughters."

Two weeks later, I was in the choir singing on a Sunday evening when Mr. Petty came in just shortly after service started. With him were his wife, two teenage daughters, Letha and Eva, and two younger sons. Letha attracted my attention.

I stopped singing and just stared. Noticing my obvious interest in those who had just arrived, the young fellow standing next to me asked, "What is the attraction?" I responded, "That's my girl." The dress she wore that Sunday evening was identical to the one I had seen in my dream two weeks earlier. I learned later that she had made the dress herself, which made her seem even more special.

It was not the typical "love at first sight." I was amazed and dumbfounded at first sight. Here the girl I had seen in my dream materialized into a real human being and she had just walked into my life. Of course, she did not know that yet, and a number of months would pass before she would be convinced.

After the church service concluded that evening, the two new girls joined our group for milk shakes at the ice cream parlor. True to form, in my shyness I did not rush to introduce myself. My propriety in waiting to be introduced was rewarded with someone else stepping in and Letha spent that evening talking to him. I don't think she even noticed I was there. However, within a month I had attracted her attention. We sat together during church and then went to get ice cream together. I felt I was making progress. I think she was frustrated because I tried to build a fence around her.

The Petty family moved to Houston the first week in January,

1943 and I would be sixteen years old by May of that year. I learned that Letha would have her sixteenth birthday just two weeks after mine. I also learned from Letha that she was very seriously interested in a young man in another city in north Texas. In telling me how extra special he was, she let me know that her intention was not to marry until at least age twenty-five and that the ideal man for her should be a number of years older and he had to be tall.

Maybe she was trying to get a message to me, but I did not hear it. One advantage became evident. Her special friend was in active military service and was stationed four hundred miles away. He was too far away to visit her very often and the Air Force would possibly send him farther away, and for a long time. Maybe I had a fighting chance. One thing I did not know was that habitually, after Letha had spent a brief few minutes with me, she returned home and wrote a long letter to Harold, the man of her dreams who was older and taller.

By February 1, Letha and I had become cordial, if not friendly, and I considered her as my girl. The timing could not have been better for me to show her my sincere affection. Because Valentine's Day was just a few days away, I went to a jewelry store and bought a gold sweetheart bracelet. On the top were two hearts. I had her name and mine engraved on the hearts. It was the first time for me to give a gift to a girl, and I was pleased when she accepted it gracefully. She complimented the choice I had made, thanked me and then slipped it on her wrist. The next time we met, she had a small wrapped package in her hand which she offered to me. She told me that she and her mother had discussed it, and she could not accept my gift.

I tried again in June. On her birthday, I presented her with a white gold watch with two small particles of diamond dust on the bracelet. I am not sure the diamonds were large enough to be seen without a magnifying glass, but coming from my background, just to mention the word diamond was tantamount to extravagance. This time Letha thanked me profusely, but apologized again that she could not accept it. I was crushed. The Valentine bracelet may have been offered a little prematurely as we had only recently met. But this was different. We had been dating for a number of months and I wanted her to have something nice from me for her birthday. She explained that it was not that she did not admire the watch, and she emphasized that my offering the gift was not inappropriate. It was just that she was to graduate from high school the following Spring and her mother planned to give her a gold watch as a graduation gift.

Frustration and disappointment engulfed me. I had come to the end of my world. I was seriously in love with a girl who had rejected me twice. Apparently it was time to move on. But I was too stunned to move, much less move on. Not long after that, Letha came to church one evening and it was obvious she had been crying. She had received a letter from Harold telling her he was sorry about her feelings for him because he had considered her more of a sister than a sweetheart. The letter also included mention of the news that he had just been married. I really did try to console Letha and make her know how concerned I was for her in this difficult situation. It was possibly the most masterfully performed hypocrisy of my life. To state it mildly, I was elated. After Letha received that fateful letter, I was certain things would change for the better, but I was wrong. True, Harold was married to someone else, but I was still just two weeks older and five inches too short.

The situation worsened. In mid-Summer, Letha told me of her plans to go away to Southwestern Bible Institute in Waxahachie, Texas for her senior year of high school. The Bible Institute was a ministerial training school and it also had a high school division in a very good atmosphere. That meant she would be gone for nine months with the exception of a few vacation days at Christmas or mid-term break.

A year earlier, my older brother, Wayne, had enrolled in a ministerial training course at the Church of God Bible Training School (BTS) in Sevierville, Tennessee. In September, he returned for his second year. My second brother, Tex, also decided he would go with Wayne and finish his senior year of high school. Al Statum, who would later marry my sister, went with them. I don't know why Al went, except that he and Tex were inseparable buddies. To say the least, when they all left at the same time, I was lonely.

After about two weeks of this loneliness, I announced to my parents on Sunday night that when I was praying at church, the Lord impressed me to go to Bible School. In a strange display of that wisdom possessed only by moms, she immediately concluded that my sudden interest in going to Bible School just might have some connection with the fact that Letha was in a Bible Institute for her senior year of high school. Mom inquired, "Where do you plan to go?" When I replied I would go to Sevierville, Tennessee to the Church of God Training School, Mom concluded that maybe I did hear from the Lord, because if the decision had been based on my feelings, I would more likely have been inclined toward Waxahachie, Texas. Looking back, I am not altogether certain it was the Lord who impressed me to go to Bible School, or if it was a very normal reaction on my part to the fact that my two older brothers, a very good friend and the girl I loved had all gone and I just felt left out.

While I had been selling ice cream at the shipyard, I had more than enough money. I enjoyed wearing nice clothes and maybe I spent inordinately for clothes now that I could afford to because I had always dressed so shabbily before. I kept an adequate amount of money for personal things and going out with Letha. Of course, I paid tithe and gave to the church substantial offerings besides. Whatever was left, I gave to Mom. I knew she managed very carefully the paycheck Pop handed her every week. I also knew there was usually a lack. It was not required of me: I just felt it was the right thing to do. To summarize, when I decided to go away to school, I had almost no money.

After a brief family planning session, it was determined that I would leave within a week for Sevierville. Mom would take over my business at the shipyard. I think she intended to drive the truck and let the high school boys continue to sell the ice cream as they had done in the past. As it turned out, Mom went early every day to the ice cream plant and packed the truck. She then made a circuitous route past a number of high schools to pick up her sales crew. When they set up the distribution stations outside the shipyard gate, Mom "manned" one location and sold just like the boys.

Going away to school, I would not have any need for a car, so I sold it. Or maybe I gave it away unintentionally. A friend wanted to buy the car, but not having the ready cash, he requested terms. His offer was that if I would accept monthly payments of $15.00, he would pay me the same price I had paid for the car some months earlier. That sounded to me like an exceptionally good deal. I bought the car for $135.00, used it for six months and now I was getting all of my money back. Naivete, ignorance of human nature, or stupidity (or some of each) caused me to believe I would get the money. I accepted the $15.00 he offered as a down payment and readily gave him a clear title to the car, confident I would have $15.00 on the first of every month to buy the few miscellaneous things I might need at school.

It may be taking up space unnecessarily on this page to report to my readers that the $15.00 I received as a down payment became the entire purchase price of the car. When I moved 900 miles away, the friend who had my car with a clear title felt little incentive to mail me the money and he apparently had no compunctions about driving a car for which he had not paid.

As soon as I had settled "all of my business affairs," I packed my clothes in a borrowed suitcase, bought a bus ticket and was on my way to Tennessee. Never mind that the school term had started two weeks earlier, and never mind that I had not made contact with the school to inquire if I could register late. Neither did it enter my mind that they might be over-crowded to the extent I could not be accommodated.

Another minor incidental item that had not even occurred to me was the matter of charges I may be asked to pay when I should register. Having given Mom whatever money I had at the end of each week while I was making a substantial income, I was not prepared financially to do anything. When I had bought my ticket and boarded the bus, I did not feel any discomfort caused by sitting on an over-stuffed billfold.

At the Sevierville bus station I entered a taxi and told the driver to take me to BTS. Having never before ridden a taxi, I had no idea about fares, not to mention that I was completely ignorant about tipping. When we arrived at the school, I inquired as to the amount of the fare. The driver replied, "Thirty-five cents."

I offered a dollar bill and waited for my change. I thought I detected a strange expression on the face of the driver when I accepted from him all of the change, deposited it in my pocket, and walked away with my suitcase.

It was late afternoon when I arrived so the offices were closed. Upon inquiring, I learned that Wayne, Virgie and their one year old son were living in a room in the men's dormitory. I went to their room and announced my unexpected arrival. Wayne observed the room directly across the hall from theirs was occupied by three high school boys, all juniors. Because the rooms each had four bunk beds, he suggested that I take the vacant bed for the night. I don't recall that I was ever officially assigned to that room, but it became my residence address for the remainder of the year.

Registration for classes was no more structured than getting my dormitory room assignment. When I had completed my sophomore year of high school in Houston, I was only seven credits short of graduation. I registered as a junior and signed up for four courses. That left three to be taken the next year to graduate. I calculated that the four high school courses would occupy my time until noon. Inasmuch as I had traveled so far to enter a Bible Training School, my priority was to include some Bible courses in addition to the basic four high school subjects.

I asked a few questions and received some interesting information. By utilizing the official class registration forms I found on a table in the Registrar's office, I was able to enroll in additional classes. I learned that Bible School subjects and college subjects met on Monday, Wednesday and Friday or on Tuesday and Thursday. To fill my afternoon, I managed to select three Monday-Wednesday-Friday courses and three Tuesday-Thursday courses. As I entered the various classrooms, I gave the registration slip to the instructor, told him/her I had enrolled late and went to a seat.

When report cards were issued, it became apparent that I had a full four credit high school load plus fifteen hours of studies that would generate credit toward graduation either from college or the ministerial training course.

A question was raised and I was called in to explain how I had managed to register for so many classes. I simply recited how I had arrived late and was given very little assistance the day I registered. This was the result. When the dean determined that I intended no violation, he agreed that I could maintain this heavy schedule as long as I did acceptable work and received good grades.

BTS was a small school with fewer than 400 students and as I learned later, operated very conservatively on an extremely limited budget. All students were expected to settle their accounts in advance at the beginning of each semester, or make acceptable arrangements to submit payments monthly. In light of these restrictive budgetary guidelines, it must have been more than a strange coincidence that I was not asked to make any payment when I registered, and neither was I billed monthly for any charges. That might be explained as the expected consequence of the manner in which I registered for that first year, although I made no effort to avoid making payment. The subject just never came up. This had to be a confirmation that God did direct me to go to BTS when I had not the slightest inclination to become involved in Christian ministry as a life work. At the end of the year, my account showed no payment made.

It was my thinking that I would return to Houston, locate a job and within a few months settle the account. Things did not turn out exactly like that, as we will notice shortly. With an unexpected detour, I did return to Houston but there was not sufficient time to earn enough money to settle the account completely. As it happened, I did not return to BTS until two years later.

CHAPTER SEVEN

FROM RAGS TO RICHES

The seventeenth chapter of I Kings reports the amazing account of Elijah, a prophet in self-imposed exile. His residence was a water-front property in a resort named Cherith. The land owner had provided Elijah a lease for a number of months without rental charges. The leased property was more of a picturesque campsite than a condominium. That was in an era prior to the gross disrespect for environmental concerns, so the prophet had access to an uncontaminated water supply that the property owner provided for his use without a fee.

Possibly the most intriguing condition of Elijah's respite at the resort was the meal catering service. This was not just a week-end luxury. Twice every day freshly prepared food was delivered to the prophet. Admittedly, the method used to bring in the food was unique. Every morning and every evening, a large bird would appear with a sandwich clutched tightly in his talons. When he neared the clear, inviting waters of Cherith, he descended to the bank of the brook to drink. Following the pattern of action originally designed by his creator, the bird spread open his talons preparatory to lighting on the ground. The unavoidable result of releasing his tight grip on the food in his talons was that he deposited it gently on the ground. With profound gratitude to God and the raven, Elijah picked up his meal and dined.

It seems the use of carrier pigeons had not yet come into vogue at the time, so the owner of the resort dispatched a raven for this delivery service. It may be only unfounded conjecture on my part, but I have a secret suspicion that the raven had located the palace of the king, where every morning the room service catering crew prepared food in the kitchen for formal distribution to members of Israel's royal household. There may be those who question such fantasy, but consider that there was a drought in the land which led to a scarcity of food. With the prevalence of famine conditions, it is highly probable that the source of food found by the raven certainly was the royal residence.

Typically, in that period in history, homes in the Orient had a kitchen detached from the main house. I trust you were watching carefully as a young man emerged from the kitchen with a large serving tray balanced high above his head. Meticulously arranged on the ornate tray was a generous assortment of aromatic sandwiches, each one individually prepared of freshly baked bread, a generous portion of the finest cut of meat, and garnished with condiments appropriate to tease a king's palate. As the server walked from the kitchen to the royal dining hall, it went undetected that a bird swooped down and took a single sandwich from the extravagant supply. If my speculation is correct, King Ahab was unknowingly delivering breakfast in bed to Elijah every morning.

If you will allow my speculation to continue, I might suggest that a raven was selected for this dispatch instead of a carrier pigeon because, a raven would naturally select a much larger portion of food than would a pigeon, and this food was being catered for a rugged outdoors man with a hearty appetite.

When the bird descended for water (and unwittingly dropped its food), it is totally reasonable to conclude that the bird returned to the precise place where it had found the sumptuous supply earlier in the day. Can you see the raven circling over the palace grounds as soon as there was any indication of activity in the kitchen toward preparing the king's evening meal? When the first delivery of food to the royal dining hall exited the detached kitchen, the hungry raven was waiting. Swooping down swiftly, he selected a sandwich sufficient for his **raven**ous appetite and soared away satisfied to locate fresh water to complement his feast.

You're right. The raven made a repeat performance, by dropping its food when it lighted on the bank of the brook for a drink. Because the meal schedule in the palace had to be exact, Elijah knew precisely what time to expect his afternoon meal to be delivered to his hide-away resort residence.

If it has not yet dawned on you, that was a miracle!

God has never performed a miracle to display the sensational. His miracles have always been a supernatural intervention to meet a specific need that a believer could not manage even with his best resources.

Never has a bird brought me lunch, but my life has been interspersed with numerous miraculous events of a different sort. My first registration at BTS seems to me at least to border on the miraculous. To be allowed to complete the entire year of studies, as well as have my accommodation and food provided, without the advance payment of the first dollar was an undeniable miracle. Similarly, that I could later find work and pay the entire cost of a year's schooling within only a few months was amazing, if not miraculous.

With the heavy academic load I carried, there was little free time. The homework assignments for ten subjects kept me busy for a few hours every evening, and when the day concluded, it found me at the desk writing a letter to Letha. Except for my longing to see her, I experienced no loneliness, even though this was my first time ever to be away from home.

From the time I took my first job at age twelve, I always had some money. As mentioned earlier, when my first entrepreneurial exercise flourished, I had considerably more than I needed, so I gave most of my money to Mom to help maintain solvency in the family budget. One day I found a fascinating billfold. It was made of clear plastic. It displayed an imitation $100 bill, clearly visible. I liked it and I bought it. I went to a local bank and exchanged some smaller currency for a $100 bill and a $50 bill.

By folding the bills I could have a $50 bill showing on one side and a $100 bill showing on the other side. That was a part of my adolescent fun. Those days were gone, and not very many days after I arrived at BTS my funds were totally depleted.

I had no way of earning any money as I had more than a full load of studies. I did have one source for a few dollars each month to buy miscellaneous items such as tooth paste, razor blades, deodorant, etc. The $15.00 monthly income from the installment sale of my car would be very helpful for these things. The only problem is that none of the payments was ever sent to me. Very likely, Mom could have sent me some money occasionally for these basic things, but I was far too proud to ask for anything. She wrote about once a week, and sometimes enclosed two or three dollars, which helped.

I did swallow my pride and wrote to Mom early in December and mentioned that Christmas vacation was scheduled for the end of the third week in December and I would like to come home for the holidays, but did not have funds for the bus ticket. She sent me the money.

I was very happy to be home for a few days, and still happier to see Letha who had returned from Southwestern Bible Institute about the same time. It goes without saying that I was more interested in our being together than she was, but we did have a very pleasant Christmas vacation and spent many happy hours together. A popular song titled "Paper Doll" had only recently been released by Perry Como that attracted my attention. The lyrics included the words, "I'm gonna buy a paper doll that I can call my own: A doll that other fellows cannot steal." When I opened Letha's Christmas gift to me, I was exceptionally pleased that she had given me a large color portrait of herself. Fifty years ago, portraits were usually black and white only, so this was very special. For the remainder of the school year it hung over my desk in the dormitory.

When the Christmas vacation ended – all too soon – it was time to tell family and Letha good-bye and return to Tennessee. Letha was scheduled to return to Waxahachie, Texas the same day I was to leave. When she arrived at the bus station about five o'clock in the afternoon, I was waiting for her. When her trip was called for departure, I walked to the bus with her. When she boarded, I boarded also. She thought I was going to see her to a seat. She was more than a little surprised when I handed the driver my ticket. Rather than going directly back to Tennessee, I decided I would much prefer to go by way of Waxahachie.

Mom had given me a sufficient amount of money for my ticket to Sevierville, and a little extra for food on the way. When I bought two tickets, the cost increased a little, and also the detour added a few extra miles, which meant I had enough cash for both tickets, but almost nothing left for food for two days. I did get snacks for Letha and myself at one rest stop on the way to Waxahachie. That used up my little reserve, so I had to wait until I arrived in Sevierville for my next meal, but it was well worth it.

Riding the bus from Dallas to Knoxville, I sat beside the same man for the entire trip. After about the third rest stop, when I did not get any meal, he boarded the bus and handed me a snack. He had apparently noticed that I had not eaten all day. Believe me, those peanut butter crackers and Pepsi Cola constituted a gourmet feast. Arrival in Knoxville was early morning and the entire area was under a blanket of snow. The weather was cold. I was exhausted. I did not have even a nickel which then would have secured a cup of hot coffee.

Being unfamiliar with the streets of Knoxville, I inquired as to how to get the correct highway to go to Sevierville. After walking more than a mile, I saw a welcomed highway marker which indicated I had located the proper highway. I put up my thumb in an effort to hitch a ride, but met with almost no response. As a result, I walked well over half of that last 30 mile segment of my trip and arrived at the school well past noon. Reflections on the 250 mile bus ride with Letha helped make those miles I walked on a frozen Tennessee highway seem considerably shorter than they were.

Bible Training School was a meaningful experience. It was constant Bible study, prayer before every class session, committed Christian instructors, and a student body that was more an association of believers than a fraternal group. The effects of such an environment had to be spiritually stimulating. For me personally, that first year at BTS helped me emerge from the cocoon where I had spent most of my childhood and adolescent years. However, it wasn't Heaven.

Because we existed in an isolated environment, there was a tendency to spiritualize everything. This was an institution where young people were in preparation for clerical service. To some extent, it was the norm to be a ministerial student, and it was expected that upon leaving BTS the appropriate thing would be to find a position somewhere in Christian ministry. This was as it should have been, but some well-meaning students were undoubtedly caught up in an emotional atmosphere which caused them to want to get involved in a life profession for which they were neither suited nor called. More times than a few, I have concluded that I may be one of these persons. Let me explain:

Toward the end of the school year a popular subject of conversation was the church-related activities anticipated during the summer months, whether it may be conducting Vacation Bible Schools for children, serving as an apprentice on a pastoral staff, or possibly preaching revival meetings as an evangelist. I didn't enter into any of those discussions because I had no plans, I did not know anyone who might be able to help me plan church-related activities, and I hardly considered myself in any way prepared or ready for such responsibilities. In addition to all of these reasons, I felt I should return home to find employment where I could earn enough money to pay for my past year's schooling and return again in the fall.

It was less than realistic of me to think that in three months, I could earn enough to pay all of my obligation for the school year just concluded and also accumulate enough to pay for the coming year. Actually, I had not even considered my 'immediate' problem. The harsh fact was that the end of the school year was rapidly approaching and I did not even have the few dollars to purchase a bus ticket to return home. I could have followed the course taken by most of the young students — simply write home and ask for the money necessary to return, but I still had much more pride than common sense. I reasoned that my parents knew I would need expense money to return to Houston and if they were not going to offer it, I certainly was not ready to put my hand out for help. The only logical solution seemed to be to walk out to the highway and hitch-hike home.

The fateful day came. Seniors had graduated and were celebrating their achievements. Others were selecting the choice dormitory rooms and laying claim to them for the coming semester scheduled to start in September. Everyone else was occupied with goodbyes to friends. The campus was rapidly beginning to look deserted. I still had no definite plan even for today or tomorrow.

Standing in front of the dormitory doing absolutely nothing and with my mind idling slowly, I was approached by Reverend Howard Statum, a pastor I had known from Texas, who inquired about my plans for the summer, to which I responded honestly, "I am not sure." Immediately, he invited me to return to Texas with him. "You can conduct a revival in my church and then in other churches on my district," he suggested. Because his was the best offer up to that time, I accepted.

It could be fair to presume that a goodly number of young people left the campus that day planning to preach during the summer who were neither called nor prepared to preach. With a tinge of embarrassment I acknowledge being in that group, even though in my case it was involuntarily. Without question, I believe the Lord spoke to me in a vision on that Sunday evening you read about in the opening chapter of this book. Looking back more than fifty years later, I am also completely convinced that we humans sometimes add to, or take from, God's perfect plan. I made the perfectly logical error of equating God's call to mission service with being "called to preach."

I was licensed as a minister at age seventeen. Since that time, I completed my theological schooling. I have preached in youth camps. I have been billed as an evangelist in numerous cities. I have pastored five churches, I served as a foreign missionary for fourteen years. I have conducted Bible conferences in more than a dozen states and some foreign countries. However, searching the recesses of my memory, I have no recollection that I ever experienced a definite call to be a preacher. Further — I do not consider myself to be a preacher. In spite of repeated attempts, as enumerated above, I don't believe I was intended to be a preacher. I do have an inclination toward teaching, and have given attention through study and practice to improving that propensity. If I have any gift or any calling from Heaven, I am a teacher.

It is a sad commentary that some of us spend a lifetime doing things other than that in which we could excel. The day my pastor friend invited me to return to Texas with him to preach revivals to the churches on his district, it seemed right so I made an unwise move in that direction.

An interesting side note: After I had agreed to go with him, Pastor Statum, who also was a masterful salesman, informed me he had bought two cars and would like me to drive one to Texas for him. Another student had also been similarly enlisted to drive the other car. Reluctantly, and somewhat fearfully, I agreed to drive one of the cars. My driving experience prior to going to BTS had been only a few months after I had reached age sixteen. During the immediate past nine months, I had not driven at all, but I had agreed, so I was put behind the steering wheel of a nearly-new Pontiac and instructed to follow the pastor and the other student. Driving at high speed in the last car in this caravan, I reasoned, "That preacher is not too smart to let me drive this expensive car with my limited experience."

Reverend Statum had family in Birmingham, so he made that city his planned destination the first day. We had traveled quite a distance and reached the north side of Birmingham well after sundown. Traffic moved at typical big city pace, and bright lights glared in my eyes from the oncoming traffic. Not being an experienced driver, and also dividing my attention between driving my car, watching the out-of-control traffic all around me, and keeping the car ahead of me in view so as not to get lost in a strange city, I arrived at our destination completely frightened and exhausted. The pastor possibly sensed my anxiety that night, because the following morning he announced to me he had sold his brother the car I was driving and I could ride the remainder of the trip to west Texas with him. Without question, that was one of the wisest decisions he ever made.

For the remainder of the trip I rode silently with Pastor Statum. He seemed to be in a pensive mood as he apparently focused his attention on driving. Taking advantage of the quiet environment thus created, my attention moved forward a few days when I would be expected to conduct a revival as an evangelist "fresh from Bible School." I prayed for direction and searched my paralyzed memory for something as subject matter for those sermons the people in Borger, Texas would be expecting from me. Whether Pastor Statum was even vaguely conscious of my awful fright and anxiety, I have no idea. The totality of my "preaching" experience until that time had been one "sermon" I had given to the BTS Homiletics class as an assignment, and one "sermon" I had given when invited by my pastor in Houston during the Christmas vacation a number of months earlier. Needless to say, this was far from adequate experience and I was understandably nervous as I pondered what was just ahead.

We arrived in Borger late Friday. All day Saturday I envisioned making a fool of myself the next day trying to pose as an evangelist, which I definitely was not. The pastor said nothing to me about plans for the next day, but because he had invited me to his church to conduct a revival, and because I understood that conducting a revival meant the evangelist was to preach, and because I was there, and because the following day was Sunday, I made the proper conclusion that I was expected to be prepared to preach.

I wasn't!

Sunday morning arrived. With no word from the pastor about the church service, I left the parsonage early and went next door to the church to pray in anticipation of my assignment, as yet still undefined. Prior to the start of the worship hour, the pastor invited me to join him on the platform. With my big Bible in my hand, and trepidation in my mind, I followed obediently.

While the worshippers prayed and sang hymns preliminary to the morning sermon, every minute had 120 seconds, except the last five minutes, each of which had 180 seconds. The time to preach was now imminent, and I waited for the fateful moment like a convict contemplates his execution. Pastor Statum went to the pulpit and mentioned to his congregation that a special visitor was seated on the platform. He invited me to join him at the pulpit to be introduced. Somehow my uncooperative nervous knees stopped shaking long enough to allow me to walk the distance of about ten feet from my chair to the pulpit. I was introduced as a young student from Bible Training School who would be speaking to the youth group on Friday evening.

Reprieved and what a relief! When I returned to my seat still clutching my big study Bible, I noticed the leather cover was wet. I could not see where all of the moisture came from, but the palms of my hands were wet too. If the anticipation of preaching had affected me like that, what should I expect when actually called on to perform? On Friday night I was to find out.

I went to the youth service prepared to preach as had been announced. I was more than a little disappointed to see a very small group of teenagers who had gathered. To add to my dilemma, they seemed much more inclined toward socializing and having fun than participating in worship. How could I be expected to preach in an atmosphere like that? The flip side is that because the adults were not in attendance at the Friday evening service, I was not subjected to total humiliation before the entire church.

It amazed me that I could have spent so many hours in preparing a sermon that I could preach in about 12 minutes. I was given a grade on my assignment as soon as I finished my brief sermon. I was disappointed, although not at all surprised when the pastor announced immediately after my valiant effort that I would be preaching in youth services at other churches on the district in the next few weeks. Quite obviously my feeble attempt at preaching had given him reason to reconsider having a revival in his church with me for the evangelist.

I walked disconsolately out of the church that evening chagrined and humiliated, but I could not argue with the pastor's prudent decision not to subject his entire congregation to a repeat of what I had done that evening. Although he had met me at BTS and invited me to accompany him to Borger where I would conduct a revival in his church, strangely that subject was never discussed again.

My inclination was to go home the following day, but I was six hundred miles from home and did not have two nickels to rub together in my pocket. That left only one alternative. Find a job!

Early the next morning, I walked out of the parsonage. Somehow I seemed not to have an appetite... Or was it that I did not want to be seen. I started walking with no certain destination in mind. One block from the parsonage was a gasoline station. Only because it was the first place of business on my way, I stopped and asked for a job. Maybe because the manager thought of me as energetic to be looking for work so early in the morning, he hired me and said I could start to work immediately. My work was pumping gasoline for the customers who entered our facility. Possibly only my older readers will recall, but in 1944 when a customer bought gasoline, even if it was only five gallons @ $.15 per gallon — we checked the engine oil, topped up the water in the radiator, checked the battery, inflated any tires that appeared to be low and washed the windshield.

Actually, servicing the cars was my secondary responsibility. Most of my time and all of my energy was assigned to tire repairs. At any time, there would be from six to ten huge truck tires waiting for repair. At five feet seven inches and 130 pounds, I was hardly the man needed to remove those monstrous tires from the steel rims for repair. Most of the tires were larger than I, and that was before the era of pneumatic tools, so it was not at all unusual that I would struggle for an hour or more to remove one tire. Removing the tire and fixing the puncture in the inner tube proved to be the easier part. The real difficulty was re-mounting the tires because this large commercial type tire had so much steel near the rim so they could withstand the heavy wear they were designed to take.

Yesterday I had been an evangelist. Today I am a service station attendant. A year ago, I had owned my own business and had income up to $20 a day. Now I was doing much heavier work for $20 a week. Incidentally, there were six 10 hour days in a week then.

The school term had ended the last week in May. Most of the month of June, this young 'evangelist' spent repairing truck tires. Very soon I tired of tires. The Church of God had its annual state convention and camp meeting in Weatherford, Texas the last week in June and I wanted to attend as I had in previous years when I accompanied my parents to this annual spiritual retreat.

Even though I had failed miserably as an evangelist, the pastor made me welcome to remain in the parsonage and my meals were furnished with no mention ever made about cost. Most of my $20 weekly income was put back for my expense to go to the camp meeting. First I took the tithe out of my pay, plus a modest offering each time an offering was taken in church services. On an average day, I allowed myself a soft drink mid-morning and another about mid-afternoon. Coca Colas then cost a nickel, so my mad money was about $1.00 a week. The remainder, I carefully saved.

A few days before the State Camp Meeting was scheduled to start, the pastor told me I could ride to Weatherford, Texas with him, and of course I would not be expected to make any payment for the ride. That was better than bus fare—and more comfortable. Next he invited me to accompany him to go buy a new suit for the occasion. I did not own a suit. When I worked in Houston, I spent quite a bit of my income for clothes, but they were sporty and casual styles, and after a year at BTS my wardrobe had diminished drastically.

At the men's store, Pastor Statum told the clerk he would like to see a nice grey suit. When he made a selection and had been properly fitted, he asked to be shown a brown suit. After he had selected two suits, the sales clerk told him of some suits that were being offered at a good discount, which resulted in the pastor's buying one more. Next he went to the shoe department and selected some black shoes. Although I believe I was able to conceal my feelings well, when he requested to see some brown shoes, I was seething inside. I did not own a suit, and I was required to accompany this preacher and watch him buy three suits to add to the generous wardrobe hanging in his closet. I had one pair of patent leather shoes (leather on the top and pattin' the ground on the bottom), and even though this pastor had some very nice shoes, he felt he needed another two pairs.

Fortunately, I did not express my feelings about the apparent inequity I had been observing. When the pastor completed his shopping, he said to the clerk, "Find a nice pair of shoes for my friend." I was overjoyed that I would have shoes to attend the convention. When the shiny new shoes had been put on the counter to be wrapped, Pastor Statum turned to the clerk again and said, "I believe this young preacher could use a nice suit." Overwhelmed, I had difficulty controlling the moisture that kept demanding release from my tear ducts. Undoubtedly, that suit was the best I have ever owned. Let me tell you why.

Two days later, we were traveling toward Weatherford, Texas. Upon arrival, Brother Statum inquired as to where I planned to stay for the week. True to form, I had no plans. (Only those who have the necessary funds can make plans.) Having a number of acquaintances in that town, he drove to the home of some friends and told them he had a young preacher with him who needed a room for a week. He waited while I put my few belongings in the room and then drove over to a small improvised restaurant on the camp site where he talked briefly with the manager. I was offered a job to work there between the convention services, when the delegates would want to get a quick snack. My pay would be $10 for the week and my meals would be without cost. I was learning that God looks out for the innocent and the ignorant. Reasoning that the $10 would be adequate to pay for the room for a week, I accepted the offer with gratitude.

If I could have had my preference, I would have chosen not to work those hours when the convention was not in session. There was something else I would rather be doing, but my economic circumstances dictated the wiser decision.

Fully six months had elapsed since I had ridden a bus seated beside Letha from Houston to Waxahachie. To say I was eager to see her at that meeting is an exaggerated understatement. I knew she planned to attend this meeting. She arrived with her parents the same day, but I did not see her until after the opening service, which I felt that night was much too lengthy. Even though I had tried to court Letha's affection for a year and six months, she remained aloof and feelingless toward me. That evening I had worn my new blue suit. She told me later that it was absolutely the best color for me because it brought out the deep blue color of my eyes. Later in the week, we had some time alone and I was shocked at how warm and pleasant she acted. She told me she did not understand what had happened, but didn't want me to leave her. She climaxed the unexpected conversation with, "I believe I have fallen in love with you." That didn't start an argument from me!!!

Later, when I wore that suit, Letha would often comment favorably about how well it fit me and especially that the color was perfect for me. More than once she reminded us both of the fact I was wearing that blue suit when her heart told her she loved me.

Perhaps it is coincidental, but isn't it interesting that I saw Letha in my dream before we met and she was wearing that fabulously attractive royal blue dress. Eighteen months later, a kind preacher friend had given me a new blue suit to attend a church convention. What he did not plan, neither did he know, was that he provided the suit I would be wearing when Letha would tell me she had an interest in sharing my dreams for the remainder of our lives.

That was a terrific night for me. I had the money of a pauper, but the wealth of a philanthropist. In a moment of time I moved from frustration to total bliss. As a young boy I had first person knowledge of poverty. Now, in a single day my life was changed from rags to riches. I had become wealthy!

No, I have never been served gourmet food by a raven, but many years ago I met the Master whose specialty is miracles. He has performed a series of miracles in my life. One of the most significant and one that I appreciated most was sent to me directly from heaven on that June evening in Weatherford, Texas.

To climax a week of wonders, Letha's ultra-conservative dad invited me to return with them to Houston after the convention concluded. The ride in the back seat of that seven year old Plymouth was far superior to the luxury of a Town Car stretch limousine.

Just before exiting the residence where I had spent the week to join Letha and her family for the return trip, I inquired of the lady of the house as to my bill. She said, "The man who occupied the bedroom next to yours brought me money for his room two hours ago and he said he wanted to pay for your room as well, so your account is settled."

Miracles??

CHAPTER EIGHT

THE BANANA CREW

After the unexpected exciting announcement from Letha in the afternoon, we returned to the church campgrounds for the evening service. Somehow to get from the car to a seat in the open-air tabernacle took much longer than it ever had before. Even though I was customarily keenly interested in the message from the preacher, I had no recollection, even the next day, of the contents of the sermon.

A little later than usual, I returned to my rented room that evening. The first thing I did was to locate a mirror so I could see what had happened to me. I was certain I must have grown at least an inch or two taller, but carefully scrutinizing the short image reflected in the mirror, I could not detect any physical difference.

The events that transpired during that week in Weatherford became the springboard for everything that would happen the rest of my life. Letha had told me she loved me, so in my thinking, from that day onward my life would include her and what she did would involve me. Although I was not aware of the psychological implications of the concept then, my nature and my temperament called out for companionship, and I had finally found the favor of the one I wanted for a companion. The only thing left was to set the date.

I wanted to spend a part of every day with Letha. There were some days we could not manage time together, but I made sure we had a higher than average score in that regard. What happened during that all important week transpired more than a half century ago but even now a day is incomplete if we do not share it. When I have to be away, or if Letha goes away for an evening and returns home late, I get restless. It seems a part of me is missing.

Something else of significance occurred the last day of the camp meeting in Texas. Traditionally, the concluding service of this annual event was a missions service with the emphasis on evangelism especially directed toward foreign countries. When the speaker finished his impassioned appeal, he invited us to join him in giving a sacrificial offering to this deserving cause. He mentioned a cash offering, and also suggested a pledge if anyone desired to give, but did not have the ready cash. If I had given cash that day, of necessity it would have been coins.

Since the "Vision" experience at BTS, I had continually maintained an exceptional interest in missions, so when it was suggested that a pledge could be offered in lieu of cash, I found a method of doing what I wanted to do, but was unable. I made a pledge of $25.00. That seems like such a small amount. In 1944, $25.00 seemed to me as impossible to find as $5,000 would be today. I gave more than I could afford and I felt very pleased that I had done so. Somehow that added meaning to giving. That was the start of a trend I have continued to follow.

I do not give just because an appeal is made.

I do not give simply because a cause has popularity.

I do not give because others are giving.

I do not give in response to pressure.

It is not easily verbalized, but when a need is presented that I "feel" needs my support, I give. My giving is predicated to a certain extent on a sense of responsibility. I try to be responsive to the urgency of the matter brought to my attention. But at the core of everything, I give for the sheer pleasure of helping a person or a cause that is worthy.

Yes, I am fully aware that we live in the ebbing years of the materialistic, pragmatic twentieth century, with a populace apparently driven by the motto, "get all you can and can all you get." I also understand that many are frustrated living in an economy in which income is limited and the cost of living seems to spiral mercilessly upward. My response to that sort of situation is that giving is never easy and further it is in direct conflict with our basic selfish nature.

It is not a false conclusion to believe that the problems of the world can all be solved and resolved by giving. Every problem that can be imagined stems from selfishness and greed. The antithesis of those reprehensible tendencies is love. Greed takes away, but love gives. It is possible to give without loving, but it is not possible to love without giving. Try it. It is exciting!

When Letha and I married, one of the first serious discussions we had concerned money. Not the acquiring of it, or budgeting its disbursement, not even a plan for accumulating it. Our conversation concerned giving it away! We agreed to make decisions together about giving, but if she should decide to make a donation or gift without discussing it with me first, I would respect her decision. Similarly, if I were to make a unilateral decision about giving she would not disagree. For fifty-two years that plan has been workable for us. (But, excuse me, I have jumped ahead of the sequence again.)

Nearly six weeks had elapsed since departure from BTS and not the first dollar had been sent back in payment of a delinquent bill for a full year of school tuition and living accommodations. Because of the missions pledge at the camp meeting, my financial obligations had increased and I had no source of income. The only obvious course was to locate employment. Because of the long duration of World War II, almost all industry had been converted to military-related production. I went to the shipyard where I had sold ice cream at the entrance a year earlier. This time, I went inside and was employed at full journeyman's wages even though I had little experience in my job classification and I was only seventeen years old.

The only thing available to me was night shift work. Work started at 5:30 p.m. and continued until 4:00 a.m. with a thirty minute lunch break. The pay was good which was important to me as my primary concern was to clear the slate of debt.

The facility where I found employment launched a ship every eight days. When construction was complete, a corps of dignitaries would mount an improvised platform built on a portable scaffold for the event that was broadcast throughout the entire work area. All employees were invited to move toward the area of the ship to be launched for a half hour of celebration of the accomplishment. As work progressed to release the ship from its construction berth, speeches were delivered and big bands played military and patriotic music preliminary to the christening. At the precise instant the ship started to move down the inclined way into the Houston ship channel, a bottle of champagne was broken on the ship's bow and another ship was sent to strengthen the United States Navy. Then it was all hands back to work for another eight days until a repeat of the christening ceremony.

What was never apparent to the vast throng that gathered to celebrate the launching of another U. S. Navy vessel was what transpired the two nights preceding the celebration. During construction, the ship rested on an immense number of sand jacks, which kept it suspended about eight inches above a launching track. The track was similar to a railroad track, but the distance between the rails was much greater. I was assigned to work in the crew that readied the ship for the launch. We were known as the banana crew. Working under the ship in nearly waist-deep water, we laid bananas on the two rails for the distance of about 1,000 feet. Then one at a time we released the hundreds of sand jacks which gradually lowered the ship directly onto the banana covered tracks where it rested until the moment of christening.

As thousands of tons of steel slid down the tracks, any kind of oil or grease would have been subjected to more heat than was tolerable and the grease would have become more like glue. But bananas remained soft and slippery at any temperature, so the massive ship gracefully rode our banana slide into the water. It was a beautiful sight to watch, but behind the scene it was less glamorous. Even though we wore rubber waders to stay dry as we worked, the frigid temperature of the water at night against our rubber waders was far from comfortable.

Although the work was hard and conditions nearly unbearable in the icy winter waters under the ships, I had no complaint because each week brought me a pay check, a significant part of which was immediately mailed to BTS to liquidate the past-due debt for my schooling. It goes without saying, I did send the $25 missions pledge when I received my first pay check, and subsequently, every dollar I did not need for subsistence went directly to Tennessee.

As the varied events of my life have found their way into this chronicle, it has repeatedly become glaringly apparent that nothing significant happens unless behind the scenes the "banana crew" is silently working. To a certain extent, much of my life has been spent working in the banana crew, but the nearer I come to the terminal point of my life on earth, the more I have come to understand and appreciate the fact that I have had the distinct honor of laying bananas on the tracks of programs and ministries God has chosen to bless.

CHAPTER NINE

TEENAGE EVANGELIST

The ten-hour shifts at night seemed to get longer and the work more difficult as the winds whistled under the ships causing a mist of cold water to spray the banana crew. However, every week brought a sizable paycheck and I had the satisfaction of reducing my debt to the school so the inhospitable working conditions and the discomforts of the environment were easier to accept. By mid-December the final payment had been mailed to the accounting office of BTS and the financial pressure was off. That may explain why the waters were becoming unbearably cold as we worked at least two nights out of every eight in the water under the ship preparing to launch another liberty ship.

Sick with a fever from too much exposure in the cold water, I went to work early one afternoon so I would have a few minutes to stop in at the personnel office to give notice that I could not continue to work in those conditions. I was told that it was not possible to transfer out of the banana crew as I had been employed less than six months and did not qualify for the change. I responded that maybe I should quit my job. I was not prepared for the reply to that statement. I was told that all defense work was considered essential to the war effort and employees in high priority defense projects were not allowed to make a change. The jobs were frozen. (I thought that was a very appropriate description of my job. Where we worked, both the job and the workmen were frozen.) I was told that I could quit my job if I wanted, but I would not be released, which meant I would be ineligible for employment in any other defense related job for a period of one month. I hardly wanted to be unemployed as the Christmas season approached, so I went to my work area, pulled on my waders and went back down under the ship.

With my account settled for the prior year's schooling, my attention was drawn more specifically to the fact I should prepare myself to be a missionary. In our denomination, church related ministry was narrowly defined as preaching. A pastor preached every week in a fixed location. An evangelist moved from place to place and conducted revival services for a week or two and then moved to another location. A missionary was assigned to minister in a foreign country. In every case, the activity was the same. They were all preachers. Our church sponsored a winter district convention, which was scheduled for February of the following year. It was to convene in Port Arthur, Texas. I made plans to attend. The pastor of the Port Arthur Church had invited me to remain after the convention to conduct a revival for his local church. The invitation was appreciated and accepted, but not without intense anxiety.

More than half a year had passed since my humiliating fiasco as a young evangelist in Borger, Texas. In the intervening months, the pastor in our local church was very helpful, and I was anticipating a fresh start in Port Arthur. Just prior to going to the convention, the pastor called a meeting of the church council and instructed me to attend also. He suggested that the local church councilmen recommend me to the state overseer to be licensed as an evangelist. Amazingly, the overseer agreed and issued me credentials at age seventeen. The die was cast. I was to be a preacher.

Having failed miserably one time, I went to the Port Arthur Church after extensive preparation. I felt I was ready. What I had not considered was that the convention would feature sermons from the leading pastors in the district and the final message was delivered Sunday morning by the state overseer of Texas, a brilliant speaker. I was scheduled for Sunday evening immediately following those seasoned convention speakers. One thing was certain — if there should be anything worthwhile accomplished, I would not be inclined to claim credit. It would have to be recognized as providential intervention.

In the two weeks that followed, I spent many hours each day in preparation for the evening service. I prayed, I read my Bible, I borrowed the pastor's personal library and read. Then I prayed and read my Bible again and read more of the pastor's books. An abundance of suitable material had been stored in my mind to deliver a masterful sermon each evening, if only my brain did not sit down just as I stood up to preach. On the final night, the pastor invited all who had given their lives to Christ during the revival to come to the front of the church as a testimony of their commitment. Eighteen came forward. Since then, many times as I have attended church services in various churches in Texas, I have met one of the young men who came forward to testify that evening. He has often reminded me that he was born again during that revival. It is a genuine gratification for me that he has been a pastor in Texas most of his life.

My next revival was scheduled in Texla, Texas. The name of the community is the result of its location on the border of Texas and Louisiana, just a few miles from Beaumont. I was there for three weeks. The pastor there was a wonderful man, and he made my stay there very enjoyable. He was not formally educated, but had an innate wisdom which made him effective in working with people. My three weeks with Pastor Gus Byrne in Texla was equivalent to a semester of college in Practical Theology.

When I recall the revival in the Texla Church, one seeming negative is clearly etched in my memory. Many days, the pastor's wife did not prepare any meals for us. I still cannot understand why a church would allow its pastor to suffer like that wonderful couple did, but the fact remains they had no food in the parsonage and because I stayed in their home, I ate what they ate — or didn't eat. One day the good-humored pastor said to me, "Brother Heil, I have been preaching for more than thirty years, and I have never missed a meal. Of course, I have postponed quite a few." During my visit there, he postponed quite a few meals, and I helped him. In three weeks I lost fifteen pounds. The motivation for that fast was not at all spiritual. It was the unavoidable result of having no alternative.

Upon my return home, my weight loss was very evident. When a person weighs only 135 pounds at normal weight, the loss of more than 10% is very apparent. Just maybe, it was a good thing that I appeared so undernourished. Letha told me later she had been shocked to see me so thin and that it was of great concern to her. My reply was that I had no one to look out for me and the result was obvious. I told her I could not think of anyone I would rather have looking after me than she to be certain I would be cared for properly as I would continue to travel. Then I told her, in a much more romantic and affectionate way that I wanted her to marry me.

You won't believe her answer! She said, "I'll have to ask Mother." With that sort of reply, being the pragmatist that I am, I took her home immediately. I went with her into the house, without the customary delay on the front porch and waited silently and motionlessly as she tried to decide how to broach the subject. If Letha's answer to my proposal was highly irregular, her mother's reply to Letha's question was amusing. She simply stated, "I'll have to talk to your dad." To which Letha responded, "What do you think he will say?" Her mother said, "You know what he will say." Six weeks later, we exchanged vows at the altar.

It was not really all that simple and in fairness, I need to take you with me to the courthouse where I would apply for a marriage license. I would be 18 years old in May and Letha would be 18 two weeks later. Texas law required parental approval for marriage of anyone under age 18, so I cautiously invited my mother and Letha's mother to accompany me to the Harris County Court House to apply for the license. Looking very somber, they followed me into the clerk's office and I apprised the clerk of the purpose of my visit, telling her that the ladies with me were my mother and the mother of my bride-to-be. I think the clerk detected a little uncertainty about me, and I have to admit to being nervous. After all, this was the first time for me to apply for a marriage license.

(As I am writing this, I just looked at a photograph of myself taken about the time of the conversation recorded in the paragraph above and it is not difficult to understand why the clerk raised a question about granting me a marriage license.)

The clerk looked at my mother with the comment, "You just say the word and I won't issue this license." Mom replied, "I think he has his mind made up, so I am agreeable." She issued me the license and recorded it in her book.

Looking back, I have sometimes wondered if the reason that court clerk questioned whether I should be issued a marriage license may have been that she had an unhappy marriage. If it were possible to find her, it would be an interesting visit to take with me my bride of more than fifty years. With us would be my beautiful Janice with her handsome husband Terry and their two children, Terry II and Daniel. Also our successful son, Ron would accompany us with his devoted wife of 25 years and their two sons, Chris and Israel, and the pride of my life, their daughter, Heather. I would simply like to tell her that my mother did not make a mistake when she signed the application for my marriage license and I had just dropped in to present to her the irrefutable evidence.

Chapter Ten

Meet Mrs. Heil

Having just returned home from a three week meeting at a church where I had lost fifteen pounds as a direct result of the fact that there was little available to eat, it goes without saying I did not bring home any large sum of cash either. Circumstances could have been better. Actually, things did become much better!

I had proposed marriage. Letha had accepted. We agreed on a wedding date of April 15, which was barely six weeks away. I had no money, and we were both too young to realize that was a problem. Of course, not being aware there were problems, it is understandable we made no effort to find the solutions.

I did realize there would be some expense involved, so I worked for Pop the next six weeks and put together enough money to pay for a marriage license and buy a suit and shoes for the wedding. I saved back a few dollars for flowers to decorate the church and a small honorarium for the pastor who would officiate the ceremony. The day before the wedding my brothers assisted me in building a latticed wooden arch, which we intertwined with greenery and roses. The small church sanctuary was simply decorated and the ceremony was neither elaborate nor expensive.

No circumstance is so sacred, and no picture is so beautiful as when a young man stands at an altar of commitment watching a beautiful virgin girl clad in white lace approach him to vow her undying devotion and affection. His unequivocal vow to provide for her every need, material, emotional and spiritual, is given to her with equal sincerity and the vows are sealed. That is the record of what transpired for us. It was so simple and ungarnished, but no ornate ceremony or display of ostentation could have improved it.

When we left the church, I took home my beautiful bride, and I loved her not only for her beauty but even more for her purity. Without hesitation I add that I also went to the wedding altar to meet her as my first lover. Accepting the risk of seeming overly emotional or melodramatic, I can say emphatically, "It doesn't get any better than that." Old fashioned and prudish as it may seem, I can highly recommend this as the best basis for a lifelong happy marriage.

We married on Sunday afternoon and took off two days from work to get acquainted. Wednesday morning we both boarded the city bus and returned to work. There was no honeymoon trip. Having no money to fund even the simplest trip, we could not have imagined then that our life together would be a continuous honeymoon covering more than half a century, including some of the world's most exotic locations and extravagant accommodations.

After a brief time of adjusting to our new life together in Houston, we scheduled a number of revival meetings and began an itinerant ministry. In June we had a revival in Dallas, and from there traveled to Weatherford for the annual state camp meeting, the place rich with nostalgia from a year earlier. We attended that meeting as a musical evangelistic team — I with my Bible and Letha with her accordion. One evening we were scheduled to sing and were introduced by the State Director of Youth and Christian Education, who mentioned that immediately prior to coming to the camp meeting, we had concluded a two week revival in the Oak Cliff Church in Dallas. He was complimentary of our work and recommended that the pastors throughout Texas engage us to visit their churches. The Oak Cliff Church was the largest church in our denomination in Texas and we had been recommended by one of the highest ranking ministers in the state.

With my appointment book in my pocket, I readied myself for the barrage of requests that were certain to result. The book remained in my pocket and at the end of the week, we had no place to go.

On returning to Houston, Letha applied to be reinstated to her former position as a secretary in a children's institution. I faced a dilemma. Having been ordained as an evangelist, would it be proper for me to put on carpenter overalls and return to my former job? Possibly there was something else more in keeping with my new position. Searching the employment section of the Houston Chronicle, I found what seemed to be right — an advertisement for a Bible salesman. I applied for the position and was hired. Actually, anyone who applied could be hired. It was commission only, with no advances and no benefits, so the company was happy to hire as many as would accept those conditions. I believed the Bible, and I was learning to preach the Bible, but I did a poor job of selling it.

Three weeks into my sales career, I was approached by a sales manager from a competitor company, who told me that selling Bibles was a tough job because people who had an appreciation for the Bible already had one or more, and those who did not believe or live by its teachings were hardly prospective buyers. Having convinced me I was selling the wrong product, he offered me a job selling magazine subscriptions. Maybe because the cash outlay was much smaller, I had a little more success. However, when Pop approached me to inquire if I would return to work for him in construction, it did not take me long to decide that I was better suited to building than selling.

With two incomes we started to save toward returning to school, but September came too soon and our pitifully small nest-egg was woefully inadequate. As a result, we postponed returning to school and concentrated on working and saving our money. As it turned out, we did more working than saving.

Being a builder, Pop had trained all of his sons to become his clones. Letha's dad was also a builder. He had two sons but at the time I married Letha, both sons were quite young. So Dad Petty approached me and said, "Bud, your dad has five sons working with him and I don't have anyone. I would like you to consider working with me."

There was one slight problem: he was on a union job and my dad had an open shop. Even though I was only 18 years old, I had become fairly skilled as a carpenter, and pop paid me first class carpenter wages. The union scale was 7 1/2 cents an hour more, and Dad Petty reasoned I could use the additional money to pay the initiation fees to join the union and my net income would be virtually unchanged. I accepted and went to work on a union job where my father-in-law was foreman.

After a few weeks, Dad Petty's job slowed somewhat, so his employer transferred me to another job. It was not at all a pleasant job. We were assigned to put a new roof on a cotton warehouse. The size of the building was not measured in square feet, but in acres. I was the only carpenter on the job, assisted by about ten laborers. They rolled out long strips of asphalt roofing felt. I fastened the strips with roofing nails every four or five inches. The laborers mopped on hot pitch and rolled out another strip. Then I nailed it.

Monotonous?

This job was less than ideal for three reasons. Working with hot pitch on a black roof under a scorching Texas sun was unbearably uncomfortable. Secondly, the boredom of crawling on my knees, looking at a vast black surface with no change but those little half-inch shiny nail-heads mercilessly reflecting the bright rays of the scorching sun in my bleary eyes was becoming intolerable. Finally, I was just one person trying to keep pace with ten laborers. I started fresh in the morning, but within an hour, I was exhausted and stayed fatigued for the entire day.

On Friday of the first week the foreman arrived at the end of the day to pass out checks. When he called my name, I reached for my check, but he interrupted me, saying that he would need the number from my union card on his payroll record before I could be paid. I responded that I had left the card at home. He lectured me about the importance of keeping my card in my pocket at all times. After the severe reprimand, he gave me my check with a warning that there would be no check the next week unless I had the union card in my pocket.

I struggled through another week on the torturous hot roof. On Friday afternoon I had my union card ready. I also had something else ready! I had been silently practicing a little speech. I intended to tell the foreman that I could not keep up with ten laborers, and I would request that he add at least one more carpenter to the crew.

I never made that speech. When I handed the foreman my union card, he scrutinized it and told me he would have to get a new check for me as the rate of my pay had been calculated incorrectly. My union card indicated I was a first year apprentice, but the payroll records showed I was receiving journeyman's wages. The difference was $.75 per hour.

At the rate I had been offered when I accepted the job, my weekly pay should have been $55.00. If I were to be paid as a first year apprentice, my pay for the week would be $25.00. I reached out one hand to take the $55.00 check and with the other hand I offered the foreman my union card. I told him he could keep it because I would not be back Monday morning, and I certainly did not intend to look for another union job where I would be expected to do the work of two skilled carpenters but be paid at the rate of an apprentice.

Monday morning I was unemployed. I could not go to work with Dad Petty because I had just severed the tie with his company. I had left Pop about six weeks earlier to take this job and my pride hindered me from asking for my former position. I decided to look for a job. What happened must have been amusing, if not hilarious. Looking very much like a schoolboy, I went to a number of residential building sites and asked for a job — without success. I am sure some of the contractors smiled quietly when I told them I could do anything. They were simply not impressed.

I approached one job site just as the shingles for the roof were being unloaded. I found the builder and told him I would like to apply the shingles on his roof. He looked at me quizzically and asked, "Sonny, are you sure you can do it?" My ready reply was,

"If my work doesn't please you, you won't owe me." My youth-ful appearance had been a detriment, but he was apparently convinced by my ultra-positive attitude. I got the job!!!!

When the builder agreed to let me apply the roof, I repeated, "If my work is not satisfactory, you won't have to pay me." Then without pausing for a breath, I continued, "But if I do a good job, I want all of your work." I was in business.

It was not easy to find enough jobs to keep busy. Most builders would build about one house every sixty days, but I could put the roof on in two or three days. That meant I would have to get sub-contracts from a dozen or more builders. Always I met with the same response, "Sonny, have you had any experience?" Maybe my baby face was against me until I fell on an ingenious plan. I decided not to shave more than once a week, so I would appear to be at least the 18 years old that I was. I think that helped some, and because of a conscientious effort to do the best work possi-ble, I soon had more jobs than I could handle. Working fast and steady, I was able to develop an income approximately double what I had been earning for an hourly rate at top wages. It was a good lesson for me. I learned early that quality and diligence in any work will bring a better reward than could be expected by performing at the minimum acceptable level.

With an overabundance of jobs I could not keep up with the calls from the builders whose work I had secured. Pop's work had slowed a little, so I contacted my older brother, Wayne, and sug-gested that he and I work together so we could keep pace with the jobs as the builders would call. Wayne liked the idea, especially when he learned that my income as a subcontractor was approxi-mately double what he had been earning as a foreman. The part-nership we formed was not exactly sophisticated. I suggested we work together, he accepted and from that point forward we were a team. Wayne doubled his income and I solved my dilemma of having more work than I could manage alone. Wayne was a very good partner for me. He worked steady and fast. The quality of the work he did never required any correction, and no job was too difficult for him.

Strangely, Pop's work continued to decrease while Wayne and I had difficulty keeping current with our jobs. We invited Pop to join us as a partner. Shortly thereafter, my second brother, Tex, returned from the U.S. Navy where he had served during the final months of World War II, and we suggested that he join us. It was a unique situation. We had no boss and no employees. Just the four of us working on sub-contact jobs, which we expanded to roofing, siding, remodeling, and then some complete homebuilding.

Before my nineteenth birthday, I had started a business, taken in my father and two older brothers as equal partners, and we were all consistently earning more than double what we would have been paid for similar work on an employee basis. I had not started with any intention of developing a leadership role. Basically, it was my nature to enjoy a challenge. I loved the satisfaction of excelling. Then too, the remuneration for doing a better-than-average job was gratifying. Could it be that I just did not want to be perceived as being "too short" and winning made me stand a little taller?

Possibly the volume of detailed information in some of these earlier chapters has seemed redundant or unnecessary. The intention has been to provide a personality portrait and an awareness of the attitudes that have molded the activities of my life and the reactions both to successes and failures. It is hoped that having been exposed to this somewhat mundane information, the reader will properly comprehend what is related from this point forward, which actually is the real story that needs to be recorded.

CHAPTER ELEVEN

THE VISIONARY
BECOMES A MISSIONARY

During the years of World War II, many things were in short supply because of having been diverted to military use, and had to be rationed. Significantly impacting the general public was the scarcity of building materials this caused. For this reason, the building of new homes and the improvement of existing homes hardly occurred between 1939 and 1945.

The climate immediately following the end of World War II was conducive to the establishment of any new business in the home building or home maintenance fields and ours continued to flourish. We were never without work, and the income was such that we could save consistently toward school expenses.

Having been away for two years, we were eager to get back to missionary training, which was to be our life's work. In September, 1946, Letha and I both enrolled in the Bible division as first year students and were able to make full payment in advance for the first semester. I had not yet finished high school, so in addition to the full Bible course, I registered for two high school credits.

Having nearly depleted our resources to pay for the first semester of tuition, books, boarding, etc., I knew it would be necessary to have an income supplement. With my background in building, I applied at a cabinet shop near the school and was employed on a part-time basis. The pay rate was not attractive, but the owner was very flexible in allowing me to work at my convenience. Averaging about 20 hours a week, my earnings were sufficient for miscellaneous expenses and we saved a little for the next semester.

During the Christmas holidays, we visited our families in Texas. On our return to Sevierville, Tennessee, my employer explained that in the winter, building had slowed and he would not need my services at least for the coming few months. I looked everywhere for employment but I could not find any job on a part-time basis. Being a very skillful seamstress, Letha filled the gap by doing alterations for a number of the students. On occasions when the ladies used formal dresses for drama productions, musicals, etc., our income improved a little. Not being able to find any work, I volunteered to help Letha with the alterations.

A secret peek into our dormitory room on those occasions would have brought a smile to your face. As a college coed stood on a table, I measured the floor-length hem line. Next I would cut the seemingly endless fullskirt of satin, lace and net. Then Letha finished the job on her sewing machine. It was far from a "macho" job for me to work as an assistant to a seamstress. But the income was sufficient to provide us with a few of the bare necessities — most of the time.

During the summer of 1947, Bible Training School (BTS) moved from Sevierville, Tennessee to Cleveland, Tennessee. The name of the school was changed to Lee College, a memorial tribute to Reverend F. J. Lee, an influential church leader in the formative years of our denomination. Prior to leaving school in May, I had secured a job in the maintenance shop of Lee College for the coming year. By working long hours in the summer in Houston, I accumulated some funds which allowed me to enroll. And then with the steady income from my job in the maintenance department of the college, the economic outlook was considerably improved.

Because of moving the school about 100 miles from its former location, at the beginning of the new school term the school president found himself without a secretary. Letha was offered the position, and she decided that rather than enroll as a student, it was better to accept the job offer. This proved to be a wise move as we were exposed to a number of church leaders who would later impact plans for us to be missionaries.

Of particular interest were the frequent visits of Stewart Brinsfield to the office of the school president. When Reverend Brinsfield had business with Dr. Simmons, the college president, he made it a practice to walk into the reception office, right past the secretary and on to the president's private office. As often as he attempted these unceremonious visits, Letha stopped him. His explanation was, "I am Stewart Brinsfield, and Dr. Simmons is expecting me." With the typical candor of an uninhibited 20 year old, and not being aware of Stewart Brinsfield's position, she frankly told him it did not make any difference who he was, the policy of that office was that he was to be cleared at her desk and she would arrange for a meeting with Dr. Simmons.

What Letha was to learn later was that Stewart Brinsfield was the Executive Secretary of the World Missions Department of the Church of God. He was favorably impressed with the way Letha protected the privacy of Dr. Simmons' Office to the extent that when it became known Dr. Simmons would retire at the end of that school year, Stewart Brinsfield offered Letha a position as his private secretary in the World Missions Office. In that capacity, she became acquainted with many persons connected with missions as well as executive level administrators in the general church offices.

When the general missions board met for official business, Letha prepared their agenda and made the minutes of their deliberations. What an ideal way to make the acquaintance of the men who were in position to affect our future as missionaries. Of course, while Letha was busily involved in the high level activities of the church internationally, I was occupied with classroom studies, and in every other available hour, I dedicated my efforts and expertise to patching together the deteriorating school properties. The Lee College campus was new to us, but it was the former campus of another college that had developed new facilities.

Understandably, because the college that formerly occupied the campus was moving to new facilities, they did not give as much attention to maintaining the old campus as should have been the case. Consequently, I never ran short of work. Neither did I have any time to make new acquaintances or to socialize.

On May 23, 1948, I celebrated my twenty-first birthday. The next day, May 24, I received my PH D (public high school diploma, that is). In my three years at BTS and Lee College, I had completed my last two years of high school, one year of Bible institute, and 22 hours of college credit. In the fall of 1948 we returned to Houston where I took a daytime job in construction and night classes in the University of Houston. Traditionally, college is four years of systematic study following high school, but for some of us who dropped out of high school, married early or became involved in business, the pattern was graduating from high school as an adult, followed by night school and correspondence courses forever.

We resided in Houston two years dividing my time between a job and night school classes. Quite unintentionally, my activity as an employee gradually evolved until I found myself again operating my own business as a builder, this time buying land and building homes for sale. It seemed I had a natural bent for business, and frankly, I enjoyed the challenge and the rewards. It was during that two year period in Houston that our daughter, Janice, was born. She was the first of three children. (Our second daughter was born about sixteen months later. Her birth came after Letha had experienced a very difficult pregnancy, culminating in a somewhat premature delivery. We buried our little Jeanette in Beckley, West Virginia, Thanksgiving morning, 1951.)

As soon as we felt it was wise to travel with Janice, we made plans to return to evangelism. I had little inclination toward evangelizing, and I felt less interested in becoming a pastor, but as a means to getting an appointment as a missionary, we had long since become aware that I had to do so by being a preacher. I conferred with our local pastor for advice and assistance. He suggested the names of three state overseers and volunteered to introduce me to any of them. He mentioned Florida, Georgia, and West Virginia. Florida and Georgia seemed more attractive, but I decided to consider West Virginia. The contact from our pastor was made, and in January, 1951, we found ourselves in deep snow in Clarksburg, West Virginia.

After only a few revival meetings, the state overseer, Reverend J. H. Hughes, called me to his office and suggested that I consider a pastorate in a small town in the northeastern part of the state. At first I declined, but he was insistent that we should make this change and he expressed confidence we could do well there. We agreed to follow his recommendation and I became the "Parson" of Parsons, West Virginia. It was only after we completed that assignment and had moved to our next position, Reverend Hughes acknowledged to me that of the 150 churches in the state, Parsons had been his number one problem. Not being aware there was a problem, we buried ourselves in our work and enjoyed it. We found the people of West Virginia to be unpretentious and totally transparent. Their warm, cordial ways attracted our attention and won our affection immediately. We settled in and started to build up the church, which had been without a pastor for a number of months.

Less than a year after we accepted the Parsons church, Reverend Hughes, the State Overseer, telephoned to advise that he would like to make an official visit to our church. We were pleased for the privilege of having our state leader speak to our congregation. We advertised and promoted the meeting well, and Reverend Hughes preached that night to a capacity crowd. (I thought I only did what I should have done, but Brother Hughes was very complimentary of our efforts and implied that he was completely surprised to see such a large attendance.)

The next day Reverend Hughes told me he had a dual purpose in visiting us. In addition to an official visit to the church, he wanted us to consider a move. The church he offered was considerably larger and stronger than the Parsons church, so he said it would be a promotion. Additionally, his private secretary had submitted a resignation and because the church he offered us was only about ten miles from the state office, he also suggested that Letha accept the position of state secretary-treasurer for the state of West Virginia as well as serve as Reverend Hughes' personal secretary. I told him Letha was expecting our second child and that perhaps she would not be able to function adequately in that position in the months just ahead, but I mentioned that because I could type at an acceptable speed and had some experience in bookkeeping, there was a possibility I could assist her in some of the duties of that position during the time she would be somewhat restricted. Reverend Hughes felt that arrangement would be acceptable and instructed us to prepare to move by the end of that month. I would be assigned as the pastor at Coal City, West Virginia and Letha would become the Church of God State Secretary-Treasurer. As it turned out, as a consequence of the move, Letha experienced some physical difficulties and never did assume the duties of her new job. The first week after the move, I went to the state office as a substitute. Reverend Hughes observed my work for a few days and then informed me that my qualifications seemed adequate and if Letha should be unable to take the job, I could continue in the state office in addition to pastoring the church at Coal City.

In his capacity as the administrator of the church in West Virginia, Overseer Hughes traveled extensively throughout the state. On occasions when he visited churches not too far distant from the state office, he invited me to accompany him. This was not a part of my assignment, but it was a pleasant experience for me as I had exposure to some of the inner workings of the church. Reverend Hughes was an exceptionally gifted preacher and I was inspired by his sermons. As an added fringe benefit, he would allow me to be his driver. It was my first experience driving a Cadillac and I enjoyed the deluxe drive as well as the personal fantasizing it allowed.

When we made the decision to move to West Virginia, it was without awareness of the fact that Reverend J. H. Hughes was a member of the Church of God World Missions Board. In the course of my work, I found myself, as Reverend Hughes' assistant, processing World Missions business and communicating with missionaries. It would have been impossible to imagine the far-reaching consequences of our decision to move to West Virginia or to comprehend how our appointment as missionaries would develop so seemingly automatically as a result of this association. Just before the Christmas season, 1951, I found myself behind the wheel of the Cadillac driving Reverend

Hughes to Cleveland, Tennessee for a Missions Board meeting. As we traveled, my spiritual mentor told me there was already a very full agenda for the current meeting, but he felt I should meet the Missions Board at its next session and he planned to have an interview for us included in the agenda.

Although it was preposterous to imagine that we might expect a missionary appointment, we were invited to the next meeting of the Missions Board in February, 1952. I was woefully inadequate in so many ways. I was not yet twenty-five years old. My ministerial experience was limited to conducting a few revival meetings with no spectacular results and two brief tenures as pastor of small congregations. I had not qualified for a college degree. All I had going for me was an absolute assurance that I had been divinely selected to be a missionary, and a complete confidence God would make a way in spite of our inadequacies and lack of qualifications and education. No, this meeting could not generate an appointment for us — but it did.

CHAPTER TWELVE

JAPAN

Purveyors of tradition relish reciting the record of the first motor-cycles in Japan. As the story was told me, a Japanese tourist visiting Canada was fascinated by the unique two-wheeled vehicle. Certain that it would be widely accepted in Japan, he purchased one and had it shipped home to Japan. During the voyage across the Pacific, the ship encountered high winds and heavy seas. As a result, some of the cargo slipped and the motorcycle arrived in Japan with a small dent in the side of the gasoline tank. Some months later, Japan's first motorcycle manufacturer announced the release of it products for sale. Interestingly, every one of their early model motorcycles had a small dent in the side of the gasoline tank.

An acquaintance from Sweden once told me that the safety match was invented in Sweden and for a long time was produced exclusively in his home country. Consider the consternation of the Swedes when they learned that matches made in Japan were being marketed throughout the Orient. They took their complaint to an international patent court. The judge ruled that the Japanese had indeed infringed on the rights of the Swedish match industry and required that they should cease manufacturing and marketing matches until they should have obtained the marketing rights from the Swedish company for an appropriate price. To insure compliance with his judgment, he further ruled that any matches marketed outside Sweden must be packed in boxes clearly marked "Made in Sweden." Undaunted, the Japanese continued to manufacture and sell matches in the Orient — with one modification. The new boxes were appropriately marked "Made in Sweden." The next time national maps of Japan were printed, there was a small town added in central Honshu. That's right, the name of the town was clearly printed: "Sweden," Japan. If an international patent judge ruled that all matches should be made in Sweden, Japan was not adverse to complying.

As a young boy I recall playing with some very small toys. They were tiny airplanes, cars, etc. pressed out of thin sheet metal. On the back of some of the toys was the telling evidence that they were made of recycled beer cans. Sometimes it was possible to see enough of the original print on the metal to determine the toys were formerly filled with Schlitz or Budweiser. "Made in Japan" and "cheap" became synonymous terms to us.

Then came World War II. Pearl Harbor incensed America. The press fed the American public a steady diet of "Jap" bashing for the next four years. All Japanese were characterized as backstabbing truce-breakers. No Japanese could be trusted and we were taught to hate them as our patriotic responsibility.

Six years and five months after the Japanese surrender to General Douglas McArthur aboard the "Mighty Mo" anchored in Tokyo Bay, Letha and I were seated in the board room of the Church of God World Missions department. The board listened intently as I recited how I had felt a call nine years earlier to be a missionary.

The board chairman was Paul H. Walker. Twenty years earlier he was the dynamic young evangelist conducting an evangelistic meeting in an abandoned store building in Mobridge, South Dakota. He remembered well that my father and mother had met Christ as Lord at an altar in that crude store building in response to his appeal.

Who could have predicted the path or chronicled the course of our journey. I first knew Paul Walker in South Dakota when I was seven years old. Since the day we moved from the frigid north country, I had not seen him. As my early life progressed, I spent my teenage years in Texas, went to Bible college in Tennessee, attended University in Texas, then evangelized in Texas and pastored in West Virginia. It was incredible that I was now seated across the conference table from this Pentecostal pioneer from the past who had been such a significant influence in my life. (Not at all coincidentally, at the next general assembly Dr. Paul H. Walker became the executive director of World Missions, and it was our good fortune and happy privilege to work under his direct supervision for the first four years of our missionary tenure.)

The mission board spokesman informed us that consideration was being given to open missions in three countries in 1952. They were Brazil, Israel and Japan. I responded that my first interest would be to go to the newly formed State of Israel, but I would be amenable to working where they should determine. The following day we learned of their decision to offer us an assignment to Japan.

I have always considered myself to be a patriotic American, and when we were at war, I worked in a defense industry and designated a deduction from every pay check to buy U. S. savings bonds! However, I never did learn to hate the Japanese as some of my friends felt we should do as a way of showing our patriotism. When our Missions Board mentioned an appointment to Japan, I did not have to clear my mind of the war-time caricatures of small soldiers with beaver teeth, straight black hair, and inordinately large horn-rimed glasses, or of suicide pilots diving their Zeros down the stack of American military ships.

My thoughts went to a nation of a hundred million people who had lost their purpose for living. I could help fill that void. Soon after General Douglas McArthur established an occupation government in the Daiichi Building in Tokyo, he issued an urgent appeal to the churches of America to send 10,000 Christian missionaries to Japan. My reaction was that Letha and I had just been offered the high honor of joining that host of Christian ambassadors to a Shinto society. We were to become two of those ten thousand.

109

CHAPTER THIRTEEN

ORIENTATION IN THE ORIENT

In the opening pages of this book, we took a trip together to the Orient, arriving in Yokohama, Japan, August 19, 1952. Since then I have ambled on through a hundred pages of details and incidentals so we could get acquainted. Let's get focused again.

Being the first missionaries in Japan under appointment with the Church of God was a distinct privilege, but it was not without problems. We knew no one in Japan, nor had we any awareness of the culture and customs of the nation we had adopted, but had not yet seen. We did not know a word of the Japanese language. These were some of the superficial problems, the real difficulties were more complex. More on that a little later.

We were met at the ship by Reverend John Clement, a seasoned missionary serving as the field chairman of the Japan Assemblies of God. He greeted us cordially, then immediately set about the task of customs inspection of our personal belongings and clearing immigration. In these matters we were accorded obvious courtesies because that is the normal culture of Japan, and also, because Japan was at that time a country occupied by the United States as a consequence of World War II. Because we were given this priority treatment, clearing customs and immigration took little time.

As passengers in Brother Clement's Chevrolet, we traveled to the center of Tokyo, all the time on the wrong side of the street. We weren't nervous or frightened. It was something beyond that. We exited the car in a subterranean parking facility and entered an elevator. When the elevator door opened, we found ourselves surrounded by the rich marble slabs of a Frank Lloyd Wright architectural masterpiece as modern as any deluxe office building in Dallas, New York or Minneapolis. This structure was a feat of engineering genius. Constructed on land reclaimed from the Tokyo Bay, this building could not be erected using traditional engineering methods as there seemed to be no foundation bedrock. Following excavation, a basement was poured on the fill dirt that had been used to reclaim the land. Next the fill dirt was removed from below the floor and the entire basement was lowered about ten feet. On that submerged basement, a second basement of concrete and reinforcing steel was poured. The process was completed twice more and the lowest basement rested on solid rock, below the initial floor level of Tokyo Bay. The four basements provided underground parking for the tenants of the building and their clients.

On the ground floor were numerous fashionable retail businesses. We entered a restaurant with noticeably small chairs and tables a little lower than our western furniture. Our host treated us to our first Oriental meal of chicken curry over rice. He then drove us to the YMCA where he had previously arranged for us to stay a few days. From there we traveled about 25 miles to the extreme west side of Tokyo where we were escorted through the big frame house that would be our home for the next twelve months. We returned to the YMCA and our host left us, but not before he had arranged to meet us early the next morning so he could show us where most foreigners shopped for the things we considered important, but were not readily available in typical shops in Tokyo. We had shipped no furniture or household essentials, so our assisted shopping covered the best part of three days — and all of this courtesy was afforded us by a man we had never met before, and who represented a different church affiliation. We soon discovered that when a very limited number of Christians live in a totally pagan environment, we learn to build our fences much lower.

A number of years ago, Brother John Clement went on to his reward in heaven for a job well done on earth. When by the grace of God I become a resident of the New Jerusalem, I want to learn John Clement's address so I can pay him a visit to tell him one more time how very much his kindness, generosity and assistance to us were appreciated. That first week in Tokyo, I learned some invaluable lessons from that saintly statesman about true missionary service. Aware that being the only Church of God missionaries in a foreign environment could create for us a lonely life, we tried to return the cordiality. As a consequence, during our fourteen years in Japan, we enjoyed a sense of family especially with missionaries under appointment with the Assemblies of God, the Foursquare Church and the Open Bible Standard churches. Some years later, when we built the Yokohama Bible Institute to train young people for ministry, our faculty staff included missionaries affiliated with the Church of God, Assemblies of God, Pentecostal Assemblies of Canada and the Open Bible Standard church. Cultural advantage to the students also was gained from these teachers from the United States, Canada, New Zealand, Switzerland, and Scandinavia.

Traveling west from the U.S. to Japan, we crossed the international date line. It would have been so very beneficial if we could have crossed the foreign missionary line also. Apparently there is no such line, so when we arrived in Japan with a mission and a plan to change the nation, we still had no halos.

Very soon we began to comprehend what Rudyard Kipling meant when he wrote, "East is East and West is West and never the twain shall meet." Everything is done differently in Japan. We open a book at the left cover and read horizontal lines from left to right. The Japanese open a book at the right cover and read from top to bottom. They progress with reading these vertical rows of picture-like characters from the right side of the page to the left, but we work down from the top of the page. Whereas the Japanese eat rice with chopsticks, we find it easier to use a fork or a spoon so the small rice grains will not fall off between the plate and the mouth. When Japanese eat western style food, they utilize the same kind of flatware we use, but it is amusing to watch them pick up an entire slice of bread with a fork, take a bite out of the slice and then return it to the plate.

Some of our missionary friends were invited out for a meal. Their host served typical Japanese food and showed them how to eat the food using chopsticks. The missionaries reciprocated with an invitation for their host to visit them the following week. As would be expected, the missionary wife prepared American style food and set the table with forks and knives by each plate. The Japanese carefully observed the host and then imitated him by picking up a fork, but they had great difficulty keeping the food on the fork until the missionary wife detected a strange irregularity. All of the Japanese guests appeared to be left handed. Her husband was left handed and the guests were experiencing great difficulty trying to manipulate their food on a fork in the left hand.

We cook fish before eating it. Japanese people are very fond of raw fish. We flavor beans with salt, but imagine the delight you would experience when you put a large spoonful of red beans in your mouth only to learn too late they had been generously flavored with sugar.

Forty-five years ago, I could have written an encyclopedia describing the ways Japanese customs differ from our western ways. However, the longer we lived in Japan, the less their customs seemed strange and different. In fact, we came to realize that in some situations, their ways seemed very appropriate: that is, until we were introduced to the Japanese language. Even a cursory evaluation of the Japanese language will be convincing evidence of the validity of the account in Genesis of the Tower of Babel. Many linguists have asserted that Japanese is one of the three most difficult languages for foreigners to learn, ranking in difficulty with Arabic and Russian.

Just three weeks after our arrival in Japan, the Naganuma school of the Japanese language started its Fall classes. In our naivete, we had anticipated witnessing, preaching and teaching immediately upon arrival in our adopted home country. Such was far from what awaited us. In the orientation session of the language school, Professor Naganuma told the large group of foreign students assembled in the school auditorium that to get a good grip on the language, we should expect to be in school three to five years. Many of the large, older established missions required that their fledgling missionaries spend their entire first term learning the language so they can expect to be effective in real mission work when they start their second term.

I enrolled in the school and registered for classes five days a week. Janice was only two years old, so Letha decided it would be wiser to employ a private tutor to come to our home every morning and give private language lessons. Although we did not know a single word of Japanese, at the school we were introduced to our teachers in Japanese. The teachers were not allowed to use any English language during class time. Everything was done in Japanese, with a little sign language to help occasionally.

On Fridays, the last hour of the school day an instructor who had a good command of English visited our classroom and allowed us to ask questions using English. Usually, the questions centered around some technical point in one of the lessons earlier in the weeks study. Amazingly, we could accomplish the most rudimentary linguistic communication by the end of our first week of study. It was a long, tiring process, but the potential rewards justified the intense effort. A missionary who had spent thirty years in Japan outlined for me two scenarios. In the first case, he would begin evangelizing immediately on arrival with the aid of a qualified interpreter and continue using this method for thirty years. Alternatively, he would move in among Japanese people and spend twenty-nine years observing their culture and mastering their language. With the wisdom and information thus acquired he would immerse himself in evangelism for one year. In both instances, he would return to his home country and retire. Then came his unbelievable conclusion: "Knowing what I now know, I would choose the second alternative, and I am certain I would accomplish more good than if I had followed the first course."

Fortunate for me, I met that man shortly after arriving in Japan, so I buried myself in the language books ten hours a day. Following instructions given at the language school, I used what I had learned every day. Returning home from school on the commuter or subways or shopping in our neighborhood, I practiced what I had been exposed to that day. After three hours in a classroom without a word of English, I returned home for lunch and then plunged into homework assignments all afternoon. After our evening meal it was the books again until I often went to bed exhausted by 8:00 or 8:30 p.m. But there was no escape. Having crowded my mind with Japanese words and phrases all day, I dreamed restlessly much of the early hours of the evening. You guessed it. I dreamed in Japanese.

Many missionary groups assign their missionary candidates to an abbreviated course in language study prior to their going to a foreign country to determine whether or not they can expect to learn the language. That seems to have some genuine economic merit. We were not accorded that opportunity, so when I started at the language school in the beginners' course, I was the only person in my class who was totally illiterate. It was not a pleasant distinction for me.

Ultimately I was to learn this was an advantage rather than a problem. The others had some comprehension of what was being said, but having had their first exposure to the Japanese language in an American college setting, they had acquired an accent which they could not "unlearn."

After being in Japan a number of years, I was often told by Japanese people,"You have absolutely no accent." On some occasions I have spoken by telephone and was asked my name. When I replied, "My name is Heil," the person on the other telephone would respond, "Yes, I understand you are speaking for Mr. Heil, but in case I call again, I need to know your name also." It seemed quite apparent the person on the other end of the telephone conversation believed he was speaking to a Japanese. Given the difficulty of Japanese, it was nothing short of miraculous that I was able to communicate to that extent in their language. It definitely made our work more effective.

CHAPTER FOURTEEN

GREEN TEA

Prior to the time we met with the Missions Board, the Executive Director of Missions had received some correspondence from a lady stationed with the U. S. Military forces in Yokohama. She had conducted a Sunday school near the military base, and being a Church of God member, she reported her activities to our mission's headquarters. To the best of my recollection her name was Margaret Flowers. From records available, she was the first Church of God member to become actively involved in a systematic effort to impact Japan with the gospel message. I have no information as to the extent of her work or its effectiveness.

Reverend J. H. Walker, the Foreign Mission's Executive Secretary at the time of our appointment, made us aware of the correspondence he had received from Ms. Flowers. He suggested that we make an attempt to locate the group she had assembled and possibly let that be a nucleus for our first church in Japan. At the time we were provided that information, Ms. Flowers had been re-assigned by the military, and could not be located. There was no information on file in the missions department as to an address where this work had started, no name of a person in charge — if someone had been designated, nor any awareness as to whether the work was continuing to function.

Reverend Walker somewhat apologetically supplied us that skeletal information and suggested that we make an effort to find this embryonic mission. At that time, Yokohama was a city with a population of approximately one million, so it goes without saying that we faced a "needle in a haystack" kind of impossibility. We made some inquiry based on the sketchy information, but soon determined it was completely futile. In any case, based on that direction from the Missions Executive Secretary, we had subconsciously considered our mission should start in Yokohama.

As we neared the end of our first year of concentrated language study, we determined we should devote at least some of our time and efforts toward our real purpose for being in Japan. We began to formulate a program of tract distribution, personal witnessing, home visitation and street evangelism with a view to establishing a church. Following our earliest inclination that our first church would be in Yokohama, I visited a number of real estate offices in that city, which was no more than an hour's drive from our residence in western Tokyo. With my American thinking as a guide, I envisioned finding a suitable location on which we could ultimately construct a church building with a parsonage adjacent. When I made inquiry of real estate agents in an effort to locate suitable land, I learned that building lots, as I understood the concept, did not exist in Japan.

Land is measured in "tsubos" with one tsubo measuring about six feet by six feet. Most of the parcels on the market were forty or fifty tsubos in size. Forty tsubos would be approximately 30 feet wide and 48 feet long. That was hardly what I had in mind.

A typical residence in a highly populated area was a building of about 500 to 700 square feet, located on land large enough to allow two or three feet of open ground at each side and the back of the house and as much as six to ten feet from the front of the house to the property line. To make it even more difficult, many of these tiny parcels of land have no street frontage. They can only be accessed by a narrow foot path six feet wide which serves as ingress/egress for a number of other similar home sites. It was difficult for me to comprehend that a wealthy Japanese is extremely pleased to locate even 1/10th or 1/12th of an acre on which he can build a veritable mansion. As for the possibility of finding land adequate for the plans I had envisaged, I was in for a jolt I had not anticipated.

The first week I looked for land, I visited as many as ten or twelve real estate offices each day. Apart from being made aware that Japan had very limited available land, as described above, what I gained from my week's activity was only that I developed a taste for Japanese tea. Each time I entered a real estate office, a young lady brought me a cup of tea. Sometimes it was served with a couple of slices of apple or a mikan (the Japanese word for a tangerine). Sometimes the tea was served with mini-sized cookies, or sweet beans, or osembe, the Japanese counterpart of potato chips. As a special delicacy, sometimes the hostess served omochi with the tea. I can best describe omochi for you as a gooey portion of rice which has been overcooked, then beaten into a sticky paste and rolled out like thick pie crust. It is then cut into squares and allowed to harden. Prior to serving, it is slightly toasted so as to restore its extremely sticky texture. I don't know why I never learned to like it because it has virtually no taste or smell.

Regardless of what may have accompanied the tea served in the real estate offices I visited, or if it was served without any other refreshment, every time I entered another real estate office, I was given another cup of tea. If we went out to look at a property, I had two cups of tea; one when I entered the office looking for property and a second when we returned.

In some offices, the small tea cups were rinsed in hot water before being filled, sometimes it seemed they were only slightly rinsed in cold water, and there were occasions I felt sure I was served tea in a cup that had not been rinsed at all since its use by a previous customer. Whether it was served in cups that were hot washed and dried, rinsed in cold water, or not rinsed at all before use, I developed a taste for tea after I had consumed at least a dozen cups a day for a week.

So much for tea. Let's find some land.

Scouting most of the city of Yokohama resulted in finding nothing that would fit into my master-plan for a church/parsonage arrangement. We were to learn later that it would be less than ideal if we had built a church and a parsonage on one property. The church would have to be for the use of the local people, and we were thinking of a parsonage next door to be a residence for ourselves — the foreigners. Half a century ago, foreigners in Japan were viewed with a certain amount of curiosity. Even as we had a tendency to consider they did everything just opposite of what we knew to be "the right way," by the same sort of reasoning, they were either amazed or confused by many of our customs and habits.

Another factor cried out for consideration. In the years just following World War II, Japan's economy had been devastated. As a consequence the income of working people was very low and their life style simple. Our living allowance for a family of three was $225 U. S. currency, which was a meager amount by American standards, but most Japanese considered our lifestyle to be that of the wealthy. For us to try to establish a church for the Japanese in an average community with foreigners living extravagantly next door would be to invite misunderstandings and problems. Some would be inclined to resent our "wealth" and extravagant life style. Just as much a problem was the insatiable curiosity with which we would be viewed as we created an artificial American environment in our home.

Having resided in Japan for less than a year at that time, we were not aware of the fact that for foreign missionaries to live adjacent to a church whose membership was entirely of another culture, could be strenuous for all concerned. Simply because we were not able to find land large enough for the two buildings, we were spared these potential misunderstandings and problem situations. We decided to start again at the beginning; this time to find a parcel of ground on which to construct a missionary residence only.

A seemingly ideal plot of land came to our attention. It was on the main arterial highway between Tokyo and Yokohama. It was elevated about twelve feet above the street level and was large enough to accommodate a modest house of about 1200 square feet and still have yard space so we could have a lawn and some shrubs. And wonder of wonders, the price was within the limited budget that had recently been allocated by our missions board in the U. S. This land had been on the market quite some time, but the local residents did not want it. Their criteria for a desirable home site is one no more than three or four minutes' walk from public transportation, but we were located more than a mile from the nearest commuter train station, and there was no bus service. They prefer seclusion rather than street frontage. Also this land was 130 tsubo (about 55 feet by 85 feet) and it could not conveniently be subdivided. That was just too much land for one house. An agreement was reached on the price of the land, and we had it registered as the first real estate owned by the Church of God in Japan. Construction started about a month later, after we had been in Japan just about one year.

In trying to deal with a Japanese builder, I soon learned that it would not be practical for me to try to deal without an interpreter as my ability with the Japanese language was far too limited. Somehow my textbook phrases seemed not to work in this sort of real-life situation. Thinking it would be both practical and economical, I looked for a young Christian with a reasonable understanding of English, who could help me in dealing with the builder and sub-contractors, plus he could assist me in laying the ground work for a church. I contacted a number of missionaries to apprise them of this need and request their assistance in finding someone suitable. We found a young man who seemed to meet our need and I hired him.

Each morning we met at the building site and went over what had been done that may need correction or modification. We tried to anticipate what would be done that day so as to head off further problems before they developed. Each afternoon we went together to crowded areas and distributed tracts. We had stamped our name and address on each tract with a telephone number to call for further assistance. We had a few responses, and Morishita San, my interpreter and I followed up on each one. A kindergarten facility was located about a mile from the house we were building and we were able to rent it for Sunday mornings only. As soon as we advertised a Sunday School, the building packed out with children through about 15 years old.

When the large crowd of children vacated the building, a morn-

121

ing service was conducted for adults, although the number in attendance was very small. Possibly it was good practice for me, but I question that much else of value was accomplished. Preaching with an "interrupter" was frustrating. Either I would make a statement too lengthy so that by the time I came to the end of a sentence, he had forgotten the beginning. Or if I concentrated on keeping my presentation brief and simple, so the interpreter could grasp it, I tended to lose my chain of thought. Those frustrations were insignificant by comparison to the real difficulty. My interpreter had a reasonable comprehension of conversational English, but when he tried to help me preach, he was totally lost.

One Monday morning, Morishita San did not arrive at the building site as was our usual schedule, but I paid little attention to that. My conversational Japanese was becoming more nearly understandable to the builder and his subcontractors, so I managed to deal directly with them, without the aid of my interpreter. When he failed to show again the following morning, I went to the one bedroom efficiency apartment we had rented for him to learn of his condition. I assumed he may be sick and need some attention. As I ascended the flight of stairs to the second story room, I heard a boisterous conversation and loud laughing. I opened the sliding door slightly, as is the Japanese custom, before saying good morning. Try to imagine my consternation when I saw my interpreter/church assistant through a haze of tobacco smoke. He was seated at a small table with two friends. There was no convenient place to hide their cigarettes. Even if they could have disposed of the cigarettes, the evidence had already permeated and polluted the atmosphere, so it was of no use. Also on the table was a tall bottle of sake (Japanese white rice wine), which adequately explained the animated conversation and hilarity I detected as I had come up the stairs a few minutes earlier.

I tried to hide my disappointment and anger at this young man who had represented himself to me as a Christian who wanted to be involved with me in evangelism. The situation I saw hardly reflected what he had tried to make me believe when he was first employed to assist me. When I questioned why he had not come to work for two days, he seemed shocked that I would want him to work on his birthday. His friends had arrived the day before for his birthday celebration, and it seemed they prolonged the happy situation into the second day. It had not entered his mind that he should have told me in advance. He intended to explain it to me when he would return to work. I next inquired about the tobacco and the wine. His response was that as a Christian he would not drink, but in Japan it was customary to celebrate any special occasion with some good wine and his friends would not at all understand if he did not serve them wine when they had gone out of their way to visit him on this special day. This was a "one time thing" and after his friends' departure, of course, he would not be drinking any more. He hoped I could understand.

I understood, and when I told him I could no longer use his services, I hoped he could understand also. I explained that it was not as much the tobacco and the wine, but the deception that was of such concern to me. He had represented himself as a fundamental Christian and told me when I hired him that he did not use tobacco and that he did not drink.

I finished the construction of our residence, dealing with the building contractor without the services of an interpreter; and having no interpreter to assist in our newly started Sunday school and church endeavor, I felt it was not wise to try to continue at that time.

We were back to square one!

Chapter Fifteen

Whom Ye Ignorantly Worship

With the loss of Morishita San, I was again reduced to a foreigner with no ability to communicate. In some mysterious way, news does travel and the word was apparently circulated that I had need for an interpreter. I never did learn how he became aware of my need, but one day a young man appeared at my door and introduced himself as Shimada Toshihige. Actually Shimada was his surname and Toshihige was his given name. Backward again!

We called him Shimada San. The word 'San' added to ones name means mister. The same word 'San' also means Mrs. or Miss when used in speaking of a person of feminine gender.

Shimada San told me he understood I was in need of a Christian worker who had a good working knowledge of English. He presented himself as a graduate of the TEAM Bible school. (TEAM is an acronym for "The Evangelical Alliance Mission," a respected evangelical mission, but definitely not Pentecostal.) Shimada San apparently had done his homework prior to his coming because he knew of my Pentecostal belief. Accordingly, he informed me that he had graduated from the TEAM Bible Institute but his belief was Pentecostal and further, he had received a Pentecostal baptism.

We were both considering the same situation. He needed me and I needed him. That was our common ground, but it later developed that the one thing we needed most but did not have was any genuine commonality. I wanted an interpreter who would help me evangelize our community with a view of developing and establishing a church. He wanted to become the pastor of a church and he wanted a foreign missionary with money to provide that church.

Even though we had some theological differences, we were both young and energetic. If persistence and hard work alone had been sufficient, we would have been one of the more successful teams anywhere to be found. One very important plus was that we shared a deep concern for Japan's unevangelized. Our days were spent in passing out tracts and gospel portions. Every piece of literature given away had our address on it with an invitation for a response. How many tens of thousands of tracts we distributed, I cannot even guess. I do recall vividly that we had very few responses. However, everyone in Japan seems to be obsessed with acquiring knowledge, and any time we passed out tracts in a passenger car of a commuter train, it was not uncommon to see a large percentage of the passengers reading them as we traveled toward their destination. Very soon we discovered that the number of responses did not seem to justify the time, effort and expense of such a large scale literature distribution, but we prayed that by reading the message, some would be inspired to believe and accept Christ. Whether they became a part of our fellowship or affiliated with another church was only incidental to our main purpose. We wanted to establish a Christian church in our community, but of far greater importance, we were concerned that our Japanese neighbors may know Christ.

We personally called on the residents in our neighborhood and informed them of our desire to establish a Christian fellowship and ultimately build a church in our community. The process was painfully slow, but occasionally we had a positive response.

Not having any facility suitable for worship services, we invited our neighbors to meet in our living room for a Sunday morning Christian service and a midweek Bible study. For at least two reasons there was a positive response to our invitations. At that time there were very few Westerners living in Japan (except military personnel who lived in clusters on secured government bases), and hardly anyone in our community had seen the interior of a western house. Some attended our services to satisfy this curiosity. Secondly, the services were conducted in Japanese, but anything I said was necessarily translated from English. Because there was a prevailing intense interest in learning English, many attended for this exposure to an English lecture and some stayed behind after the meetings were dismissed so they could practice their English in conversation with one who spoke English as his mother tongue. The English language capability of most of them was limited to what they had learned in high school or college and the instruction had been given by a Japanese teacher. To decipher what they were trying to articulate was sometimes nearly impossible.

In the Japanese language nearly every symbol in the alphabet is a combination of a consonant and a vowel. They experience difficulty in speaking some English words because their language does not contain some sounds commonly used in speaking English. In many cases, their substitute for the letters 'D', 'L' and 'R' are virtually the same. So when they ask for rice, their pronunciation of the English word may sound more like lice or dice. The word love then may sound like rub or dub.

Incidentally, there are fifty characters in the Japanese alphabet, and to make it more complex for us, they use one phonetic alphabet, but two written alphabets, Hiragana and Katakana. Both sets of written characters are pronounced exactly the same, but there is absolutely no similarity in their written form. One set of characters is used to write Japanese words and the other is employed when they incorporate a foreign word into their language. Present day Japanese includes many words taken from German, French, Spanish and English. When they are written, it is obvious they are foreign words because they are written with the "Katakana" alphabet.

Oh, did I forget to mention that these two simple alphabets of fifty characters each are only a minor adjunct to the main written language which is a modification of the Chinese characters. Traditionally there were 10,000 of these Chinese characters used

127

by the Japanese. To make the language more practical, an abbreviated form was devised utilizing only 3,000 characters. Then happy day! After World War II, streamlining was achieved by a reduction to a "bare bones" minimum of only one thousand eight hundred characters.

Whether our Japanese neighbors came to see the interior of a western home to gain exposure to foreign culture, or to practice conversational English, the fact is they came and we were gratified for the opportunity to present to them the message of hope in Christ.

Our residence soon became too small for the large number of children who attended our Sunday school, so again we rented the kindergarten building we had used in our first attempt to start a church. The adults continued to meet in our home, and ever so gradually, a tiny nucleus of a church started to develop. A small number of our group professed faith in Christ and were baptized as believers. We were coming to understand something of the complexity of the Japanese mind-set and their concept of religious belief. For them it was a serious matter to divorce themselves from the age-old religious traditions which touched every facet of their lives.

To us who have lived all of our years in a Christian environment, believing is a simple act of faith and acceptance. For these people, because all of their traditions and customs are so tightly interwoven into the fabric of their religion, it was a complete renunciation of family, friends, community activities, religious ceremonies, patriotic observances; and in some cases even total separation from family and their closest friends.

At the time we made our appearance on the Japanese scene, devout worshippers were celebrating the 2500th birthday of Gautama Buddha. Dating back for a similar number of years was the recorded history of the royal family of Japan. According to the Imperial Chronicles, there had been an unbroken succession to the throne of their island-based empire for more than twenty-five centuries. The history of Japan traces the genealogy of the emperor back through the centuries to the first emperor who is firmly believed to have been the child of "Amaterasu Omikami," the Goddess of the Sun. The religion/philosophy known as Shinto is closely aligned to what is sometimes called emperor worship.

Generally accepted statistics put the religion of Shinto as the preference of more than 90% of Japan's population. Buddhism also reports more than 90% of the Japanese people as its adherents. This is not considered to be a false claim of either of these two religious groups. The fact is that there is no apparent conflict if one embraces both religions as they are not mutually exclusive. (We anticipated that it might be quite difficult to explain such complexities as the unity and trinity of one god. However, that did not seem to be such an insurmountable hurdle when viewed against this backdrop of an entire nation that simultaneously embraced two religions.)

A very elementary and general explanation of the matter is that Buddhism is primarily a system of religious beliefs, whereas Shinto might be more accurately classified as a philosophy. One can begin to comprehend why there is no conflict by thinking of Buddhism as a *philosophical religion* and Shinto as a *religious philosophy.*

Buddhism was born in India and rapidly spread its influence over many Oriental nations and cultures. It is often explained as the eight-fold path to perfection. Each of these eight paths leads to being incorporated into the great impersonal force of good referred to as "nirvana." It was essentially a religion of good works. The eight paths to nirvana include good thoughts, good words, good attitudes and good deeds. The fallacy is to believe that the development and exercise of these elements of good are sufficient to make the practitioner holy and deserving of eternal bliss.

The ultimate weakness of this religious system is that the worshipper acknowledges his sin and immorality, but then purports to do all the good things required by Budhism, but he does them in his own strength. Immorality cannot produce purity. Corruption cannot produce its own cleansing.

The word Shinto comes from two Japanese concepts, "shin" meaning *truth* and "do" which means *road*. Together they form the word "shin-do." With a slight euphonic correction, it becomes "Shinto." Look at the meaning of the two parts of this compound word and the obvious emerges: Shinto is the way of truth. It is totally logical that a person can espouse a religion that provides a road map showing eight roads to eternal life, and at the same time submit to a school of philosophical thought that lights the road through life.

The amalgamation of these two religions is easy not only because the teachings of one naturally complements the other, the integration of the "goodness" inherent in both systems seems to provide a compound benefit for the worshippers.

One other precept of Shinto that must be considered is that of ancestor worship, with emperor worship at the core. If the first emperor of the current dynasty really was the son of Amaterasu Omikami, then it is no violation of reason that every direct descendent in that unbroken lineage has possessed that same inbred divinity.

In discussing this matter of emperor-worship with some of my Japanese friends, more than once I was told that the emperor is not worshiped as God in the sense that he is believed to be the "Supreme Being." Rather, the sentiment of patriotic Japanese toward their Emperor somewhat parallels the feeling of a loyal British citizen toward the Queen. Rather than worship in the strictest spiritual connotation, it would be better understood by any outsider as supreme respect and reverence.

Even though many modern day Japanese have attempted to rationalize this controversial subject for the foreign mind, ample evidence still points to the fact that the Emperor is seen as more than just a mere man. A case in point might be the dedication of pilots of the tiny "zero" aircraft used by the Japanese air force during World War II. It was commonly believed that to die in combat in the service of the Emperor was an absolute guarantee of eternal life. That conviction caused many Japanese pilots to lower the nose of their zeros in an attempt to dive directly down the stack of an American battle ship. Turning the small aircraft into an incendiary bomb with a human pilot was not considered at all unreasonable.

Assuming emperor worship does exist, the oriental concept of ancestor worship becomes somewhat understandable as a logical outgrowth. It is reasonable to rationalize that extreme parental respect logically gives birth to ancestor worship. A young man respects his father and expresses it in complete obedience during the father's lifetime. When the family patriarch dies, the young son mourns his passing, and tends to eulogize the father for his good traits. The loss of personal and business guidance, coupled with a desire for the companionship that has been taken away by death becomes fertile soil for the seeds of respect and parental appreciation to germinate into ancestor worship. The development of this process can heighten the desire for further communication between the departed and the bereaved, which seems to be accomplished at the "kamidana" (translated literally as god shelf). On the god shelf, surrounded by various small religious paraphernalia, is a photograph of the departed parent. When a member of the family goes out, he pauses at the god shelf to ask the favor of his father. On his return, he enters the house and bows again in appreciation of the blessing his father provided while he was away.

One significant spiritual problem appeared to supersede all others. Participation in religious activities seemed to be more cultural than spiritual. It was an empty ritual and the rank and file were involved primarily because it was the thing to do; not that they comprehended the ceremony or received any genuine satisfaction from it. Many told me they were seeking for peace, but could not find it. When we taught that Christ is the Prince of Peace, some wanted to add him to their many other deities. But when they accepted him as Lord, they experienced real peace and the joy that can only follow a personal relationship with Him.

When the apostle observed the Athenians giving obeisance to a multiplicity of gods, even to the extent that they had erected an altar to one whom they knew only as the "unknown," he had no option but to conclude that they were very religious. Paul also was so religious he was considered by many to be a fanatic, and even a fool. When he acknowledged that the Athenians were very religious, from that common ground he preached Christ as the one whom they tried in their spiritual ignorance to worship. We decided we could find no more appropriate basis for evangelizing in Japan, so we adopted the attitude of Paul and continued to preach Christ, even as we were surrounded by one of the world's most religious cultures.

I was confident that as a teenager I had been called to be a missionary. It may be correct to say I accepted the traditional position that a missionary is one who moves away from the comforts of his own environment and proclaims the truth of the gospel to spiritually illiterate pagans. I believe I was spiritually, emotionally and psychologically prepared to do that. What I had not anticipated was being confronted by a nation of believers who were in many ways more religious than I was. How is one to go about presenting the teachings of Christ to those who already practice many of the same principals, but packaged with a different label?

I began to comprehend more correctly the dilemma Paul experienced on Mars Hill in Athens, Greece. A lack of religious involvement was not the problem. They had too many gods! Paul took the best approach when he commended the Athenians for being very religious, but then seized their interest by calling attention to an altar they had dedicated to "the unknown god." In the city where logic had such deep roots, Paul logically concluded that if their god was unknown, then their worship was in ignorance. But he did not leave them dangling in that ignorance; rather he gave them a personal introduction to the God they had been searching for — the one true God who gave to us all life, energy and our very existence. Trying to follow that example, we preached Christ in a very religious nation.

Our Bible study groups were well attended, but to penetrate the complexity of the Japanese "mind/personality/soul/psyche" was extremely difficult. Their home life... the totality of their educational system... their patriotism... and their religious life were so completely intertwined. Their Emperor was the direct descendent of divinity... their nation was destined to rule the world... their ancient culture taught that they had eight million gods... each home had its kamidana (god shelf). As an expression of respect and reverence they regularly placed food on the kamidana for the departed ancestors. On religious holidays they visited the ancient shrines and temples with other countless millions. On certain designated sacred trees on the temple grounds, many tied small white slips of paper containing their prayers. They dropped their monetary gifts in a large receptacle as they entered the temple and shrine areas and burned incense before leaving. Without question these people were as religious as the Athenians in Paul's day. *Where should we start?*

The number of believers in our emerging church increased and soon it became impractical to try to house the church in our residence. We rented a small house and moved the church into a building dedicated only to church services so the believers would not feel they were an imposition when they stayed late after the service had concluded.

Two years after arriving in Japan, we formally organized the first congregation of the Church of God in Japan. The attendance in our new church was increasing consistently, and we had expectations of establishing a strong local church. But when we organized the church and asked the worshippers to make an open testimony of a genuine conversion to Christ and a commitment to the church, most of them were not yet ready to take such a bold step. To many of them, making an open testimony of conversion to Christ was to be disowned by family and in extreme situations, other family members considered them as no longer living. With such stringent restrictions imposed by family and friends, it is understandable that our first church was established with only eight charter members. This was significantly reminiscent of the first Church of God congregation organized in North Carolina about sixty five years earlier. The charter membership of that first local church also numbered only eight.

Today the Church of God is an international organization whose membership is counted in millions in more than 125 countries. We are pleased that although the Church of God in Japan has developed from such an humble beginning, it now stands strong as a respected partner with Church of God members throughout the world.

CHAPTER SIXTEEN

WHERE DO
WE START?

Every missionary has a story to tell. Taking one interesting incident from his five or six year stint of service in a foreign environment, one will recount his most fearful experience, when he was accosted by a band of marauders and his life was threatened.

Another may tell of the vast crowds that gathered to listen to his Gospel presentation, with pictures to substantiate his testimony.

Still another may recall a revival meeting when a large number of pagans became Christian believers in a one-week crusade.

A fourth missionary may direct his appeal to the American churches for financial support by a presentation of photographs depicting the poverty and squalor in the area where he has been appointed.

One effective way of generating support to a ministry in a missionary setting is to show a succession of color pictures of church buildings that have been built by the missionary making the presentation. Of course, there will be a group of believers assembled in front of each church building.

A picture that never fails to elicit interest and support from an

American church is a long line of candidates for baptism lined up on a river bank awaiting the culminating event in the process of conversion.

Even though all of the above may be very true and accurate, the fact usually is that each missionary has extracted a one-time incident or circumstance from his recent five-year appointment. It makes good press and it is honest and correct, except for the fact that the missionary may not have specifically emphasized that this was the exception — not the norm. The logical consequence is that the average American church member formulates a composite of the information cited above resulting in an inaccurate conception of foreign missions.

Many American Christians tend to visualize a foreign missionary as an unusual, committed, consecrated saint who has extricated himself from the comfortable environment of home. He surrounds himself with people of another culture and another language and often suffers from loneliness as he exists in a circumstance of deprivation. He learns to live in the squalor and accept the dangers that are constantly prevalent. Even so he is highly effective as he preaches to vast crowds and baptizes hundreds of converts, who then become the members of the many churches he builds. Based on the accurate information disseminated by various missionaries at different times and different places, we develop a concept of foreign missions that is totally unrealistic.

Now to get back to the real world. I was a committed missionary, but not a spiritual superman.

Having gathered together a small company of believers, pastor Shimada and I began to consider the need for a permanent facility to give the local church an identity and the possibility of perpetuation. The first step was to revisit dozens of real estate offices, where we imbibed barrels of tea. A small tract of land was located near the residence that housed our developing church. It was on the same arterial highway as our residence, about one mile north. We agreed that the location was good and should provide good exposure. Within two years of arriving in Japan, we started construction of our first church.

On the city survey maps, the land we had acquired seemed suitable for the church building we needed. On measuring the land as it was surveyed, we found that about twenty percent of the land was not usable as it was a steep bank rising nearly perpendicular to a height of more than twenty feet. We rolled up our sleeves and prepared to move a mountain — literally.

Finding our property line, we started the excavation at about 25 feet above street level and dug straight down. Because most of the property was flat and just a little above the level of the street, there was no place on our ground to discard the vast amount of dirt we dug from the hillside. I engaged the service of four men to work with picks and shovels and hired two small three-wheel vehicles to haul the dirt away. These three-wheel vehicles were a mongrelized invention that one would expect to be developed by the Japanese. It was like the front of a motorcycle with a two-wheel trailer welded to the back. In this way, they had the economy and maneuverability of a motorcycle, coupled with the hauling capability of a pickup truck. After about three weeks of faith (mixed with works), we had moved our mountain. We now had a building lot large enough for the church, but it was bordered with a sheer precipice not more than four feet from the side wall of the proposed building.

Fearing that erosion would cause an on-going problem, we gave consideration to building a retaining wall at least ten feet high to protect the building from falling dirt and debris. We struggled with the necessity of this project which could entail a large expenditure that had not been in our building budget. While we slept one night, the decision was made for us by a rain storm accompanied by high winds. Two feet from the bottom of the cliff we had created was a vein of fine sand nearly a foot deep. When the driving rain beat against that sand, it quickly washed out, leaving a gaping hole. The dirt above the sand collapsed and the next morning we found approximately four hundred cubic yards of dirt on our church building site. It was no longer a matter of choice: we would construct a retaining wall!

City Hall entered the picture and sent engineers to survey the situation and design a wall that would not be vulnerable to damage by future rains. Forty feet above the street level, houses had been built on the next higher terrace of land. With the current condition of our property, those residences could sustain serious damage and possible total loss if the problem was not corrected. The design presented to us by City Hall was for a reinforced concrete wall 120 feet long and 20 feet high. At the base the thickness of the wall would be 18 inches tapering to a thickness of only 6 inches at the top. To support that wall would be a foundation of heavily reinforced concrete 18 inches deep and ten feet wide, running the entire 120 feet length of the property.

The city code required that a licensed, bonded contractor be employed for construction of the retaining wall: and for the safety of the adjacent properties, it must be done without delay. This constituted for me something of a problem: our approved budget for the church building was $7,000 to be funded by the Foreign Missions Department. The lowest bid I could secure to build the wall was $3,000. My initial request for funding the building at $7,000 had been based on a bare bones calculation. With the money I had already spent to cut down the embankment and haul away the dirt, plus this $3,000 for the wall, half of the budgeted money was gone and the building of the church had not yet begun.

We were soon to learn that our biggest problem was not that small mountain of dirt on our church building site, nor was it the expense of constructing the massive retaining wall. The decision of City Hall to mandate construction of the wall in the interest of public safety became public knowledge immediately, and within hours we were visited by an attorney who told us he represented four families whose land joined ours. Their position was that our disturbing the natural contour of our property was the primary reason the wall collapsed under the pressure of the rain. Their logical conclusion was that we had jeopardized their properties. Further we had endangered their families in case there may be more deterioration of the land before the wall could be built to restore them to their former safety. They also claimed that their anxiety was the direct consequence of my negligence and therefore they demanded that compensatory damages should be assessed against me.

Litigation was never initiated in any court, but the lawyer and I became well acquainted in the weeks that followed his initial visit. Until the wall was completed, that attorney was at my front door almost daily. Intermittently, he threatened retaliatory conduct by the neighbors, an expensive court battle, settlement out of court and occasionally he made subtle references to an "appropriate" amount of cash as a gesture of good will to the neighbors whose property was in danger. It was really nothing more or less than money under the table. Thankfully, the funding for the retaining wall construction was provided, and the work was completed without incident. When the wall was completed, visits from the lawyer were suddenly discontinued.

From the start of excavation until completion of the wall, including the endless delays, more than three months elapsed. That one project (problem) used up 5% of our entire first five year term in Japan. That is not exactly what most church members envision as the activity of a missionary but that is how it happened to me. No, I was not that committed saint immersed in nonstop miraculous activity. I was the pragmatic laborer in overalls, wielding a pick and shovel during the day and fighting off attacks of an unscrupulous lawyer in the evenings. Looking back, I am inclined to wonder how I managed at the young age of 27, and with my limited experience, to work through some of these difficult situations.

It seems we prefer to accept the romanticized version of missions and missionaries, but more often than not, such is not the case. Rather, what you see is what you get!

After completion of the wall, construction of the church was accomplished without further incident. It was a very attractive concrete block building with the exterior stuccoed to simulate large building stones approximately one foot high and two feet long. It made a very nice appearance and we could point with justifiable pride at our first church building in Japan.

CHAPTER SEVENTEEN

LAYING A
FOUNDATION

Accomplishment is usually always followed by a sense of satisfaction or gratification. I felt good about the building of the
church, in spite of the mountain of problems that sometimes
challenged the possibility of completion. The church dedication
was the first meeting in the new building in November, 1954.
The auditorium was filled to capacity, but I was not unaware of
the fact that our local church believers were outnumbered by the
visitors who had come to celebrate with us the establishment of a
new spiritual lighthouse.

It was almost Christmas when we occupied our new facility, and
Pastor Shimada planned a special program with a view to
properly introducing our church to the community. He suggested
that I preach the Christmas sermon in Japanese rather than utilizing his interpreting, as we had always done up to that point. He
felt I had a fair working ability in the Japanese language, and further it would very favorably impress our membership and their
visiting friends if I would give the message in their language.

Knowing I could not do it, I declined, but Shimada insisted.
Being of German ancestry, I have a tendency toward stubborn-
ness. But when confronted by a determined Japanese, I found I
did not even comprehend the meaning of the word "stubborn."

Completely wearied from resisting, I reluctantly agreed to try to preach my first sermon in Japanese — with one condition. I would write the sermon and Shimada would translate it. Then I would use that manuscript as my crutch. What I had agreed to attempt was virtually unthinkable in view of the fact that I had been in Japan only slightly more than two years with just one of those years devoted to full-time language study. Many linguistic experts classify Japanese as one of the three most difficult languages, so it goes without saying, this was to be a premature attempt.

With the translated message in hand, I read it to familiarize myself with how my English sermon had survived the Japanizing process. After a half day with my bilingual dictionary, I concluded the translation had been very well done and would convey quite accurately what I had originally intended. A significant amount of my time during the first three weeks of December, 1954, was spent in memorizing my Christmas message.

Compressing this brief Japanese message into my western cranial cavity was finally accomplished after no less than fifty hours of intense concentration. To deliver the message to the church required only twelve or thirteen minutes. I am not certain about the ratio of the time spent in preparation vs. delivery, but it did seem to be counterproductive. After that, I wrote many sermons in Japanese, but that was the only one I did by rote.

By the end of our third year in Japan, we had one functioning church and two mission outreaches. We were soon brought directly to the question of how to create new churches without more workers, and how to develop new workers without more churches. As preposterous as it might seem, our small, struggling church needed a Bible Training Institute. Early experience had taught us that to send students away to a school operated by another denomination was less than ideal. When they returned (if they returned), they had a tendency to make comparisons with our small group in contrast to what they had seen of the other group.

It was about this time I met Tom Harland, a dedicated, hard driving Canadian. He had come to Japan without the sponsorship of a denominational missions board and he worked alone. He had established one church, but when he tried to start a second work, he faced the same dilemma as we, in that he could not divide his time between two congregations and be effective either place. The need for qualified ministerial associates was urgent, so he started a small school. Nine students were enrolled, and Tom Harland was the school's founder, financier, president, and the entire teaching staff. Classes were conducted five days a week from 9 a.m. until noon.

Tom Harland was a likable man and I learned to appreciate his friendship. We shared some of the same goals, as well as frustrations. Following a monthly missionary fellowship and prayer meeting, Tom engaged me one day in a conversation, which seemed intentionally to be going in a specific direction. It was. Tom told me he was getting weary with trying to serve as pastor of his local church plus teach in the school three hours every day, five days a week. Any pastor will tell you that to look after his church properly is a full time job. Try doing it with a congregation of a different culture and using a foreign language!

Classroom teaching requires that the instructor should be familiar with his subject matter to the extent that he can effectively convey information and concepts to his students. Customarily, he teaches each class only one hour per day to a group of students and then in the next hour he may use the same material but for a different group of students. As an interesting alternative, how about facing the same students for three consecutive hours every day. That means fifteen hours of new information must be presented every week, not to mention the time necessary for preparation.

Either of these constitutes a serious responsibility and a demanding schedule. For one person to do both simultaneously borders on the impossible. Now contemplate compounding the difficulty by doing all of this in a language you did not even imagine existed four years earlier and you might comprehend why Brother Harland told me he was becoming weary to the point of exhaustion. Concluding the recitation of his woes, he invited me to teach three hours a week in his Bible School. Thinking this to mean a one hour class on three different days a week, I agreed. It was not until I inquired about my schedule that I learned I was to teach three consecutive hours all in one day.

I had enough to do in trying to establish the work I had been sent to do for the Church of God, but I felt inclined to respond affirmatively to Tom's request. After all, I was in Japan primarily as a Christian and a missionary: and incidental to that I was affiliated with a specific church denomination. I reasoned I would some day possibly establish a school for our churches and working with my friend would provide valuable experience preparatory to that work at some future time. I did make one stipulation when I accepted this invitation. I would give my time, but I did not feel I should take Pastor Shimada from his pastoral duties to accompany me as my interpreter. Brother Harland informed me that one of the students was quite a capable interpreter and she would assist me. Two weeks later I was officially on the staff.

When I arrived for my first teaching session, I was greeted with the unwanted news that the interpreter was absent because of illness. I responded that I would await Brother Harland's arrival and suggest that he interpret my teaching. I had been in Japan less than three years and was completely inadequate linguistically. Tom Harland had preceded me in Japan about a year and six months and was more proficient than I, so I felt it was appropriate to suggest that he interpret. To my utter consternation, I was told Reverend Harland would not be coming to the school that day because I had been scheduled to teach.

I had two options. I could dismiss classes for the day or I could volunteer to be a fool for a day. I made the "foolish" decision. Somehow I managed to teach for three hours without any student walking out in protest. The second week I returned to the school to teach and learned the interpreter was still sick. I felt sick, too. What followed was three amazing hours when again I was able to keep their attention.

The third week I was greatly relieved to learn the interpreter was in school. I was sure it would be easier now that I could concentrate on the subject matter rather than on how to convey my message in a foreign language. This young lady had been reputed to be a good interpreter, but to say she made my teaching easier would be a gross misstatement. Some concepts she translated quite well. At other times she could not understand what I said. If she suggested that I rephrase a comment, the trend of the teaching was interrupted. Sometimes she made a valiant effort to convey what she thought I said. Because I had a fair comprehension of spoken Japanese, I knew when she was interpreting correctly and when she was improvising. In either case, I was frustrated.

After the interpreter and I had gone through about three weeks of mutual misery, some of the students apologetically approached me with a suggestion that they received much more when I taught them directly in their own language than when I tried to use the interpreter. With that rearrangement, I helped in that school for a full year, one half day a week. I'd like to believe I made a contribution to the Kingdom of God through the lives of those students. It was a rewarding experience for me and it proved to be of benefit when, a number of years later, the Yokohama Bible Institute was founded.

Quite frankly, no serious consideration had been given to initiating any plans to develop a Bible School, other than the fact that we knew some day it would become a necessity. There seemed to be no other method of effectively expanding the small work we had started. However, that had to be a part of our long-range planning.

When we went to Japan, our denomination was only slightly more than fifty years old. The first Church of God missionaries had gone to the Caribbean area about forty years before our appointment to Japan and there had been general interest and concern for world evangelization since the early years of our existence. However the fact remained, we were still a fledgling denomination. As I recall, giving for foreign missions for the entire church at that time was about $500,000 annually. It goes without saying, therefore, that having finance readily available for expansion was more an idealistic goal than a reality. We lived on a very limited budget. Even so, I don't recall ever complaining about a lack of finance and we pursued every opportunity with faith and optimism. As a consequence, a number of our friends in other denominations referred to us half-in-jest as

"The rich Church of God missionaries." This phrase had no basis in fact, but there were times it brought us some advantage.

Prior to the completion of our first church in Yokohama, I was approached by the field chairman of another mission. An elderly lady in their organization was retiring and had offered her residence for sale. Their policy provided that each missionary was responsible for generating his/her own budget, so since she had initially raised the budget for that property, she would be allowed to sell it and retain the money in her account to fund her repatriation. One missionary in their denomination expressed interest in acquiring the house, but did not have funding readily available. So the field chairman offered it to the "rich Church of God missionaries." The house was very well located in a nice residential area in western Tokyo. At $4,000.00 (U. S. currency), I thought it was very moderately priced. I asked for two weeks to respond.

Because I felt this would be an ideal residence for a second missionary family if such an appointment might be forthcoming, I contacted Reverend Paul Walker, our Foreign Missions Executive Secretary and strongly recommended that I be authorized to make the purchase. Knowing funds were very limited, I suggested that if we could not have this special allocation on such short notice, I would like a $4,000.00 loan against our monthly allotment to be repaid at $100 per month for forty months, without interest. My request for the loan was granted, and within two weeks the deed was ordered. This acquisition in no way advanced our evangelistic activities, but it was to become a vital factor in our expansion later.

We had the house. Also, my allotment the next month would be reduced by $100.00 so if we planned to eat, it was urgent that I find a tenant to occupy the house for at least $100.00 a month. With a large American presence in Japan so soon after the end of World War II, it was not difficult to find an American tenant for a western style house. I immediately signed a two year lease agreement for 40,000 yen, which exchanged for U. S. $110.00. My real estate payment was secured and we had $10.00 per month with which I started a new page in the ledger. I captioned it the "real estate fund." By mid-1956 the property loan was completely repaid and we had a small balance in our real estate slush fund —and we had property in Tokyo debt-free which had significantly increased in value.

About the time the loan against the Tokyo house was completely paid, I received a letter from the United States from a person I did not know. That letter contained a $500.00 check and the donor specified it was to be used for our Bible School (which we did not have at that time). I deposited the check in the bank and made a $500.00 entry in the "Real estate fund" ledger. It was unusual that we had no Bible School, nor had we ever solicited any support for a school, but had received this generous contribution from an unknown source. I accepted that $500 as a nudge from the Lord to explore our options and to start formulating some definite plans for a school.

With approximately $1,000 in hand plus the continuing monthly income from the Tokyo house, I started to look for a suitable location for a Bible School campus. With that limited amount of money, we were not likely to make any large purchase in the immediate future, so I decided to look around, but not to utilize the services of a realtor. Because realtors in Japan collected 5% from the seller and an additional 5% from the buyer, there was the possibility of quite a discount in cost if we could make a direct purchase.

One afternoon in January, 1956, feeling exhausted, Letha and I felt we needed to relax a little, so we took a short drive into a rural area west of Yokohama. For no specific reason I turned off the main highway on to a road that had formerly been the main thoroughfare, running parallel with the new highway for nearly two miles. Midway of that small road was a large open tract of land. The land was perfectly level and about three feet above the street. In shape, it was almost exactly square. For my American readers I should mention that in size it measured about one acre. Using Japanese measure, it was 1,300 tsubo. To the Japanese farmers, that was a very large and attractive field; and extremely valuable.

I made inquiry as to the owner and was pleased to learn he lived less than fifty yards from the property. I went immediately to the owner's house and introduced myself to him. After some small talk, he asked the reason for my visit. I replied I wanted to buy the tract of land near his house. He told me that was a major portion of the land he had under cultivation and he had no interest in disposing of it. Then in what seemed to be an afterthought, he inquired, "Why do you want my land?" My response was, "I want to build a Bible School there," to which he volunteered, "If you want to build a Bible School, then I have a responsibility to help you. I will sell you the land."

I was both dumbfounded and excited. When I mentioned price, he responded that he would need a little time to decide for two reasons. First, he owned 800 tsubo facing the street, but the adjoining 500 tsubo at the rear of the property belonged to a relative, whose consent he would try to get for me. Secondly, he wanted a few days to consult with family members as to what would constitute an appropriate price. He invited me to return after a week to get his final position.

When I returned a week later, he offered the entire tract for two million, five hundred thousand yen. I could not believe it! Two and a half million yen at the exchange rate then was the equivalent of $7,000.

Trying to conceal my elation, I calmly suggested that I give him a check for 500,000 yen (about $1400 equivalent) with the balance payable in ninety days, at which time the deeds would be recorded. I added a contingency that finalization of my offer had to be subject to approval of our home office in the U. S. In the absence of that approval, I would receive immediately a complete refund.

In 1956, international telephone service was archaic, utilizing two way radio signals and sometimes requiring three or four hours waiting time at the international telephone office until the scheduled call could be completed. Another important factor was the very high cost involved. For these reasons I had never utilized this service. But this was different. It completely justified the extravagance of an international telephone call.

I presented the situation to Paul Walker, and as expected I was given a very encouraging reply. He favored my position and offered to poll the mission board members by telephone. I should expect to know their position within less than a week. I enjoyed a meaningful rapport with Reverend Paul Walker. Both of us grew up in the Dakotas and we had similar tendencies when faced with either opportunities or challenges. He had pioneered the opening of the northwest for the Church of God a quarter of a century earlier, and I was certain he had to appreciate my enthusiasm for this proposed project. True to form, he came through strong for us. Within the week, he telephoned and instructed me to move ahead as planned to acquire the land.

It was a miracle! Less than a month after I had first seen this property, I signed a purchase agreement for land to build a Bible School. The only thing left was the formality of having the land use changed from agricultural use to light commercial building use. No one assumed this would be difficult.

I did not sleep well that night. It seems excitement substituted for rest and I spent quite a few hours conceptualizing a school for ministerial training at our newly purchased location.

CHAPTER EIGHTEEN

PATIENCE, PATIENCE, PATIENCE

Acquiring land for a school had been such a simple transaction, it put me into a state of shock. I could never have expected to find a tract of land more suitable for our need. It was large enough to accommodate the buildings I felt would be adequate for up to forty students. Being almost perfectly square, and having 210 feet of street frontage, the land would lend itself well to a compound featuring three main buildings side by side set back from the street about one hundred feet. By utilizing the unique horticultural skills possessed by the Japanese, this open space in front of the school could be manicured to resemble a city park.

Near the back boundary line, I visualized two residences to be occupied by members of the faculty. As it developed, between the two residences was a double-wide garage with a one bedroom apartment above it. Although it was not initially intended, that small building was the first building erected with the small second story apartment occupied by my family of four until the two residences were completed.

It might be accurate to say that finding and purchasing that land was one of the least complicated transactions of my life. It made me reflect on a conversation with a veteran missionary shortly after our arrival in Japan. He told me that to be a successful missionary in Japan required the development of three special traits. They are patience, patience and patience. In this instance, I was not once called on to evidence any patience to the extent I was tempted to discount the need for that good advice. I could almost see the buildings growing out of that farm field.

To locate land well situated; to find an owner amenable to our interest in procuring it; to come to a mutually acceptable valuation without one word of negotiation either to raise or lower the price; to make the entire transaction without the involvement of a real estate agent, thus reducing the real cost by 10%, etc. was a miracle. We were definitely inclined to believe that God must have been smiling on our efforts. If that were the case, then the eight months following the purchase of the land gave us ample cause to reason that there definitely is a real devil and that he intended to block our progress. We could not get a permit to change the zoning of our land. Let me explain.

Japan's population is nearly half as great as that of the United States, but its land area is comparable in size to California. Only 17% of the land is arable, including numberless hillside terraced plots that have been meticulously carved out of stubborn rocky soil, and made usable by continuous irrigating and fertilizing. With that extreme scarcity of tillable ground, it is completely understandable that this national asset must be closely guarded to insure that the population can continue to be fed.

I felt I understood the need to maintain vigilance in protecting Japan's farming properties, but I was asking for only one acre. Surely that could not cause any major upset or imbalance in the overall food production of the nation! Evidently the prefecture (county) agricultural board did not concur with my rationale. I was required to submit a request for a variance which would allow rezoning of the land from agricultural to light commercial before our property could be released from the land bank. The committee was not ready to relinquish to me such a large tract of ground ideally suited to growing food. I prepared and submitted the application for the variance with a heavy stack of papers attached as supporting documentation. Then I waited. About a month later I received a letter-packet with an official looking return address and no postage stamp attached. It was my reply from the prefecture agricultural committee. The message was brief and to the point. On the front page of my stack of documents was stamped one word. **"Declined."**

I resubmitted and waited another month. Near the end of the month, I was invited to meet with the agricultural committee, which would be in session at the prefecture office building from 8:30 a.m. until 5:00 p.m. I suggested that Pastor Shimada accompany me and further that he should be the spokesman so it would seem less like an application from a foreigner. Having been advised of a date, but not a specific time to meet, Pastor Shimada felt we ought to arrive early so if our case should be called early on the docket, we would not miss our appointment. Twenty minutes prior to the opening of the session, we were seated in a hall outside the large assembly chamber.

We were not first on the docket — so we waited. Fearing we may miss being called, we did not go out for lunch. After we had been sitting more than eight hours on uncomfortable chairs in a cold hall, a message was delivered to us. Apologetically, the committee informed us they had been working through a very heavy agenda and would not be able to include a discussion with us prior to adjournment. We were invited to meet with them at their next scheduled meeting the following month.

A month later we were there again. You guessed it. At 4:30 p.m. a messenger approached us. He was extremely apologetic about the full agenda of such important business that we just could not be worked in. But next month…

We reasoned that surely we would not receive the same cold treatment three months in a row. We had reasoned correctly — this time it was different. At 4:30 p.m., instead of sending a messenger to us, a member of the government board came out of the conference room. Professing sincere regret he gave us essentially the same message we had received twice before, the only difference being that this time we were given the courtesy of receiving the message directly from an official rather than from a subordinate.

Finally, after a four month delay, we were granted a meeting. The committee sat solemnly as our appeal was read by Pastor Shima-da. In our presence they deliberated at length, considering such things as the importance of spiritual guidance and religious education. Mention was made of the fact that we had been quite agreeable and patient for a number of months. Some of them favored granting the variance. I was very encouraged. While we listened to their discussion, I fantasized the development of our new property. I could visualize the various improvements which would make for a very attractive as well as functional campus.

In the midst of my delightful dreams, I was summoned back to reality. We were instructed to approach the chairman's desk. He advised that his committee had considered all of the evidence very carefully and they had decided to grant the variance, thus paving the way to have building permits issued. I looked up gratefully. God does care, doesn't He! After a long pause to remind us we were in an auspicious atmosphere, the chairman continued, "We will issue the variance, but we cannot in good conscience approve taking one thousand, three hundred tsubo out of agricultural production. We are prepared to release up to half of that valuable property. You select which part you want to use for your school and we will issue the variance. Then the remainder of the land must be returned to the farmers who sold it. Bring us your revised plans next month for final approval."

Before the next session convened, I received a message suggesting that the committee had devoted a great deal of time to our project, and a monetary gift in an appropriate amount to each member of the board could possibly result in a reconsideration and release of the entire property. The concept was reprehensible to me and my reply was, "Let the land rot! How can I build a school for the training of spiritual leaders on ground that was secured with bribery?"

My reply was apparently delivered back to the members of the board, because the next month, Pastor Shimada and I sat in the hall eight hours, received a brief message from an errand boy and then went home.

The anonymous emissary who had suggested the cash bribe appeared again. He apologized for the indiscretion of suggesting money under the table. Alternatively, he commented, "The men really do want to help you. As an expression of your appreciation for their kindness to you, it would be a very fine gesture if you would invite them to a nice dinner."

"Where would be a suitable place for such a dinner, and how much should it cost?" I queried. When he mentioned a price per person about ten times as much as I had ever paid for a meal, I ventured another question. "Would I be correct in assuming that such a dinner at that cost would include alcoholic drinks and geisha girls?"

"Of course," he said.

"That is tantamount to a bribe; not only of cash, but also of serving the bribe in a sensuous atmosphere. I am not at all interested. Trash-can our application, but don't ask me again to bribe anyone to get a permit to build a Bible School. I cannot build a school to teach truth if the classroom is on a foundation of falsehood!" I responded angrily. My dubious consultant did not return again.

The following month our variance was granted and progress resumed.

Admittedly, this protracted game of politics and personal power frustrated me. It may well have been best for us because we were not yet ready to start any construction on that property. By this time we had only three functioning churches, which would hardly justify the opening of a school. Then there was the minor matter of money, which was usually in short supply. Actually, the unwelcome delays imposed by government red tape allowed me time to give attention to other important matters.

When I had recommended the purchase of the land for a Bible School, I included two related matters. We had the house in Yokohama occupied by my family and we had the residence in Tokyo that had been purchased for $4,000. Almost simultaneous with my submission of an offer to purchase the land for a Bible School, the Tokyo house became debt-free. The $110.00 monthly rent income had increased to $165 after the first tenant moved. In

155

a very short time the entire purchase price had been paid by rental income and we had a nice property. My proposal included selling that property and using the proceeds to pay the balance due on the new land.

My plan provided that my family would occupy one of the residences at the new location, so our residence also could be sold with the receipts applied to this new project.

The Tokyo house had been purchased for $4,000. Because the total cost of the house in Tokyo had been returned with the rental income, our actual investment in that property had been reduced to zero. Three years after purchase, it was sold for $8,400. That was more than enough to pay off the land. Therefore this new tract of land was ours without any outlay of actual cash except the initial deposit of $1,500 allocated by the missions board.

The Yokohama house had been built at a cost of $5,200. It was sold for $7,500. Even though our permit from the agricultural department was repeatedly delayed or denied, we felt confident of the final outcome, so during that same eight month period, I busied myself with selling the two properties we owned.

When the permit was issued, I had blueprints ready to present to the building office at city hall for permits. I had money in hand to pay off the land completely and enough to construct the double garage with the apartment above it, plus adequate funds to construct one of the houses. To build the third building, I had to request $4,500 from the Foreign Missions Department, which they granted.

By the end of our first term, the three buildings at the rear of the property were completed, including concrete driveway and walks, the back one third of the land very attractively landscaped, the yards sodded and basic trees and shrubbery planted.

The total new outlay of cash from the stateside missions department had been only $6,000. What a thrill it was to transform two modest homes into two much better new homes and to have a choice piece of real estate for a school. Without intention, I was receiving graduate level education in business negotiation and real estate development, which would prove to be very beneficial in later years. While this manuscript has been in preparation, I received word that the Japanese pastors have decided to sell this property and reinvest the proceeds in local churches. After having had the use of this property for 35 years, they are offering it for sale for the U. S. currency equivalent of four million dollars.

CHAPTER NINETEEN

NATIONAL TELEVISION

June, 1957, marked the end of our first five year term in the Orient. I arrived in Japan when I was age twenty-five and five years later returned home about age thirty. Nearly everything had changed. Five years earlier, I had hair; I returned home bald. I went to Japan with an impetuous, impatient temperament. When I left, I had learned some patience and restraint. I went to Japan the father of one daughter and returned with a son who was "made in Japan." Our travel from San Francisco to Yokohama by ship in 1952 had required 19 days. We returned from Tokyo to Seattle, with a stopover in Alaska, in 19 hours.

We were gratified to leave Japan having established four small churches as a foundation of a work destined to expand in later years to impact Asia. More than we realized it, we needed the rest after five very busy and strenuous years. We spent a few weeks renewing family ties, but soon I grew impatient to be on the move again. We had returned for a rest and the Missions Department continued our monthly financial support. However, when I expressed a desire to travel throughout the nation to visit as many churches as could be arranged, I was given approval to travel as well as assistance in scheduling. During that first furlough, I conducted one night missions-emphasis meetings in more than 150 churches to solicit the prayers and concern of our American constituency for our overseas outreach.

Our daughter, Janice, was then a second grader. She had attended a Japanese kindergarten, followed by first grade in a U. S. government school which existed primarily for dependent children of military personnel. Because of these adjustments, Letha felt Janice needed her nearby. Our son, Ron, was three years old, and to travel with him, staying in a different pastor's home, or motel every night would have been difficult. As a consequence, I did most of that travel alone.

With so much activity, our one year furlough passed quickly. In August, 1958, we boarded the Hikawa Maru for its final voyage across the Pacific. For years, the Hikawa Maru had been the flagship of Japan's passenger fleet, of which they were very proud. It was now obsolete and facing retirement in Tokyo bay as a floating museum. On that last voyage, there was no suggestion of being old and worn. The crew catered to the passengers in royal fashion and made that a most memorable final trip.

Travel to Japan the first time was exciting and held much intrigue for us. This time, we knew what to expect. Within days after arrival, we were immersed in all of the activities of missionary life. At the start of our first term, Janice was only two years old. Then two years after our arrival in Japan, Ron was born, so with the care of two young children, Letha had not been able to concentrate as much as necessary to learn the Japanese language. She determined that during this second term, she would correct that.

Shortly prior to our leaving Japan for furlough, a young lady from South Africa, Joan Wakeford, joined our team in Japan. Joan was a member of the Full Gospel Church of God, a sister organization of the American Church of God. When we departed Japan, we left her in charge of the fledgling work. A few weeks before our return, Joan was made aware of a plan to close an American military base near Tokyo and that the buildings were being given to Christian missions without cost, except to demolish the buildings and remove the materials. Joan had applied for and received one building.

Once again, contrary to the picture many have of a missionary, I donned my overalls and traveled early each morning to Tokyo. Very soon the building was demolished and transported to Yokohama. Inasmuch as there was no immediate plan to develop the campus, we decided to use these materials to construct a modest chapel on the front of the school property. Of course, it would be temporary until the school should be built, which would include a chapel in the main building. This church building project had not been anticipated, so there was no budget for it.

With building materials on hand, but no money, I did the only logical thing that could be done. I built the church and opened the doors for service. I built the church entirely alone because I had no money to hire any help. Many of the neighbors were fascinated to see this building erected by one man. One neighbor contacted NHK (Japan's national television) to report this strange incident. NHK sent a news man to interview me and invite me to appear on national television. The story made national news.

During our second term in Japan, we were kept extremely busy. The four small churches started during the first five years were growing and one of my primary concerns was to provide spiritual nurture for these converts. When the churches were strengthened, the natural result was evangelism and expansion. At the end of our second term, our churches numbered eight. Because of this growth, we were made even more keenly aware of the urgency of having an educational facility that would develop leadership for these emerging congregations.

Two years into our second term we received word of the closure of another U. S. military installation fifty miles northwest of Tokyo. I was selected to act with a small committee of missionaries to allocate 57 duplexes in an officers' housing area. The buildings had been erected only two years earlier, but top brass in Washington determined the base would close, so these new buildings were ready to be dismantled and the land returned to its Japanese owners. We were the beneficiaries. The buildings were given to any registered mission in Japan at no cost. Our only expense was labor to demolish the buildings and truck the materials away. Our mission received three buildings, so I had sufficient materials to erect three buildings on our campus. It was tantamount to a mandate to build a school.

By working with a crew of craftsmen and laborers, without the services of a contractor, I calculated the cost to reconstruct the three buildings to be about $15,000. At my request, the missions department granted the allocation, and we were ready to start the project. Under huge tarpaulins was stacked enough lumber to frame and enclose our three school buildings. I acquired a quonset building in which was stored all of the windows, doors, frames, interior millwork and hardwood flooring for all three buildings.

The expansion of the number of local churches and the need for trained pastors dictated the school was a necessity. Virtually all the material needed to construct three buildings was on our property. We had an approved budget to complete the work. These factors, in combination, loudly suggested it was time to start.

It was decided that the main building should have a basement, so we started moving dirt with picks, shovels and small two-wheeled carts with human motors. It was a time consuming project. The excavation was completed and the concrete foundation was poured by early June. The timing could not have been worse. Every year in Japan it rains every day from June 10 to July 10. The farmers take advantage of this phenomenon and plant their rice during this precisely predictable time of incessant rain. It was the season for the inevitable rain and we had an open basement. In spite of the likelihood of inclement weather, we started to build.

Each morning I went outside to see the sky. Ominous clouds reminded me it was the rainy season. Sometimes, I saw where a few drops of rain had spotted the sidewalk. Realizing the farmers were depending on rain to germinate their crops, I felt that to pray for clear weather would be wrong. So when I saw a clear sky, I breathed a prayer of thanks. But when I saw signs of impending rain, I simply thought, "Wouldn't it be wonderful if it may be clear today so we can build, and then rain tonight for the farmers' benefit."

I don't claim any special spirituality or faith, but from the day we started laying the concrete block walls for the basement until the roof was decked and covered with black felt, was 25 days. Sometimes it rained at night: at times there was rain on neighboring property, but during those 25 days, my workmen did not miss ten minutes work time because of rain. While the men were putting the felt paper on the roof to waterproof the building, about 2:00 p.m. on the 25th day, it started to rain. I sent the men home early with a full day's pay and walked in the house feeling keenly that God does care.

Certainly it was more than coincidental that so many provisions were made and so many details dovetailed. I was convinced we were doing the right thing. As the project progressed, one young Christian and then another in the local churches told me of his desire to be enrolled in our first classes. By my count, we would have ten students registered for the first quarter. Of course, I realize ten students does not constitute a large student body. We learned later that missionaries from other groups would drive by our property and seeing the construction progressing, made comments about Noah's Ark being built again. The uncomfortable fact is, they were quite right.

As we neared completion of the buildings, I began to devote much of my time and consideration to the opening of the school, the curriculum to be offered, who would be on our teaching staff, and a myriad of related matters. I anticipated with enthusiasm this new phase of our work. If I have any innate inclination toward ministry, it is in the field of teaching rather than evangelizing, pastoring or other types of Christian service. We came to a decision that I would devote the greater part of my time and energy to teaching and administering the general operation of the school. After all, this is the work that would most effectively contribute to the expansion and long range success of our emerging Japanese church. The pastors of each of our churches would be invited to commit to teaching one or two courses in addition to their pastoral responsibilities. This pleased them because they could have a part in the development and growth of our denomination. Also, this was a refreshing diversion for them.

About the time plans were in their final stage, I had an unexpected

163

visit from Pastor Shimada, who had been my right hand for about five years. Although we both made an effort to work together for the good of the church and its members, behind the scenes were a multiplicity of disagreements and difficulties. On the afternoon in question Shimada had brought to me numerous recommendations for consideration. (More accurately, I should state that he brought to me numerous demands for immediate approval and implementation.) I was quite busy and suggested that we set a convenient time to meet later. He was insistent that we meet immediately!

The subject matter of our conversation became less consequential to me and I was becoming more concerned with attitudes and uncontrolled displays of temper, almost to the point of violence. It became clearly evident that Shimada believed I could not function without his assistance, and he was driving hard for a more prominent (and more dominant) role. His timing was critical because we were just weeks from opening the school, and because it was expected that most of my time and energy would be given to the school, he intended to exert more influence over the other pastors and their local churches. I believe he initially intended a friendly coup d' etat, in which he would emerge as the ultimate — if not apparent — authority. As the debate continued, the idea of a "friendly" takeover became sublimated in the intent to control under any circumstances, friendly or hostile.

When his self-control had been replaced with an open display of aggression, rage and anger, I felt the time had arrived for me to do what I had known for some time ultimately had to be done. I told him quietly that everyone within hearing distance had become aware of the fact that he and I shared no mutual respect, much less a common ground for cooperative Christian ministry. I reminded him that it was I who had appointed him to pastor our first and largest church; and now he had left me no alternative but to suspend that appointment. I gave him official notice that he should vacate the church and parsonage within thirty days. I told him further he would receive the equivalent of two months' salary as severance pay and we would bear the expense of his move.

Shimada's first response was that this was a Japanese church, he was the pastor and he had no intention of resigning. Further, as a foreigner, I would face severe opposition if I should attempt to implement what I had just told him. I advised him I would take that risk, and my decision to relieve him of all duties and control had not been changed by his expressed intention to oppose it. He then changed tactics. He reminded me that every pastor in our small organization was assigned to a church and we had no one to replace him. "Then I will become the pastor," I responded.

On numerous occasions under more agreeable circumstances, Shimada had told me my use of the Japanese language was exceptional. However, at this time it seemed wiser for him to point out my limitations in the language. He emphasized that Japanese people would not attend a service conducted primarily by a foreigner speaking Japanese with a heavy accent. I knew he was correct on that score, but told him I would prefer to pastor that church in spite of my limitations than to have our Christian believers led by a person who had just proved to me he was far more motivated by selfish concerns than the spiritual well-being of his constituents. Regardless of the difficulty, in good conscience, I could not reverse my decision.

I was faced with two mammoth jobs; I was pastor of a church and doing it all in a foreign language. Additionally, I was to become principal, instructor, comptroller, student dean and yardboy in a school soon to be born.

The weight of these new responsibilities was lessened considerably one Sunday evening after the service was completed. A member of the church approached me saying, "When you spoke to us through an interpreter we got your message. Now we get your heart." I could not have been more complimented or more encouraged.

The school term in Japan starts in April. As the announced date for the first term of classes at Yokohama Bible Institute approached, a number of letters of apology were received from individuals previously registered to become our first students, explaining why their plans had required some modification. In view of the fact that our facility was adequate to accommodate up to forty students, we had decided some time earlier to accept students from other churches to the extent space was available.

165

Ten young people had made advance application to attend, but by matriculation day, every one had decided to wait until the next term, except two students from a non-affiliated church. I faced a tough decision. Should I implement a program to operate a school with a full course of study, using for two people a facility large enough for forty? And should I expect pastors to leave their responsibilities to the local churches to travel to the school to teach only two students? Was I willing to dedicate my time to teaching two students, who might graduate and then return to pastor a church for another group? I think I started to comprehend the feelings Noah had. Maybe my critics had been closer to correct than I had been willing to acknowledge.

I made the decision. Yokohama Bible Institute opened its doors in April, 1961. Less than nine years earlier, Letha and I had arrived in Japan. Since then, we had acquired a relatively acceptable working knowledge of the language. We had eight functioning churches or mission outreaches (some admittedly very small). And now we have a school!

A school?? With two students???

CHAPTER TWENTY

EMPHASIS ON YOUTH

Just a few weeks prior to our arrival in Japan for a second term, Mary Grace Comans made a quiet debut in Tokyo. Having grown up in a rural setting near the tiny town of Sebastapol, Mississippi, she had been exposed to little of the superficiality sometimes referred to as life in the fast lane. The two most significant influences in her early years had been her high-principled father and the small rural church near Sebastapol. It followed, therefore, that Mary was extremely sincere. She had a quiet sophistication and was totally unpretentious.

Mary Comans was a civilian employee of the U. S. military as an elementary school teacher for dependents in Tokyo. Her employment was to impart the three R's to American children, but her underlying compelling concern was to impart faith to Tokyo's youth.

Mary spoke no Japanese, but she communicated well with a pleasant personality and a warm temperament that did not require a translator. With her infectious smile, she attracted the attention of many young Japanese who were interested in association with Americans and an exposure to English conversation. Capitalizing on this ever prevalent interest, Mary made many acquaintances and then invited them to her apartment. Within a very short time, her living room was crowded every Saturday evening with about 20 young people eager for exposure to anything western. They wanted to learn English. Mary wanted to talk about spiritual things. She read to them from her Bible and invited their comments and discussion in English. With this arrangement everyone was pleased.

Within a few weeks, Mary's modest living room was not able to accommodate the growing group. Mary soon solved that small problem by dividing them and inviting the collegians to continue to come on Saturday evenings and she formed a new group of high school students to meet on Tuesday evenings.

It was only a matter of weeks until both meetings were over-attended. Undaunted, Mary simply divided them again. Tuesday evening was for high school level; Thursday evening was college level. A new advanced class started meeting on Saturday evenings intended for business people and graduate level university students. As the demand dictated the need, a fourth group was formed. This was all happening in Mary's living room. The meetings were basically social and educational in nature, except for the fact that the text book for English study was the Bible. But Mary was more interested in offering her new-found friends spiritual values than educational. When anyone expressed interest in a clearer understanding of what had been discussed in the class session, or when one had personal need, she arranged an individual interview, or possibly a meal together. As a result, Mary cultivated many lasting personal friends and not a few of them chose to share the vibrant faith she exuded continuously. Without specifically intending to do so, Mary was preparing a foundation for what was to become our largest church in Japan.

As the group grew and demands on her time increased, Mary became aware that this intense involvement four evenings every week, in addition to her forty hours weekly responsibility to her primary employment was becoming increasingly difficult. Her first appeal for help was directed to Joan Wakeford, our missionary associate from the Full Gospel Church of God in South Africa. Joan assumed responsibility for the high school class. Later she called on Letha and me for help. We volunteered to take the Saturday evening business level group. It was a good diversion for us. My work required me to communicate almost exclusively in Japanese, and this weekly meeting conducted entirely in English was like releasing a pressure valve.

Since late 1956, my family had resided at the location intended to become the Yokohama Bible Institute. By April, 1961, construction of the physical facility was completed and occupied by two students. Admittedly, I was embarrassed and humiliated having this commodious compound and only two students, but I did what I was convinced was right. In the months that followed, we received six applications for late enrollment into our school. Not being stringently structured, and not being restricted as a fully accredited school would have been, we approved all of those late applications. By the end of our first term, enrollment had "swelled" four hundred percent! In other words, Yokohama Bible Institute had a spectacular beginning. We possibly were the only school in the world that had twice as many faculty members as students. After the phenomenal influx of late registrations, this ratio was diluted to one faculty member for every two students.

Our young mission was still painfully small, but that was not attributable to a lack of activity. As we neared the end of our second term, between Letha and me, we were conducting nine services a week. This was in addition to the fact that I was in a classroom at the school from three to five hours a day, either teaching or interpreting for a missionary who had not yet developed sufficient language skills to teach in Japanese.

With eight young students in the school preparing for Christian service as their life work, we had not only a responsibility to disseminate information and instruction in the classroom, but also to provide hands-on training in the real world. To facilitate this, we acquired a tent and four or five times during a school year conducted evangelistic campaigns. Students covered an area with gospel tracts and printed invitations in the afternoon. In the tent that evening students conducted the early part of the meeting, including welcome, singing and prayer. The sermon was given by one of our pastors from a nearby church or a missionary.

One specific evening in the tent remains vividly in my memory. Bob Midgley, a dedicated evangelist from New Zealand had affiliated with our mission and he contributed greatly in the school classroom. Also, he was a very effective speaker in our tent meetings. On the evening in question, he was to be the speaker. Arrangements had been made for an interpreter to work with Bob. During the early minutes of the service a few seats were taken and there was a restless group milling around outside the tent. When it was nearly time for the sermon and the interpreter had not yet arrived, Bob Midgley became visibly nervous. With no better alternative, I offered to serve as Bob's interpreter.

Bob was announced as the guest speaker. He walked to the podium. I followed him. Bob greeted his audience in English. I translated it into Japanese. The restless crowd outside became quiet. They had been attracted by the novelty of an American interpreting an English message into their understanding. As if mesmerized, the individuals scattered outside gravitated into the tent and remained spellbound during the entire service. At the conclusion there was a good response to the message presented. Because this unique method of teamwork was so effective, Bob and I employed a similar pattern of team preaching on numerous occasions, always with similar results.

Our small mission continued to develop. Joan Wakeford had been sent to Japan to assist us from our South African Church. Mary Comans was a special gift delivered to the right place at just the right time by the United States Government. Bob Midgley was sent to Japan from New Zealand by the Slavic and Oriental Mission. Strangely, Bob had been given no instruction or guidance as to what he should do. When we met, he was studying Japanese with a private tutor, but having no sense of direction, he was frustrated to the point of resigning and returning home. I invited him to visit our home and while there to be a guest lecturer at our emerging school. From the first day, it was a perfect match. He enjoyed teaching these future leaders of Japan's churches, and they loved his teaching.

Within a few weeks, Bob inquired of me as to whether we could make a place for him on our team. If it could be arranged, he said he was prepared to mail to the Slavic and Oriental Mission a letter of resignation he had already written. I contacted our home office, recommending that I be authorized to accept Bob's application for affiliation, which was approved. His talents complemented mine exactly. Everything I could not do seemed to be Bob's area of specialization.

Having gone to Japan as a very young and inexperienced novice, I did not know what to do or how to do it. Basically, I busied myself with what seemed the right thing to do, and often while I floundered, it appeared God was working out His plan and purpose for me. We had started a school, which everyone thought was destined to be a complete fiasco. Bob Midgley was the ideal person to impart information and spiritual leadership to the students who were to become pastors of churches not yet organized. In the first year two students increased to eight. The second year, enrollment increased to 16. What was heralded as a colossal albatross at its inception was getting positioned to prove its critics incorrect.

While this welcome metamorphosis was taking place at Yokohama Bible Institute, the youth meetings in Tokyo continued to expand. It seemed every time we met Mary, her one item of conversation was the need for a Youth Center to facilitate the activities of the existing groups and to extend the work among Tokyo's youth. My standard response was usually a hollow, artificial agreement. Did Mary not understand the high cost of land in Tokyo? Further, just when we were completing a costly project in Yokohama did not seem to me a propitious time to request a budget for land and a building in a place as expensive as Tokyo.

While I was constantly busied with trying to coach Mary to exercise some patience, I awoke one night and the whole plan unfolded before me. I addressed a letter to Dr. Cecil Knight, who was at that time the General Director of Youth and Christian Education, worldwide. In my letter to Dr. Knight I provided a brief review of the development of our youth work in Tokyo and then something about the need for a facility designed specifically to attract Tokyo's youth to a center concerned with youth ministries exclusively. I concluded my letter with a suggestion that in view of the fact this proposed center would focus all of its attention on youth, this should be a good project for his department.

My recommendation to Dr. Knight was that some advance

brochures be mailed to churches all over the United States apprising them of a planned concerted effort on a single specified day of youth throughout the entire denomination to sponsor a center for Tokyo's youth. With a plan of this sort, it would not create a hardship on anyone, but at the same time, with every church participating, we could conceivably fund the entire project with just one offering from each participating youth group.

The following week, I received a telephone call from Cecil Knight. He was elated! What he told me was exciting. He related that the General Youth Department was in the middle of a project to build a church in Brasilia, a new city not yet in existence. Their method of raising the money and sponsoring the project was precisely what I had suggested in my letter. Dr. Knight went on, "I like your proposed plan for a Youth Center, and when the General Youth Board meets next week, I will make them aware of your letter and will recommend that they designate Tokyo as our target for next year. As soon as I get a response, I will telephone you."

A week later, Cecil called to tell me that the Tokyo Youth Center had been accepted as the National Youth Department's challenge for 1962. Brasilia was the first project and Tokyo would be the second. Actually, due to many complications in developing this new city in the jungles of Brazil, even though it was the first nationally sponsored youth/missions effort in our denomination, the Tokyo center was the first facility to materialize.

When that single offering from all of the churches was counted, it was nearly $18,000. I was extremely grateful for the nationwide support of our youth groups, not to mention that I was also pleased for the money they had gathered together for Japan's youth. One major problem loomed large. I knew it would not be possible to make this plan a reality with $18,000. However, so that I could be prepared to discuss the matter intelligently, I surveyed a number of areas in Tokyo. I located one small parcel of land near the city limits of Tokyo's south side. It was available for six million, five hundred thousand yen. At the rate of exchange effective at that time, that was the equivalent of U. S. currency $18,055.

I made contact with the Missions Department and requested

authorization to secure that land, spending the $18,000 received from the Youth Department. Further, I submitted a request for an additional $20,000 with which to construct a suitable building. Approval was forthcoming and I contracted for the land. Next I had an architect to prepare blueprints for the building.

From the time construction of the Yokohama Bible Institute was completed, there was not time for my tools to collect even a little rust until we were back at it again. With such limited finance and such an ambitious plan, every cost had to be held to the absolute minimum. Thankfully, we were able to build a nice sanctuary with a second floor to accommodate a complete training center and space for social functions. The center was completed and dedicated just one month before my family and I departed Japan for our second furlough to the U. S.

This new facility functioned as a Youth Center for a time, but ultimately it became evident that it could be better utilized as a church and the program and method of operation was modified. Today it is by far the best church in our denomination in Japan. When we visited Tokyo just a year ago, the pastor told us about their current schedule of services, including outreaches. As I recall, this one church conducts nine services each week.

CHAPTER TWENTY-ONE

SAYONARA

At the completion of our second term in Japan, we returned to the U. S. traveling west instead of east. Our trip took us through a number of countries in Asia and Europe, but my main purpose for routing that way was to visit the lands of the Bible. We had a most interesting and inspiring two weeks in Egypt, Israel and Greece.

Our second furlough was essentially a repetition of the first, and our third term in the Orient was basically a continuation of the first and second terms, so to include that information here would be redundant — with a few notable exceptions.

Spanning the second and third terms, I made a number of visits to Korea. In the latter 1950's, our World Missions office received reports of the personal witnessing activity of a young U. S. Army sergeant. Dr. Vessie Hargrave, then the General Director of World Missions, instructed me to travel to Korea to check on these reports and attempt to make contact with the young soldier, Joe Comer. Before my arrival in Seoul, Joe had been assigned to a different duty station. However, I did meet with two Korean Christian laymen who were keenly interested in associating with our international church with a view to developing an extension in Korea. One of these men, David Kim, had spent some time with Joe Comer and had a limited awareness about the Church of God. A very enthusiastic, almost impetuous man, David strongly favored an immediate action to establish our church in Korea. The other person, Young Chul Han, was more reserved, but definitely positive.

From our first meeting we enjoyed a meaningful friendship and soon a cooperative working arrangement evolved. Between 1958 and 1964 I made six trips to Korea. On one of those trips we located a small tract of land in Seoul, which we later purchased. It became the site of the first Church of God in Korea.

Roughly eighteen months into our third term to Japan, Letha went to town for some shopping. When she stopped at a traffic light, the driver behind her apparently did not notice the light was red, resulting in a collision. Letha sustained a severe whiplash. That injury, coupled with an acute nervous condition that had been developing for quite some time, incapacitated her for a number of months.

The last time I went to Korea, I accompanied Dr. Leonard Carroll, our General Overseer. A highlight of that trip was the dedication of the first Church of God in Korea. Because Letha's physical condition following her automobile accident continued to deteriorate, we were compelled to request an emergency furlough shortly after I returned from Korea. The result was the termination of our missionary service and our return to the United States early in 1966.

Approximately two years later an unpleasant situation developed which made it advisable that the Church of God discontinue further association with David Kim. At that time he opted to affiliate with a different church group.

Young Chul Han became the National Overseer of the emerging church and has done a phenomenal work for Korea with scores of churches throughout the nation. He has also initiated and directed the development of a Bible college in Seoul. At the time of this writing an application for university status has just been approved by the Department of Education with full recognition of the Korean Government, effective as of January, 1997.

Not only has the church experienced gratifying growth in Korea, under the leadership of Dr. Young Chul Han, they have sent out missionaries as far distant as Libya in North Africa, as well as Manchuria and Mongolia in extreme northeastern Asia.

Prior to our departure from the Orient, I had submitted a request for a six month emergency furlough, which I felt would be adequate time for Letha's recovery. My request was approved as submitted, and we left Tokyo in February with plans to return to the Orient in August, immediately following our denomination's General Assembly.

When the General Assembly convened in August, the World Missions Board also was in session. We were invited to meet briefly with the board. I presumed we were to finalize plans for our return to Japan. As it turned out, our meeting with the missions board was somewhat of a courtesy to us, but there was no discussion about the possibility of our return to Japan. They felt Letha's condition would be worsened by returning to Japan.

On the final day of the General Assembly when all executive appointments were announced, my brother, Wayne, was seated beside me. My name was called out as the Superintendent of Japan. The missionary who had been directing the work in our absence was announced as the Assistant Superintendent. Of course, I was pleased when I heard the announcement of our re-appointment.

At that time, Wayne was a member of the World Missions board. He had been instructed to be with me during the reading of the appointments and to explain what had been done. He and I immediately went outside where he told me we were not to return to Japan, but rather the appointment was made in recognition of what we had done in pioneering the work for the Church of God in Japan. The appointment would stand for two years, but I would be the Superintendent in Absentia during that time. Wayne told me this had never been done in the history of the church and it was intended as a very special commendation by the board.

Our missionary career had abruptly ended. I was paged to meet Reverend W. E. Johnson immediately following dismissal of the session. Reverend Johnson informed me of my appointment as pastor of the prestigious church in Logan, West Virginia.

Logan was one of the three leading churches in the state. In its fifty year history, Logan had been served by some of the outstanding clergymen of our denomination. In fact, Reverend Johnson told me he was a former pastor of the Logan Church.

There was one major problem. I had begun to see myself as a missionary, but I was never called to be a pastor. The next two years would serve to prove that fact.

Arriving in Logan, we located a large, beautiful church on the main arterial highway through West Logan. It was an imposing structure of traditional design with a red brick exterior. The full daylight basement served well as an educational facility as well as various social events and celebrations. A comfortable living accommodation was provided for us in the parsonage nearby. The church I had been assigned to pastor was a fellowship of some of the most caring people on earth. Undoubtedly, God created an exceptional class of people, from which he populated the mountains. When we parked our Rambler in the driveway of the parsonage, we were greeted by a group of these people. Their friendly temperament was infectious.

Logan was good to us. Some of God's choice children were members of our congregation. Thirty years later, we still receive letters and telephone calls from these special people in the mountains of West Virginia.

But I had reservations...

I thoroughly enjoyed serving the church as director of the worship services. Teaching was always a pleasant assignment for me and to be totally candid, my preaching basically consisted of camouflaged teaching sessions.

It may be that I tried too hard to be a good pastor but could not measure up to my own expectations. I felt I must relate to the individual needs of each member who called for help. But lacking personal experience, it was not possible for me to be honestly empathetic. Often when I tried to relate, I felt artificial and hypocritical.

In our small town setting, it was expected that the pastor make visits to the homes of church members on a regular basis and counsel with them about all of their concerns. I did make the visits, but I never felt I was very effective with the counseling.

The Logan church was fifty years old and many of the members were of advanced age. That meant wakes and funerals. When I became pastor of the Logan church, I had been a clergyman with credentials for 21 years, but had never conducted a funeral. Although I was from a large family, we had not had one death in our immediate family, so death and funerals were foreign concepts to me. In those two years, I attended many wakes and officiated at numerous funerals. However, having had no personal prior involvement, again I had difficulty trying to relate.

Much of my work consisted of visiting the sick and infirm in hospitals. But I had never been sick in my life and I just could not empathize. I learned to say the right words, but I am sure they conveyed little encouragement to the hospital patients.

The second half of the twentieth century is correctly characterized by failed families, love triangles, and marital infidelity. In this area also, I had difficulty offering solace. I do not propose putting my family on a pedestal as an example of the perfect family, but our marital compatibility has been noticeably above average and our children have never embarrassed us by lewd living or involvement in alcohol or illegal drugs. So when I was confronted by the crying wife of an unscrupulous husband who had forgotten his marriage vows; or when distressed parents wanted me to visit their wayward son in the penitentiary, I did not have the right answers.

Often I was sought out for counsel and assistance by church members with financial difficulties. Having lived most of my life without the luxury of money, I lacked the credentials to offer any sound advice in this area. Occasionally, I offered a few lame suggestions, but facing crisis and ruination, they were searching feverishly for solutions that made dollars and sense immediately. Simply stated, I was not the man with a plan.

Even though I made my best effort to be a good pastor, I felt I was the prime player in a real-life game of charades. Constantly I had the feeling that I "didn't fit"; the church in Logan deserved better than I could provide. They did not need a professional with a French cuff shirt and a pin-striped suit dispensing good theology for their spiritual needs and hackneyed solutions for their down-to-earth difficulties. There are often times when hurting people need a refreshing cup of cold water. I had access to the water supply, but my cup was too small.

After having made my best effort for more than two years to be the pastor that the Logan Church of God had a right to expect, as a favor to the congregation, and to extricate myself from a circumstance where my inadequacies far outweighed my capabilities, I resigned the Logan pastorate.

CHAPTER TWENTY-TWO

GOOD FOR NOTHING

Many times during the less than successful years of trying to pastor the Logan church, I was convinced I was not intended to be a pastor. On the other hand, many of the constituents had convinced me that my preaching was acceptable and had been helpful to them. Often they made genuine compliments about the sermons and the teaching sessions. Based on that premise, I began to give consideration to making a serious change in my life work. I would become an itinerant Bible teacher, conducting Bible-based seminars for spiritual living in an unspiritual environment.

I once heard a comment comparing pastors to laymen. It was stated that people expect a pastor to be good. He gets paid to be good. But the layman is good for nothing. For most of my years

Note: The events recorded in the next three chapters cover a time span of about ten years. The information included is based on memory recollection as no formal records were kept with an intent to write this biographical report. However, every effort has been made to make this information as accurate as possible. Certain persons and businesses are mentioned incidental to this biographical record. Reference is made to some persons as contributing to the problems and failures experienced by the writer. Even though numerous negative situations are cited as events that actually occurred, so as not to place blame or make any derogatory inference toward anyone, in many cases the names of those businesses and persons as they appear in this book are fictitious.

as a professional clergyman, I suffered from a sense that I did not belong. Maybe I could be a good layman, and as such, make a meaningful impact in my small corner of the world. I reasoned that it is far more important that we do some good while we live in this world than how we do it.

This new circumstance I was considering would be more of a modification than a complete change. My decision was not to leave the ministry. I would do that part of clerical work to which I seemed best suited, but not be involved in those things toward which I had no inclination. I had been a clergyman long enough to learn it is expected that preachers should be poor and humble. Well — at least poor! Realizing I could not expect to generate enough income from these proposed meetings to support my family unless I should schedule meetings back-to-back, it became apparent that another component was essential to complete this new equation.

I would need to schedule my meetings out of town not more than two weeks of each month. In the remaining time I could occupy myself in some way that would supplement my income. I believed I could do that in a business I would create.

As a young man I had learned about building from Pop. If I could somehow find funds to purchase a building lot, I would build and sell a house. When that house should sell, I would build another. In this way, by creating my own job, my work schedule would not be controlled by someone else. I could work when I was home, and when I had to be away, I could have sub-contractors at work.

Janice had graduated from high school in May and had applied for admission to Lee College in Cleveland, Tennessee, the town where our church is headquartered. Because there are hundreds of local churches within a few hours' driving distance, which should facilitate scheduling my meetings, and because Janice would be there for the next four years, we felt it might be prudent to make Cleveland our next home.

Twenty years earlier when I attended Lee College my total cost for schooling with all living expense included was $400 per school year. When Janice registered, I learned the cost would be $4,000 per year. I had no cash reserve, but thankfully, Janice had done well in high school, so we were able to locate some scholarship money and a student loan. What impacted me abruptly was the fact of such an extreme increase in those twenty years. It caused me to realize that I had been very immature in not making any financial preparation for the future of my family. I could have justifiably rationalized that because I had been on such a small living allowance during those years as a missionary and as a pastor, it had been impossible to save anything. That is not necessarily true! I have since concluded that one is not necessarily spiritual simply because he gives no attention to anything material.

I came to a very important decision to give proper consideration to my financial future while at the same time continuing in a work I considered basically spiritual. I would continue to entrust my future to God, but no longer ignore the need to make some preparation of my own as well. I had resigned the pastorate at Logan and given a thirty day notice for the church to find a replacement so there was little time for the transition. Two of my brothers, Gebo and Dean, were in the construction business in Houston. I called Gebo and arranged to borrow $2,000. That would buy a building lot in a modest sub-division in Cleveland and even though I had no surplus fund in case any unexpected expense may develop, I was confident I could make this new venture succeed.

When the last weekend service in Logan was concluded, I had my final week's salary of $160 in hand plus a small savings account of less than $600. With that much money, I could rent a trailer to move our few personal belongings and pay the first month's rent on a small house. However, we had no furniture and no money to buy any, so we settled on a mobile home as a viable alternative.

Through the introduction of a mutual friend, we met a mobile home dealer who was very considerate of clergymen. He agreed to deliver and set up a home for us in a mobile home park. He discounted the price to the extent that we could finance the entire cost. Having lived with a very restricted income for so many years, we had never done installment buying for anything except a car. As a result, we had no bad credit. It seems that no bad credit is the same as good credit, so we qualified for the loan.

Traveling one day and unloading the U-haul trailer completed the move into containerized living. During those final weeks in Logan, I had made advance arrangements for a number of one week Bible conferences, so having settled the family into our pre-fabricated castle, I was off to Michigan for two weeks.

How quickly life can change. Last week I was an unknown pastor in a tiny mountain town in West Virginia. This week I am being introduced as a Bible lecturer with international experience. It is amazing how much I had changed without even being aware of it.

Before departing for Michigan, I had submitted blueprints to a bank for a loan commitment and interim financing to fund the job during construction. I had also requested a building permit from City Hall. While I was away, I had a lawyer prepare and record the deed for the building lot I had purchased. Upon my return, these various things were completed and I was in business.

Even before construction was completed on my first house, I had tired of mobile home living. We had a sixty-five foot long deluxe model with an eight foot by sixteen foot expansion in the living room, but it was still compartmentalized living. Sharing this residence with a teen-age son could only be tolerated if there had been a working traffic light in the hall (which was not a standard feature on the model we bought). As the house I was building neared completion, we placed two classified ads in the Cleveland Daily Banner. One advertised a new three bedroom brick bungalow for sale. The other offered for sale a deluxe mobile home that had been occupied only four months. It could be had for a token down payment and assumption of the note. We had decided to accept the first realistic offer for either property; sell it and live in the other. Then I prayed the mobile home would sell first. Within ten days we had a buyer for the mobile home and we prepared to move again.

To my amazement construction of the houses I was building

progressed well even when I was out of town about half of the time. Houses sold as fast as I could build them and soon I was receiving calls to build custom homes. My travels in ministerial activity in the first three years in Cleveland took me from Florida to North Dakota and from Maryland to Texas. I also had engagements for conventions in Japan, Korea, Costa Rica and Nicaragua. In fact, I had some invitations I had to decline because my schedule was just too full. Those were extremely good years for me. My ministerial activities were in demand and the building business was flourishing. From my ministerial activities, I received spiritual gratification. From my business I showed a profit on every job — and was pleased for the success.

When I came to Cleveland I had faith, confidence and a plan. Within four years, I was told by one of the corporate owners of the largest building supply company in Cleveland that I was their largest volume customer. If I was the largest volume customer of the largest supplier, it seemed reasonable to assume that I had an enviable share of the business in this growing town. At the peak, we were building one residential unit a week. A unit may have been a private house, or one unit of a multi-unit building.

As I developed more satisfied customers, word circulated that I put up a quality building for a reasonable price and that I could be trusted. Of course, that was a good formula by which to increase business.

I was developing quite a reputation.

Some of the information being circulated was not altogether factual, but it sounded good. For example; there was some speculation that I was a millionaire. At first I was shocked by the sheer extravagance of the statement. Any time this was mentioned to me, I denied it because it was not the case. I felt embarrassed that anyone would have imagined an idea so far from the fact.

When I couldn't squelch the rumor, I decided to ignore it. If some chose to believe the 'millionaire rumor' even though I had emphasized the fallacy in the statement, there might be some benefits.

To my absolute amazement, bankers were starting to speak to me with courtesy at a chance meeting in public places. I was invited to the banks to discuss business plans and projections. In the past, I had entered banks cautiously and with trepidation. Anytime a banker approved a loan for me, I expressed my appreciation profusely, spicing my statements with numerous superlatives. That was changing. Bankers actually wanted to do business with me! I was incredulous. I was riding high and relishing the ride. Possibly I was enjoying it too much.

One day a pastor friend said to me, "Brother Heil, I don't necessarily admire you because you drive a Cadillac. Rather, I admire you because you look like you belong in a Cadillac." Actually, I had bought a large car for its comfort and safety. It was within my budgetary capability to have it. I had earned the money honestly and paid taxes on my income. Further, I put the tithe and offerings into the Lord's work, as well as some giving to local charities. I had made the purchase legally, so when I bought the Cadillac, really nothing wrong had been done.

Later, reflecting back on my defensive response to that totally innocent comment by my friend, I can see the possibility of something secretly sinister and seductive. Comforts, conveniences and possibly an occasional extravagance are not wrong in and of themselves. It is how we treat these things that can make them right or wrong. If my motivation for having this above-average car was to astound people with my success and create in the minds of people incorrect impressions, then I was venturing onto thin ice.

There is nothing wrong with owning nice things. Certainly it is not improper to appreciate a compliment — maybe with even a little flattery included. In my case, I very likely placed too much importance on such recognition to the extent my real purpose in life was diminishing. I had been divinely directed to be a missionary. My primary concern should have been seeking out hurting people to whom I would provide a cup of refreshing water. I was still a believing, practicing Christian. That is, I still had access to the Water of Life, but some place I had lost my cup. Of course, it goes without saying, *cups of cold water for the destitute are not customarily dispensed through the window of a Cadillac.*

Sometimes it is well to remember what we do is not as important as why we do it. In the sixth year of this construction/real estate business, my financial statement showed my net worth to be $500,000. I started to reflect, "If I could start with $2,000 of borrowed money and develop a net worth of $500,000 within six years, it is not unrealistic to believe that starting from this base, and with a thriving business already functioning, I could be a millionaire within four more years." By that time I would be 50 years old. This was not an obsession, but I must admit, I reviewed the data and the potential frequently.

For some time, when I traveled away for Bible conferences, I did it without any personal remuneration. Following an established tradition, the churches provided me with an honorarium, but I did not keep it. On some occasions, if the church was small, I gave the money to the pastor. In some cases, I gave it to another itinerant minister whose travel expense may have been high and his income low. I was unusually blessed in that I did not need the money, and I always had a good feeling when I could find someone in need and give some help.

As I considered the fact of continuing success in my business and occasionally reflected on the possibility of becoming a millionaire by age fifty, I reasoned that with financial security, I could travel more extensively, conduct more Bible conferences and ultimately bless more people. A plan for expanding the "cup of cold water" enterprise was crystallizing in my mind. Or was it?

We will never know precisely the answer to that rhetorical question, because I did not experience the expansion and success I had envisioned and I was not a millionaire at age fifty.

Somehow, it is easy for us to lose perspective. When I thought of business success, financial independence, retirement at fifty, giving my services full time without compensation, helping the needy just because they had needs, and just because I had the ability to do so, it all seemed so right.

I didn't discuss these things with anyone — not even my family. They would remain my private musings until the details could be worked out, and then the fully developed bright-colored butterfly would emerge. Much of what I pondered was not realistic, but it was pleasant to contemplate the possibility.

The development of my business was a non-stop process of success and profit. Hard work can be very pleasant when it is flavored with success. Because I totally enjoyed my work, it was not unusual for me to work much longer hours than most people but not get tired. If I was doing the right things, the result of all of that extra work had to be extra profitability.

There were times I sold properties to clients who had a shortage of cash, so I made numerous sales when I accepted undeveloped property in lieu of cash for all or part of a down payment. Almost without realizing what was happening, I had amassed numerous properties in four different counties in Tennessee and some property in Florida. Other times, I accepted a smaller, less expensive house in trade for one I had built for sale, using the equity in the smaller house as part of the down payment. Then I would sell the smaller house and retain my profit in the form of second mortgage. Because I had little invested in that sort of property, I was under no pressure to make a sale, so I usually sold them without engaging the services of a real estate broker, thereby retaining as my profit the 4% or 5% customarily paid as sales commission.

One day while a real estate broker and I were at lunch together he told me he had checked the records at the court house earlier that day and found that I had transferred more properties in the past thirty days than any real estate firm in the county. The interesting thing is that I was not even real estate licensed. This volume of transferred real estate was totally the selling of my own properties, which did not require a license.

I soon learned that businesses do not grow and succeed without constant monitoring and supervision. As my business burgeoned, of necessity I devoted more time to it. I saw the actual growth and in my fancy, I saw what was developing behind the scenes. There really did seem to be a possibility that I would be able to retire in dignity, with assets, at a much earlier age than most. It was a fascinating fact! As I watched the profits continue to accrue and the assets increase, I was intrigued with all that was happening. I continued to have those occasional quiet moments when I was alone with my thoughts. As the business flourished, it is understandable that my thoughts logically turned to my favorite fantasy.

The strange, but disappointing development was that I gradually thought more about the comfortable retirement I would enjoy than about my original intent to travel to churches where I could help them, but they would not need to compensate me. I thought more about the fact that I would be debt free and have accumulated assets to fund that comfortable early retirement than I thought about the fact that I would have resources enabling me to alleviate some of the ills of suffering humanity. I thought more often about such things as travel to exotic destinations and leisurely vacations than I thought about travel to remote areas, either domestic or foreign where I would have to get my hands dirty as a self-sponsored short term missionary.

Yes, success was happening. Realization of my dream was coming more sharply into focus. Everything was coming together right. While I was enjoying every day of an adventuresome life, something unexpected occurred. My fast train to the land of Oz derailed. What happened, I don't know. When it happened, I was not aware. How it happened, I have yet to figure out. But why it happened, I believe I know now. While I was busy in an imaginary paradise, my vision dimmed. My priorities got rearranged. Inconsequential personal goals became more important than a major concern for others. In short, my values became skewed. When my world lost its balance, I fell off. A simple verse I read as a teenager may be appropriate here:

> **It's not what you would do with a million**
> **If riches should ever be your lot.**
> **It's what you are doing right now**
> **With the thirty-five dollars you've got.**

Chapter Twenty-Three

Opportunity Knocks Only Once

In November, 1968, we moved into our mobile home in Cleveland. It was shiny and new. The furnishings that came with the home were inexpensive — with quality that matched the price, but it was color coordinated and tastefully decorated, so we were pleased in our new situation.

Anticipating that I would develop a successful business that would potentially expand to include things other than just home building, I selected a generic sort of name and registered my new business as East Tennessee Enterprises. East Tennessee was quite a large area, so the name I had selected suggested growth. Even though there were no plans to expand anywhere at that time, just the selection of a name that would permit extension and outreach was an indication of my optimistic inclination.

In President John F. Kennedy's inauguration speech, he said, "Some people look at things as they are and ask why. Others look at things as they could be and ask why not." That comment expresses well the sort of attitude which has always been a driving force in my life.

Optimism, enthusiasm, ambition, diligence, determination and faith are concepts I learned and adopted early in life. At this juncture those traits and beliefs served me well. From my first month in business, I began to show profit. I had no large obligations, so there was no need for me to take out of the company an excessive salary or benefits. I operated the building out of the trunk of my car and the business from the top of my tiny dining room table. I was careful to keep complete and accurate records so I could properly measure my accomplishments. I always started the construction of a house with the attitude that one of my friends may buy this house and I wanted them to be totally pleased with what they bought, even long after the new had worn off. In short, I did the best work I was capable of doing. Possibly this explains, at least in part, why we never ran out of work. Also, I made a sincere effort to use only good quality materials, work with reputable subcontractors to the best of my ability, and build quality into every part of each home I offered for sale. I felt that integrity was one of the most important items I could offer to those who purchased my houses, and I determined to build a house that I would not be unhappy to occupy if it didn't sell. That very philosophy quite likely is the reason that my houses did sell quickly and the clients for whom I built custom homes were quite well satisfied.

Somewhere I had heard it is not possible to be honest and succeed in business. I did not think that was necessarily factual and I set about to prove the cliché to be a falsehood. In the process, I came dangerously close to proving myself to be woefully inadequate for the tough, competitive business I had selected. From my youth I had been involved in building and had developed some degree of skill in the areas of architectural design, concrete finishing, carpentry, painting, plumbing and landscaping, so I could build a nice house. My weakness was in creating, funding and managing a business. I did ultimately learn by the trial and error method (I made a lot of tries and a lot of errors).

As the image of success started to develop, I was occasionally approached with opportunities for joint involvement in a variety of ventures. I was flattered by the invitation to be a partner with successful people, so in me they found an easy sale. The first venture I accepted was a land purchase about fifty miles from Cleveland. The three hundred acres had a good stand of timber and engineering assays had established there was a very shallow vein of coal suitable for strip mining. That was represented to me as evidence that the property had value beyond its price. Gullible as I was, I accepted the pitch at face value and agreed to become a partner. It was easy. No money was required. Each of the four buyers signed a note at the bank. This was more attractive than the hard labor of building a house. I just signed my name and immediately I had a 25% ownership in a large tract of land, with potential wealth from a lumber and mining operation.

While I was still on a high about the easy success and the prospects of good profits, a real estate "dealer" telephoned early one morning to invite me to join him for breakfast. After we had finished eating he picked up the meal check, but as it turned out, I believe ultimately I paid for the breakfast.

We got in Roger Hanson's Mark III and drove to his office where he told me he had just been selected to market an exceptionally valuable property in Florida, which he knew I would love to own. It was a package of three properties. One existing 12 unit apartment complex and two duplexes situated on one tract of land. Adjacent to the older buildings was a 40 unit complex, less than one year old. Rounding out the attractive property was an 80 unit apartment complex under construction, targeted for completion and ready for occupancy within 90 days. The price — only two million dollars!! I protested to Roger that he was obviously not aware of my financial limitation. It was just not possible for me to consider acquiring a property with such an exorbitant price attached. He was sure I could qualify to assume the debt on the property and the down payment was only $75,000. He suggested I give it some thought and he would call back later in the afternoon.

When I was alone, I reflected on what had just transpired. I was considered a likely buyer of a $2,000,000 property. I knew it was 50% flattery and half salesmanship, but I was intrigued. I also knew I was considering a total impossibility, but I experienced a twinge of excitement just recalling Roger's certainty that he could get me approved to assume the loan and own the property. This was much bigger than anything I had ever dreamed of.

I drove to the office of Roberts' Real Estate and met with the principal broker, Winston Collins. He and I had been casual friends for a brief time. I recited for him my conversation with Roger earlier in the day. Winston seemed to have some interest in a joint ownership. When I mentioned the $75,000 down payment, he said he would have no trouble in coming up with his half.

As planned, Roger and I met later the same day. I recounted my discussion with Winston, concluding we would take some time to consider the matter and get together later.

Two days later Roger telephoned to inform me that he had three first class round trip tickets for a flight to Florida. He felt Winston and I should see the apartments. He had arranged for the owner to meet us at the Tampa Airport the following morning and drive us to Lakeland to view the properties. When I agreed we would accompany him to Florida, he casually replied, "Why don't you get a $75,000 cashier's check so just in case you like the deal, we can make a contract while we are there and avoid another trip." I agreed to the suggestion, then went immediately to Roger's office for a face to face discussion to be sure we were on the same wave length.

I told Roger before spending the cost of three first class air tickets, he should reconsider the fact that I would most likely not be approved for assumption of such a large debt. He remained positive and committed to go. Then I advanced another bit of bad news. I did not have the cash for my half of the down payment.

At that point, Roger told me the seller did not want a down payment. The $75,000 was to be his commission. He volunteered to defer part of the commission until the end of the year (nearly eight months away). We settled on a down payment of $40,000 cash and a $35,000 note due at the end of the year.

I went back to see Winston at Roberts Real Estate Office. Within five minutes we decided we were ready to go to Florida the following morning. I gave Winston $2,500 which he took to his bank with his check for $37,500 and he purchased a cashier's check for $40,000. I prepared a promissory note for $35,000 payable to Roger. He marked an envelope "earnest money," inserted my note and put it in his desk drawer. The next morning in Lakeland, he told the seller he had $35,000 earnest money in Cleveland. As it was arranged, I would pay $2,500 down and become a 50% owner in a $2,000,000 property.

We traveled to Florida, ate breakfast with the seller, went to the apartment site and surveyed the entire property. Next we visited with the president of the bank that furnished the construction money and had committed to the permanent financing as well. We had been in conference about fifteen minutes when the bank president excused himself. When he re-entered the conference room, he suggested we go for lunch, and he would have the assumption papers prepared by 1:00 p.m. ready for signatures. He told us he had made two telephone calls to Cleveland and spoken to the banker that handled Winston's business, and another banker where I had my accounts. He said both bankers told him we have perfect credit and advised that he do business with us.

Winston and I signed more notes that day than a music composer and went home each $1,000,000 deeper in debt. You might say we were property rich and cash poor. It was my first transaction in the big league.

Somewhere I heard a tidbit of philosophy that opportunity only knocks once. I was beginning to doubt the validity of that comment. I already had one business that appeared to be successful, and the events of recent days had thrust me faster than I could calculate into another multimillion dollar business. The irony of it was that my total up-front cash investment was $2,500 and I became the president and owned 50% of the stock in the corporation that was formed to hold this asset.

When our daughter, Janice, was a college senior, a handsome young man occasionally visited my home. I was relatively sure he didn't come to visit me, because he never stayed more than a few minutes. I recall the time he telephoned me and with a very professional sounding voice requested that I set an appointment when he could come to my house. Strangely, he had never before thought it necessary to clear with me prior to coming. He simply showed up, and within minutes he and Janice left, again without consulting me. Why this sudden concern for formality?

We set a time and Jeff came over. He began to discuss a plan that had been forming in his mind, and now he wanted to discuss it with me if I would be a sounding board for him. He and two other college seniors were interested in forming a diversified corporation which would have its home base in the small town of Cleveland, but would have interstate objectives. They envisaged a corporation so strong and successful that it would some day have offices nationwide. Jeff told me he was interested in some hands-on practical experience in the real work world. His primary reason for the discussions with me was to ascertain whether I may be interested in serving as a consultant for this emerging company during its initial formative development. Simply stated, Jeff felt my years of experience in the business world could be of value to him and his friends. Jeff's friends were David and George.

On our second visit, Jeff told me there had been a change in his thinking. He suggested that he and his friends wanted to form a corporation, and rather than have me serve as a consultant, they would be pleased if I would join them as an incorporating member of the new company.

As we discussed various options, I noticed that two of these young men definitely showed promise. The third did not impress me, but he was a friend of the others and they wanted to stay together, so I did not object.

We made an agreement and applied to the State of Tennessee for a corporate charter. Four years earlier, I had decided to name my business East Tennessee Enterprises, so I could expand throughout the eastern part of the state. Following a similar thought pattern, but with a more aggressive twist, we elected to do business under the name "Dixie Development Corporation."

I planned to continue my building business under the name East Tennessee Enterprises. This new entity would be my corporate toy. However, very soon I detected my young associates had in mind something more than my concept of a diversion from my work in the real world. They wanted to play hardball. It was their intention literally to impact the entire southern part of the United States. It would actually spread throughout all of Dixie.

When I found out how serious my partners were about our new enterprise, I decided it would be difficult to direct my own business and at the same time be involved in the ambitious plans they were making for Dixie Development. Rather than try to divide my time and interest, I offered to integrate East Tennessee Enterprises into Dixie Development and I would become its first full time employee. Until that time, Dixie Development was an entity, but I was not aware of exactly what we did. I knew we had meetings twice a month and discussed developing a monumental company, but we didn't "do" anything.

Of the three, David was the idealist. He thought we had to do everything like a big city corporation so we could project an image. The first thing he did was to contact a large legal firm and sign a contract with them that they would direct our development and represent us whenever we had need for legal service. Cleveland was so small and Chattanooga was only a moderate-size city. David reasoned we should not have a little known legal firm from a small town as our official representative. The firm he engaged was based in Atlanta with offices in Washington, D. C. and New York. The firm was comprised of 135 lawyers.

After contracting with a prestigious law firm, his next step was to negotiate with an accounting firm of similar stature that would set up our financial records appropriately so when we should make Dixie Development Corporation a public company, we would have all of our minutes and financials in order to present to the Securities and Exchange Commission in Washington without any worry about getting our public offering approved. Of course, he used the professional counsel of our newly appointed attorney in deciding which accounting firm to select.

At the next meeting of the Dixie Development Corporation board of directors, David took great pride in announcing he had consummated working contracts with a very influential law firm and an accounting firm of similar caliber. It goes without saying, a part of his agreement was that we put both firms on retainers. That meant we would have their services whenever there may be a need. To me, that meant we had put two expensive firms on our payroll, whom we did not presently need, nor could we afford.

197

David went on to report he had submitted to the legal firm the name of our corporation and instructed them to research public records to determine that there was not another company with the same name, as that could potentially be a problem when we would later expand into other states. When they should have completed this research, David instructed them to develop a logo for the new firm.

Some six weeks later that work was completed and David brought with him a sample of our new stationery. "It is very unique and professional," he said. It was a faint ivory color parchment instead of plain white paper like ordinary firms use. At the top was the designation in sophisticated black block letters Dixie Development Corporation. A little below the corporation name and to the left side of the page was a one inch circle enclosing the letters "DD." One letter was blue and the other letter was green. He had been able to get this deluxe stationery printed (including the designing of the logo) for a modest sum of only $4,000. I knew then we were in trouble.

When we had incorporated Dixie Development (and before I came to know of David's ridiculously extravagant inclination) I spoke to my brother, Gebo. He is one of the brothers who loaned me the initial $2,000 to start East Tennessee Enterprises. When I told him three acquaintances and I had just formed a new corporation, he expressed interest in joining with us. At that time, he and my older brother, Tex, were operating a rather successful light commercial construction company in Houston. The original four incorporators had invested $1,000 each. When I told Jeff, David and George that two of my brothers were interested in joining us, they reasoned that three brothers could conceivably control the corporation, so they were not too favorable. However, they offered a concession to allow Gebo and Tex to come in with a number of shares equal to ours, but for an initial payment of $10,000 each. This would infuse some operating capital and would not dilute the voting strength of the original corporate officers. Tex and Gebo agreed to these terms and became investors and shareholders in Dixie Development.

The first major decision reached by our board of directors was that we needed an imposing home office if we expected to attract the investors to make this a significant corporation. A location was selected one block south of 25th Street and near I-75. It had good visibility from 25th Street, but minus the noise. The location was good, the design was attractive, and I projected I could build it for at least 25% less than appraised value, so we had no trouble in getting a commitment for permanent financing. We took the commitment to a Chattanooga bank and were approved for a construction loan for 100% of the commitment amount. About six months after ratification of our corporation charter, the 15,000 square foot headquarters office building was under construction. At completion, a sign on the front identified it as the Dixie Development Center.

I was the only full-time employee working for Dixie Development as the others had employment elsewhere. However, a few months after forming the corporation, Jeff offered to resign his other employment and dedicate his time to our newly formed corporation. When Jeff affiliated with Dixie Development in an employee status, he became the Director of Development. At that time, we had East Tennessee Enterprises, as a homebuilding division, but other than that we were not "doing" anything. This literally meant Jeff could move in any direction to expand the company. We had no defined direction, except that we wanted to be a big, impressive, interstate company.

One weekend Jeff and I, with our wives, went to Gatlinburg, a phenomenal resort town at the edge of the Great Smokey Mountain National Park. Jeff was intrigued with the natural beauty of the area and also with the commercial value of the real estate there. The Smokey Mountain National Park was reported to be the most frequented park in America, with about six million visitors every year.

Within a relatively short time, Jeff had scouted the area and located some resort property that appealed to him. It was a small lodge with two duplex cottages, one house that would accommodate eight and a larger building with a capacity of sixteen, plus kitchen and dining facilities adequate for the occupants of all four buildings. This made it a suitable facility for small camping groups, or each building could be rented separately. The owner was in the process of a divorce, which made him quite a motivated seller. He had priced the property right and was willing to carry most of the financing. When Jeff presented the package to our next board meeting, we voted to acquire the property. We used my financial statement to qualify for the purchase. Dixie Development had expanded into Sevier County, approximately 100 miles from our home base. It was our first step in blanketing Dixie!

Jeff's next project was a motel on Interstate 75 in southern Ohio. I am not sure how he started in that direction, but finding attractive real estate, a well known franchise name and records that suggested high profit potential, Jeff set to work to determine how we could acquire and operate that motel as the first in a network of hotels we would ultimately operate. When Jeff had completed about a month of research, writing reports, making recommendations and all the other things professionals do to justify their salary and expense account, he presented it to the corporate officers. We decided that Jeff and I would go to inspect the property and the records.

Upon arrival, I learned that Jeff had made quite an accurate report and the motel did seem desirable. We met with the manager and he opened the corporate books to us, including the occupancy log and the profit and loss sheets for the previous year. With a little scrutiny, I found that the motel did not show a profit from the room occupancy. Being on a major interstate, a large part of the traffic was truck drivers. The carpet and furniture had been subjected to too much grease and mud from the boots of drivers, which made maintenance inordinately expensive. The overall operation did reveal a profit, however. There was a well appointed dining room that stayed open around the clock seven days a week greatly enhancing the net revenue. The basis of the profitability of the restaurant was the presence of live entertainment and the sale of alcohol from the bar. Not wanting any connection with the sale of liquor, I recommended that we take no positive action toward acquisition of the motel.

The next project was a shopping center. We located a seven acre tract of land on a busy intersection and drew preliminary plans. Through some creative financing, we acquired the land and paid cash for it. An insurance company agreed to lend funds for long term financing, but required two anchor stores as a prerequisite to releasing any money to start construction. We did consummate some conditional leases, but never did get the two anchors, so the shopping center was never built.

While Jeff busied himself with trying to develop a viable list of tenants for the projected shopping center, David was checking out fast food franchises. He was certain Dixie Development would be recognized as a strong corporation if we could develop a chain of fast food outlets throughout the South. For some reason he determined Dunkin' Donuts would be good for us. This was a totally unknown concept for me, but the others strongly favored investigating the possibilities. I was learning the difference in owning my business and being a part of a corporation. Simply put, I was no longer allowed to decide what I would or would not do. The following month I found myself, with two of my young corporate officers aboard an airplane bound for Boston. We were met at the airport by a Dunkin' Donuts vice president and driven to the home office of the famous New England Donut Company. As we entered the ornate offices, David was carrying his briefcase filled with important-looking documents and computer studies intended to impress the upper level management of Dunkin' Donuts of their need to do business with our corporation.

We emerged from the executive offices in Boston near the end of the day with a working agreement. We were the area franchisee for the greater Nashville, Tennessee area, extending 75 miles in every direction with the exclusive right to develop up to ten Dunkin' Donut stores. Prior to our meeting, Dunkin' Donuts had already decided to put up a company operated store in Nashville. All preliminary work was completed and they projected construction would begin within less than a month. That would become our first store according to our area agreement. We would open our first outlet within approximately four months. Incidental to the signing of the ten-store franchise agreement, our corporate checkbook was no longer cluttered with large, cumbersome numbers. We had succeeded in trimming it down to a clean, manageable small figure. In 1973 Dunkin' Donuts franchises could be procured for a modest $25,000 per location. Dixie

Development Corporation was to own and operate up to ten outlets in the Nashville area and one in Cleveland, Tennessee.

Almost before the ink on our corporate charter was dry, we were becoming visible with a very impressive home office building, a resort lodge in Gatlinburg, two Dunkin' Donuts stores, a home building division that produced a house a week and a newly developed division selling and installing residential swimming pools.

We apparently were making a good appearance, because one morning Winston Collins, my corporate vice president in the Florida company walked into my office. He proposed putting Roberts Real Estate Company into Dixie Development. Roberts Real Estate was totally owned by Winston and his wife, Joanne. Winston put a price on his company of $250,000 and volunteered to take the entire amount in Dixie Development stock. It was a paper transaction, so I accepted it with one condition. Winston would have to continue as broker for a minimum of two years because we had no one in our firm who was real estate licensed. He accepted that condition and the ownership of Roberts Real Estate was transferred to Dixie Development. Another facet had been added to our growing company.

PICTORIAL REVUE

My Tribute to Mother and Dad

Every person is special and unique — each being the handiwork of God. But only a few men and women can be called truly "great." Everyone's life is filled with stories to tell, but not all are stories to which others desire to listen.

It was welcome news when Mother told me she had finally convinced Dad to write his autobiography. I was certain this was a wise decision because the stories he has to tell are genuinely noteworthy and I am sure will be of interest to many people. As I reminisce, I view this record as more adventurous and exciting than fiction. It is filled with exploits of intrigue and adventure at every turn. It is numerous biographical glimpses at a man of humble beginnings, who followed the path which God mapped out and who now travels a road about which most can only dream. It is a path that has lead literally around the world.

My Mother and Dad were missionaries to Japan during the 50's and the first half of the 60's. To report the events of those years would require volumes if all of the details were included.

The chronicling of business triumph and the failure which occurred primarily in the decade of the 70's would also make for interesting reading. This portion of Dad's experiences shows the unpredictability of life: how one can be at the top only to topple in the next instant. It emphasizes the value of putting our trust in something bigger than ourselves — of having our security in the One who created us.

The record of Mother and Dad's life since 1980, when A. L. Williams, an innovative financial services company, became a part of them, could be viewed as a composite of many stories in one. It involves perseverance and faith, coupled with hard work which led ultimately to success.

Success is viewed by some as the acquisition of wealth, honor and power. Mother and Dad now have all three. However, in my opinion, success is so much more. It includes having purpose and meaning in life that establish significant relationships, possessing the gift of wisdom, following the path of integrity and having strength of character. Interestingly, success can be characterized as the ability to discern that giving is more wonderful than receiving. Especially, success is maintaining a personal, intimate relationship with the Creator God. In all of these qualities, my mother and dad are rich.

Without contradiction, the biographical record of my parents, both in success and failure provides compelling reading. It is the story of a truly "great" man and woman.

Dad, I am so pleased you have written this book so others can share the multiple meaningful stories of your life. Without question, many will be motivated and encouraged because you have made available to us the legend of your life. I count it a privilege and an honor that I can call you and Mother my parents.

Affectionately, your daughter,

Janice (Heil) Leach

This is the little boy, who was short, too young, and bashful. Born in the remote prairies of South Dakota, he experienced poverty first-hand during the Great Depression of the 1930's.

Ed Heil at age sixteen

At age twelve, he took his first job in the competitive Big-City atmosphere of Houston. At age fifteen, he embarked on his first entrepreneurial enterprise, which would thrust the diminutive boy into the scene of tough competition. At age fifteen, he bought his first car (paid cash out of his own pocket).

This is the little boy who would develop the largest newspaper route in the city of Houston for the "Houston Press."

Having dropped out of high school to engage in his business, Ed completed the last two years of high school, one year of ministerial training, and one year of college all in two years.

At age twenty-four, Ed Heil was appointed to Japan as the first missionary in his denomination, the Church of God. Seven years later, while still serving in Japan, he was assigned as the first Church of God missionary to represent his denomination in opening a new work in Korea. He was never succeeded by another missionary. Rather, the work in Korea was set up as an indigenous church under very capable national leadership.

Who could have imagined the future? In fourteen years, this unlikely young missionary registered his denomination in Japan, established eight local churches and founded a ministerial training school (Yokohama Bible Institute), of which he was the principal for five years. Incidentally, Ed personally built all of the church buildings, parsonages and Yokohama Bible Institute.

When his missionary career was abruptly terminated due to his wife's being injured in an automobile accident, he returned to the U. S. to start over again. Using $2,000 borrowed money, he established a new business. In six years, he became one of the largest volume home builders in Cleveland, Tennessee.

At age fifty-two he moved again to unknown territory with Primerica Financial Services. In his fourth year in that business for which he had no training and no background, he was paid $100,000. In his thirteenth year, annual income increased to $500,000.

This is the bashful, backward boy who could not take his bride on a five day honeymoon trip, but was later to take her to such exciting destinations as Honolulu, Hong Kong, Jerusalem, Athens, and Cairo. They stood amazed at the incomparable beauty of the Taj Mahal. They marveled at the huge golden gods in Bangkok, Thailand. The list is long — London, Munich, Rome, Paris, New York, Amsterdam, Washington. They have been there!

This is the unlikely boy from the prairies who was recognized before 38,000 of his peers in the New Orleans Superdome when he was inducted into the PFS Wall of Fame.

This is the high school drop-out who completed requirements for a college degree as an adult and was later recognized by his alma mater with an honorary doctorate for his accomplishments in foreign missions.

This is the man who was photographed with the President of the United States.

That all came later. When he was sixteen years old, he had only one aspiration — to win the favor of Letha, the girl of his dreams…

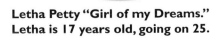

Letha Petty "Girl of my Dreams."
Letha is 17 years old, going on 25.

Married April 15, 1945 at age seventeen.
Age was not a factor. Marriages built on
true love, trust and devotion will last
whether you are young or old.

Teenage evangelist on
the road again: this
time with his new
bride. (Chapter 12)

Embarking for Japan as missionaries with daughter, Janice, in 1952.
(Chapter 12)

Our little "blonde" Japanese girl at age four.
Yokohama, Japan

Ronald Paul was
"made in Japan."
1954

Living in the country, Janice's playmates were all Japanese.
There is no language barrier between children.

Ron attended
Japanese kinder-
garten. He was
the only Ameri-
can among 160
children.

First organized
Church of God
in Japan.

The church
Ed built single-
handedly.
Yokohama, 1958
(Chapter 19)

When news of a missionary building a church without any help came to the attention of NKH (Japan Broadcasting Company), Ed was invited to appear on "Wa ga Himitsu ga aru" — Japanese version of "I've Got a Secret." (Chapter 19)

Following Japanese custom, Ed is seated on the floor teaching a Bible study in the little church.

The three buildings for Yokohama Bible Institute. (Chapter 19)

YBI faculty and student body in front of classroom building in 1963.

Mary Grace Comans.

Mary Grace Comans, a civilian employee with the U. S. Military in Tokyo, held English Bible Classes in her living quarters several evenings a week. (Chapter 20)

Tokyo Youth Center — Presently this facility houses our leading church in Japan.

A tent meeting held in Korea with Yongi Cho, who now pastors the world's largest church. 1959

During our furlough to the U. S., Janice and Letha dressed in kimonos when we conducted mission emphasis services throughout the States.

Pastor Cho with his mother who was miraculously healed of cancer. Seoul, Korea

Biding farewell to family and friends to return to Japan for our third five-year term.

213

The little mazda Letha was driving when she had an accident which brought us home.

Ron, his wife Diane, and their son, Chris (our first grandchild). Cleveland, Tennessee

Ron and Diane had two more children — Ginger and Israel.

Diane was named "Most Congenial" in the 1983 Mrs. Tennessee Pageant.

A Tribute to My Wife Letha

*More than fifty-two years ago we met. Immediately, I was attracted by
your beauty, and fascinated by your pleasant and happy disposition.
Two years and four months later, I stood at the altar in a small
chapel in Houston and saw walking toward me in white lace the
most beautiful young lady I had ever met.*

*I walked into the church a teenager with no earthly possession,
and I exited a wealthy young man because that Sunday afternoon your
father gave you to me. We had nothing to give, but even so we pledged to
each other everything: which included nothing more than love and hope.
Thankfully, that has not changed. Fifty years have passed, and
we have had many occasions to reflect on that memorable day and
what transpired for us both. It has been a rich and rewarding fifty
years together.*

*Today is our golden celebration! Just like I told you in the company
of our family and friends then that I loved you, today we have invited
family and friends who again have assembled here to help us celebrate,
and in their presence I want to tell you again "I love you."*

*Fifty years ago I could not give you even a small diamond, but you
became my beautiful bride even without that time-honored symbol
that I had pledged to you my undying love. Today, it is my great thrill
to correct that inadequacy by placing on your finger a gold ring
ornamented with fifty diamonds. I want you to wear it with pride
remembering that each diamond reflects the brilliance of a year
I have had you as my bride.*

*In the fifty years since we stood before our friends to pledge our
perpetual, mutual love, I have met many beautiful ladies: some
friendly, some educated, some sophisticated, some talented, and many
of them very attractive. If in some mysterious way I could have known
all of them fifty years ago, I still would have gone to that same small
chapel on Sunday Afternoon, April 15, 1945. I would have stood
impatiently at the altar. I would have been enraptured as I saw you
walking toward me in that pure white lace. I would have thrilled as the
pastor instructed us to join hands. Then I would have felt I was the
most privileged person alive that I could look at you in all of your
purity and beauty — and say "I do."*

215

Janice met and married Terry
Leach in 1978.
Cleveland, Tennessee

Two more grandsons were
added to our family —
Terry II and Daniel Leach.
(The boys were proud that they
had dressed themselves.)

Janice and Ron at our
40th Anniversary in
Honolulu, Hawaii.

Ginger having a Hawaiin lei
placed around her neck by her
two brothers.

As a National Sales Director in A. L. Williams, we were honored to have our picture made with our favorite president, Ronald Reagan, at a political rally in Atlanta, Georgia 1986.

Supporters of Pat Robertson's campaign to become the next president. (Chapter 27)

As an added advantage for above average production, we drove a Shaklee Bonus car for six consecutive years. (Chapter 27)

217

Promotion to Regional Vice President in A. L. Williams by Senior Vice President, Ronnie Barns, in 1981. Honolulu, Hawaii. (Chapter 32)

At the 1984 convention, Dan Heil (pictured with his wife, Jerri) was one of the Top 20 Recruiters in the nation. To be one of the top twenty in the company with more than 100,000 agents is outstanding! In Dan's third year, he was paid $170,000.

Charles Whitener with his wife, Reiko. They have been leaders in my organization from the beginning. In Charles' first month with PFS, he was paid $5,000. After sixteen years with this company, Charles has offices in ten states and has a personal income of $400,000. Charles has trained more successful leaders than anyone on my team.

Rene and Carol Vargas worked with us to enter Guam with A. L. Williams. They are pictured here with Lt. Govenor, Edward Reyes. (Chapter 34)

218

Art and Angela Williams, being presented this Bronze Bust of Art in Atlanta by some of the company's top leaders. (Chapter 35)

Angela Williams and Ed on deck for a life-boat drill on a Carribean cruise. (Chapter 36)

Twice, we were awarded a five-day cruise on "Lady Angela," the private yacht of Art and Angela.

PFS was founded and led by Art Williams for the first thirteen years of its existence. Art was a crusader with a cause. He led us like a totally committed Commando General. Together, we won many skir-

Joe Plumeri with his very personable wife, Nancy.

mishes. The current CEO of Primerica Financial Services is Joe Plumeri. As a crusader, Joe parallels Art in intensity and committment. Additionally, he brought to PFS the benefit of nearly thirty years in financial services and a polished professionalism that has been of inestimable value.

Our home is located just off Gulf Shores Parkway, halfway between Mobile, Alabama and Pensecola, Florida.

A place to relax and enjoy the singing of the birds.

The "Prophet's Chamber" for our Shadow Ministry.
(Chapter 40)

At the celebration of the golden wedding anniversary of Ed and Letha Heil, their son, Ron, read the following tribute. Stating so succinctly in a few lines how their lives have impacted his, it deserves a place in this biography.

A Tribute to my Parents

Most of us are familiar with the poem "footprints in the sand." When I think of Mom and Dad's life together, I see the essence of that story played out over the last fifty years. Footprints from South Dakota to East Texas, from Japan to Tennessee, from Hawaii to Alabama, with West Virginia squeezed in a couple of times.

"The steps of a good man are ordered by the Lord: and he delighteth in his way. Though he fall, he shall not be utterly cast down: for the Lord upholdeth him with his hand." These verses from scripture reverberate in my mind when I think of my parents.

I realize that close beside the steps of a good man are the smaller, yet equally important steps of a good woman. For those who are unmarried or have only been married for a short while, let me clarify.

Two years ago my mother-in-law had some minor surgery and my wife, Diane, was to spend just one night with her at the hospital. I came in from work that evening and was taking a shower when I realized I was overwhelmed by a feeling of depression and gloom. Not being one to have feelings of that sort more than once or twice in a decade, I tried to figure what could possibly be wrong. Then it dawned on me — Diane was not going to be home until tomorrow morning. It made me aware of how very much her presence means to me.

About ten years ago Mom was diagnosed with operable breast cancer. When the doctor told them, Mom related to me later, the look on Dad's face was of utter despair and calamity. You need to be aware of some of the setbacks my father has taken in stride — financial devastation; being cheated by business partners; basement walls collapsing from mud-slides — you name it. I've seen Dad tried in the fire. About the most horrendous exclamation ever to come from him was, "Oh my, what a disappointment." But when the health of his companion, his number one cheerleader, his bride of fifty years, the queen of his castle was involved, it shook him to the foundation. No, most of us would not progress very far on the path of life without our God-given partners.

Most of us grow up thinking our Dad hung the moon, and that is as it should be. In my case, I recall Mom was always there to help him get it centered exactly.

When I reflect on Mom and Dad's life, I see an adventurous journey like very few mortals get a shot at. I see humor and sadness, elation and near tragedy, some setbacks and great victories, Dad's optimism and quick wit, and Mom's naivete and blind faith and trust.

I remember when Dad cooked a piece of cotton cloth inside the pancakes of a visiting evangelist and watched innocently as the poor fellow tried to cut through it with a fork.

I remember going early in the morning to the trout ponds in Karuizawa, Japan. When we brought home the rainbows, Mom cooked trout and waffles. Later in the afternoon we would crank homemade ice cream with some missionary friends.

And I remember traveling from Houston, Texas to Logan, West Virginia with everything we owned in a U-haul trailer that seemed larger than our Rambler. As we were going down a long, steep mountain, the trailer seemingly got bored with following and decided to change roles with the car. As we fish-tailed from one shoulder to the other, Dad — clearheaded as ever — knew better than to apply the brake and jackknife the whole rig. Rather he accelerated to outrun the trailer to the bottom of the hill, then coasted to a stop on the opposite upward slope. I was rather enjoying the lateral roller coaster ride until I noticed Mom, white knuckled, clutching stuff and praying "Jesus, help us. Help us, Lord." That was one of the many times there was only one set of footprints in the sand.

On occasions I think back on the hours I wasted trying to win just one game of chess against Dad.

There was the time Mom made two beautiful cherry pies (no one could rival Mom's pies). She dropped one of them face down on the kitchen floor. I don't know which was more crushed, Mom or the pie.

I recall when I fell from the kitchen counter top and damaged a vacuum cleaner with my nose. It was bleeding profusely — my nose, that is. Dad picked me up and ran up the stairs so fast it was like being airlifted. If I ever saw Dad lose his head in a crisis, I can't remember it.

Once I came home from school to find both of my parents sick in bed. A student from the Bible college told me they had almost drowned that day. On a school outing, they were all in small row-boats. Mom and Dad's boat capsized, spilling them into the lake. Mom slid right out onto Dad's shoulders, bringing the waterline just above Dad's glasses. Since Dad's nose is below his glasses, he couldn't breathe.

Realizing this situation was getting him nowhere fast, Dad went down to get out from under Mom (who couldn't understand why he was letting her down, literally). Wearing one of those Lucille Ball full skirts, Mom bobbed around in the water like a colorful pleated buoy, but Dad nearly drowned. I would say there was only a single set of footprints on that beach, wouldn't you?

Years after the fact, Mom told me that when they were at the bottom of the heap financially, sometimes she had to search for coins in her purses to buy groceries. Even then, Dad continued to put $50.00 in a tithe envelope every week. Oh, that the rest of us would have that kind of spiritual integrity.

When Dad's business failed, his attorney told him to file bankruptcy and he could come out smelling like a rose. Dad stood up, looked him squarely in the eyes and defiantly replied, "Not as long as I'm breathing." Is it any wonder God has prospered my parents?

Besides the recession in 1976, Dad had some partners in his business who stole from him, and his secretary/bookkeeper wrote herself extra checks now and then. Once his carpet layers left town, having just received a $5,000 advance to buy carpet for a large job, which they never installed. We did try to find them to retrieve the money, but Dad would take no legal action against them.

By 1978, Dad's building business had failed, and even though he despised remodeling old buildings, he found himself doing remodeling and odd jobs. He had fixed up one house real nice and several months later it was partially destroyed by fire, so he was re-remodeling it. It was summer and very hot outside, not to mention in the attic where he was replacing each charred rafter individually without removing the roof decking — singlehandedly!!

I had stopped by after work to bring him a cold drink and to see if I could help. As we sat under a big tree with our cold refreshment Dad said he didn't know how he was going to make it. The interest on what he owed was putting him $150 deeper in debt every day. For what work he could find, he was earning only $10.00 an hour. He was in financial high gear reverse!

I often noticed two slogans Dad kept on his desk. One stated, "The difficult we do immediately: the impossible takes a little longer." The other, "We have done so much with so little for so long, we are convinced we can do absolutely anything with nothing at all in no time flat."

I suppose I believed my father could do anything because I told him, "Dad, you're going to make it. You did it once and you can do it again."

Was I right or what?

In December, 1979, Dad was introduced to Art Williams, the founder and president of A. L. Williams and Associates, and the rest is history. I have always believed Dad could sell fleas to a dog. In short, Dad didn't wimp out. He paid two hundred fifty thousand dollars in past debts, plus interest. He met Art Williams when he was age 52, and starting from the bottom of a very deep pit, climbed his way out. No doubt, God has blessed him richly for his integrity and his efforts during that time and since.

I have to credit Mom too for standing with him during these difficult times. She told me years later that after they moved to Hawaii,

224

she worked part-time at a small co-op vegetable & fruit market without pay, other than that members could buy their produce at a discount. That's above and beyond the call. Don't you agree?

The Bible yields words of wisdom and admonition to men and women equally. But, have you ever noticed there is no counterpart to Proverbs chapter 31? I have often wondered if my father's life story might be Proverbs chapter 32. Maybe Solomon is writing that chapter even now.

Recently I said to Diane, "Being the children of our parents and the parents of our children, isn't it wonderful to be us!"

I have seen both of my parents live a life of integrity, wisdom, unselfishness, sacrifice and Godliness. I have also seen God bless their efforts, reward them richly and fill their hearts with joy unspeakable. And that's just in this life!

Mom and Dad, I love you both and am undeservingly proud to be your son.

Our Fiftieth Anniversary picture, 1995

CHAPTER TWENTY-FOUR

HUMPTY DUMPTY

In a nursery rhyme, Humpty Dumpty (an egg) tried to sit on a wall. It is not possible for a round egg to sit very long on the flat top of a wall without exposure to the danger of falling. A very important teaching hid in that child's verse is that an egg cannot expect to survive a hard fall.

With so much growth so quickly, I resembled the famous egg sitting atop a high and narrow wall. My wall had been erected before the concrete foundation had time to cure, so if it leaned just a little, that should come as no surprise. Further, my wall was not thick enough to provide a safe place at the top for an egg to sit and it was evidently built too high. It was an attractive facade, but it lacked substance to reinforce it. As the wall became higher, but still resting on an inadequate foundation, my place on top of the wall became progressively more precarious.

To the uninformed, my wall may have appeared to be well constructed. But take a little time to evaluate some of the stones used in that wall. A glimpse at each segment in the previous chapter can be quite telling. My first venture into expansion was a grievous error in three ways:

I.   The project was presented as a highly-profitable, risk-free, no-money-down bonanza. Believe me, if any promoter actually has such a project, he is not going to offer me part of it with nothing invested. It was offered as a get-rich-quick opportunity that shouldn't be overlooked. That was exactly what I was looking for. The whole project was a farce, but a slick promoter had found a dumb buyer and the deal was done. ·

II.   A large tract of mountain land with potential future profit in timber and coal mining had nothing in common with home building. In no way could my building business be bettered by my 25% ownership in that land.

III.   Even if this had been an exceptional opportunity, because my primary business was still in its infancy, it was very unwise to divert any money or credit to an outside investment. Admittedly, we did not invest any cash, but when the note came due at the bank, we did have to come up with the cash. And because our entire purchase price had been paid with a note, the added interest was causing our actual cost to accelerate faster than the value increased.

I had been convinced we could later sell this property for an enviable profit. Since we had no cash invested, all of the net money received at the time of sale would be profit! If there was such a certain profit when the property should be sold to the right buyer, why had it not sold already to someone in timber or strip mining? The answer is obvious. It was not a good buy. It was a good sale, but not a good buy.

Look at the second stone in my wall. Isn't it a beauty? Without question, we acquired a valuable property in Florida. It was incredible that Winston and I were able to make that large purchase just five hours after we first looked at it. Had we taken time to investigate, we may not have bought it. Also, if we had known to prepare a more detailed contract, it would have been money and time well invested. There were some serious discrepancies!

The man we met in Tampa represented himself as the owner of the properties being offered. The facts later revealed that he and his three children (and their spouses) owned it. At first the children agreed that since their father had contracted to sell, they would not oppose it. Later, they refused to allow the sale to finalize. They increased the price and gave us two alternatives. Either we could accept the higher price and consummate the transaction, or they would return our down payment and cancel the purchase agreement.

The fifty-six existing apartments were all occupied. The renters had made a fully refundable security deposit when they occupied the premises. The seller had those fifty-six deposits in his bank account. He agreed that when we should assume management of the apartments, this account would be transferred to us. When we requested this money (approximately $9,000) at the closing, the seller told us the funds were in his wife's account and that he would get her to make a check for us later in the day. We never did receive that $9,000.

Another major problem developed regarding the kitchen appliances in the 80 units under construction. When we made our initial visit to Lakeland to inspect the properties, the seller told us there would be a refrigerator, range and a dishwasher in each of the new units. However on the day set for final closing, Winston and I walked through the newly-built apartments and noticed there were no appliances installed. We were told they were on order, but there was a little delay because the seller had experienced a cash-pinch as construction neared completion, and the order had been submitted late. We were assured they would be installed within days. Believing the seller to be a man of integrity, we executed all of the documents and closed the loans. The appliances were never delivered. Winston and I had to borrow an additional $80,000 to install these appliances before the apartments could be offered for rent.

And how about that nice mountain resort near Gatlinburg? Wasn't that quite a find for a newly formed corporation? Chalets in Gatlinburg were some of the most desirable real estate to be had. There was a perpetual demand for these cabins, which kept the rental rates high. And because we secured our cabins from a highly motivated seller, our debt service on this property was such that a high occupancy would produce a good net figure.

One item of major importance had been overlooked. Only chalet property affiliated with a major reservation system has a good program for advance bookings. Many tourists in that area drive into Gatlinburg or Pigeon Forge trusting they will find lodging after arriving. Therefore, in order to succeed in renting chalets, one must have affiliation with a major reservation system or an office on a front street for easy visibility. We had no front street office. Neither did we have any one resident in Gatlinburg to handle this business. The small number of units we owned did not justify a full-time manager, but without a local manager, our cabins remained totally unoccupied many nights even when tourists were being turned away from motels.

I had a friend, Bill Jones, who owned a 50-unit motel just about a mile from our cabins. Bill's wife offered to act as our agent in renting the cabins for a modest fee. This was a great help to us, except the fact that our cabins usually were not offered to customers without reservations who stopped in at the Jones' Motel until after all of their rooms had been occupied. In essence, our cabins served as their overflow in case they had a caller after having completely filled their own rooms. On nights when there was not a heavy demand, our cabins remained unoccupied.

The next stone I used in building my Humpty Dumpty wall was actually only a man-made simulated stone. That soft stone was Dixie Development Corporation. Rather than being a building stone, it was more like a marshmallow — attractive to the sight and pleasant to the taste, but really it was only sweet fluff.

When I took the time to make a realistic evaluation, I realized, too late, that I was the only one in this new company who had any money. I had some money and my corporate associates had a plan. What was not obvious to me in the beginning was that their plan apparently was to get my money.

The expensive Dixie Development home office building should never have been built. It comprised 15,000 square feet, of which we used only 1,000 feet for our office. We did not need that much, but it was impressive with the top of the line massive mahogany furniture David had unilaterally selected and ordered.

It was our plan to rent out the space we did not use to generate more than enough cash flow to service the debt on the building. The offices were completed and ready for occupancy by Spring of 1973, just when we were in a steep recession. Existing businesses were reluctant to relocate and new businesses that did contract to use our space usually could not survive. They moved out without paying their rent. At our best time, the building was 40% occupied. We had a commitment for permanent financing, but the insurance company would not close the loan without at least 80% occupancy. Not only did we lose our commitment which had cost us $16,000, the bank that furnished construction financing was pressuring us to move the loan from their bank. For the three years we owned the building, our average deficit was $3,000 every month. Because we could not find a buyer, we ultimately conveyed the property to an investment group for the balance of the loan.

There was some viable business being conducted by Dixie Development, but virtually no project was adequately funded. Standing alone, most of our projects could have been completed without difficulty. The problem arose because a portion of top management cost was assessed against each project. In every case, we experienced cost overruns. To be totally candid, the top management cost was extremely disproportionate with the size and strength of our corporation. Within months of forming the corporation, Jeff, David and George were all employed by the corporation. Being employed did not necessarily mean they worked. It meant they collected a salary. Exactly what they did, I am not sure. I do know I was the only corporate officer working to bring cash into the company's bank account, while the other three spent the bulk of their time trying to develop more plans to spend money.

Even though I was convinced the corporation could not support executive-level salaries and benefits for four corporate officers, I had only one vote on the board, so it was not possible for me to control what was happening. Of the four salaried executives, three were involved in "planning" for expansion. That may have been acceptable if we had been flushed with capital, which definitely was not the case.

When Dixie Development was less than two years old, the death knell sounded. It was not a loud sound, but it was very definite. When it occurred, I do not know. Exactly where it happened, I am not aware. Who initiated it, I can only speculate. The only fact of which I am sure, is that there was a clandestine meeting of the officers and directors of Dixie Development Corporation. In the corporation records, I was listed as the President and CEO. Also I was Chairman of the Board of Directors. However, by some small, innocent oversight, I was not apprised of the agenda, nor invited to attend the meeting.

At that meeting, two momentous decisions were reached. The first item of business was increasing of salaries and expense accounts. I was never made aware of any details of the discussions: I only learned later, in quite an unexpected way, of the action taken. The corporate officers were to receive an increase in salary; plus all company-related expenses were to be reimbursed from company funds at the end of each month. The unusual oddity of this action was that salary increases and expense accounts were approved for those in attendance at the meeting, but I was neither made aware of the projected increase, nor did my checks show any change. I can only presume they must have based their action on the fact that I was directing the building projects in overalls, and for that unsophisticated type of work, I was being adequately compensated. The other three officers were the "think-tank." What they did was certainly deserving of a larger remuneration, so they put their salaries above mine.

Following this historic corporate ignominy, the bookkeeper was instructed to write larger salary checks to Jeff, David and George. Each of them also prepared expense accountings for themselves and collected additional funds. I was to learn later they had sternly required that in no case was the bookkeeper to make me aware of what had been done, at the risk of losing her employment. Also, she was to lock up the checkbook and corporate records to insure further that this information would be kept from me. I would learn of the second item of business to come out of that shameful meeting later, quite by accident.

When funds seemed always to be insufficient to meet our expenses, one day I went into the office and told the secretary/bookkeeper to bring me some records so I could try to determine why the perpetual shortage of funds. My first surprise came when I observed the large salary checks for my fellow board members. It is an understatement to say I was shocked to see one expense reimbursement check for $4,200 for one man for one month. When I instructed the secretary to bring me the supporting receipts, vouchers, etc. for this expenditure, she was unable to produce any backup documents. It was then she told me she had been forced by the other directors to conceal information from me.

Not at all pleased by what I had learned, but also curious to know if there might be any other strange secrets, I pursued my search. I found a check written to William Isaacson, a person whose name I did not recognize. The check was marked for travel expenses from New York. I found two more checks to the same name in the amount of $1,000 each and marked "retainer fees." The next day, I confronted Jeff for an explanation. If you find it difficult to believe what Jeff told me, I will understand. Here is his story.

"A number of weeks ago, David called George and me to suggest we get together to discuss some matters of mutual interest. He proposed that we were underpaid, and there should be some adjustment. The salary increase and the payment of company expense are legitimate and we should have them.

"At first, I opposed this action, but when David insisted, George and I followed his lead. In order for Dixie Development to become the success it must be if we are going to make it a public company, we need to project a winning image. Of course, that does require more money.

"Next, David introduced for discussion his meetings with a Wall Street stock broker, William Isaacson, who could take our company public and in the process make us all instant millionaires. We decided to fly this broker into Chattanooga and show him our operation. Then we would follow his advice for preparing to offer the Dixie Development stock publicly.

"The broker flew to Chattanooga. I met him at the airport and drove him to Cleveland. He went through our office building. We showed him a number of homes we have under construction. We also looked over the proposed shopping center site and the blueprints for its development. We went through the Dunkin' Donuts store and I told him we have another store in Nashville, with franchise rights to open nine more. It was not practical to travel to Gatlinburg, but I told him about the resort cabins we have there. He was favorably impressed and told us we definitely have the core of a public corporation.

"William then outlined what is necessary to make a successful public offering of our stock. He said, 'You already have six divisions with (1) your office leasing and shopping center space, (2) home construction, (3) swimming pool sales and maintenance, (4) Dunkin' Donuts as your fast food division, (5) resort properties for lease in Gatlinburg and (6) Roberts Real Estate, which can be expanded to market real estate in numerous areas.'

"William went on to recommend that we make additional purchases of a number of small companies in different types of business so as to give the impression of a completely diversified, interstate company. He suggested buying a lumber supply company and possibly a concrete mixing company or concrete block manufacturing facility, which would very well complement our home building division. It might also be conceivable that we open two or three more real estate sales companies in other nearby cities, all under the aegis of Roberts Real Estate and using Winston as our principal broker in all offices.

"The last thing William advised we do was to be sure to buy a small public company. That is, one that has already been accepted by the S.E.C. In that way it will be possible to eliminate the long and expensive process of getting our company approved. We were advised to secure a small company with little or no name recognition. Preferably, buy one that is bankrupt, so the price would be very affordable. All we were to be interested in was the shell. That newly-acquired company would then sell all of its stock to Dixie Development at a token price and Dixie would emerge as a public company. The result is, we will have a pubic company without the need to endure the pressure and expense of registering with the Securities and Exchange Commission. When we have combined approximately twenty of these small companies all registered as affiliates of Dixie Development Corporation, William told us he will develop all the necessary paperwork to make a public offering, and he will personally line up a brokerage firm that will market our stock. The stock should be a sellout within 90 days. We will be instant millionaires."

That is the story as I heard it from Jeff.

"And what will William Isaacson intend to charge Dixie Development for this service?" I inquired.

"Only the $1,000 per month retainer fee while the development is in process, plus reasonable expenses, and 15% of the company stock," was Jeff's naive response.

I looked with pity at my stupid, gullible vice president and told him, "You may become instant millionaires, but only for an instant. In addition to having a million dollars, you won't need to worry about where you will live or what you will eat. The government will provide you with those bare necessities in a federal institution without cost to you. After you have sold that artificial corporation to the public, someone will have to make it perform profitably. When a court decides that this illusion of a successful company is nothing more than a combining of unsuccessful businesses, intended to mislead unsuspecting investors, somebody is going to the penitentiary. I don't intend to be that sacrificial lamb offered on the altar of your greed. Count me out!"

Immediately I dictated a letter to Mr. William Isaacson to inform him that our corporation no longer had need of his services and that there would be no further $1,000 checks mailed to him. We never received a reply to that letter.

The next thing I did was to telephone all of the shareholders to announce an emergency meeting. When the meeting was called to order, I had only one item of business to present. It was that the corporation immediately dismiss David as a director and as an officer and that all related financial benefits be discontinued concurrent with suspension. The vote was in the affirmative. Our action precipitated a small war, in which there was no winner.

235

But that does not necessarily belong in this narrative, so we will leave David to his evil designs.

The cancer had been excised, but it was too late. Dixie Development Corporation was too anemic to survive. By our action, David was out. Within weeks, Jeff and George saw the handwriting on the wall and found employment elsewhere. Interestingly, their new employment was not in Cleveland. I was left alone to assume all consequences of the disgrace. At that time I was not aware of the severity of the collapse of Dixie Development.

In addition to the uncontrolled extravagance of my three young associates, the bookkeeper had been writing checks to fictitious persons, thereby bleeding the corporate account of what the evil vultures had not taken. It seems she decided if the corporation officers could embezzle funds and get by with it, why should she be deprived. After all she was an employee, too. So she reached her hand in the cookie jar and took what was left.

When the smoke cleared, I calculated the obligations of Dixie Development. To my utter amazement and consternation, Pan-Southern Corporation had debts totaling $250,000. We had 37 creditors, and almost all accounts were delinquent. With interest applied to the balance each month at near-usurious rates, I could not even pay the interest that was making the total of our accounts increase every month. Having no alternative, I surrendered our corporate charter to the Office of the Secretary of State in Nashville.

I arranged to meet in different locations and at separate times with my attorney, my accountant and the presidents of two banks where I had extensive credit. They all suggested I had no choice but to bankrupt, personally and corporately. I refused to follow their recommendation. The debts had been created by four persons. Three had left town, but my conscience told me the creditors deserved to be paid, and I was the only person who felt an obligation to satisfy the debts honestly.

I wrote a letter to every creditor to let them know Dixie Development was defunct, but that I had accepted personal responsibility and I would make small periodic payments until the entire amount due had been paid. I had no idea how I could pay $250,000, but I knew I had to try. My business was gone. My self-respect was destroyed, and my future was bleak.

When I was forty-six years old, I had a net worth of $500,000 and had calculated when I should reach 50, my net worth ought to be $1,000,000. Now, nearing fifty, I was broken and broke.

CHAPTER TWENTY-FIVE

ALL THE KING'S MEN

Dixie Development Corporation was no longer. Big plans had been suffocated with bigger greed. Impatience to become rich without making the proper investment in capital, planning, commitment and time, had blinded the eyes of the young management team and the business could do nothing else but fail.

Seeing that failure was unavoidable, and just maybe because the money source had suddenly vanished, my over-enthusiastic corporation directors looked for greener pastures elsewhere. Isn't it amazing how committed some people are to a cause or a project as long as they are being well compensated for their time and service? It is even more amazing how quickly those same individuals can forget their professed loyalty when things get tough.

Where my friends subsequently found employment, I am not aware. I have sometimes wondered what information they gave about a former employer when making application for a position. I was never called for a reference.

Actually, I hardly had time to investigate where they had gone. I had a quarter million dollar problem to look after. Dixie Development, as a corporate entity was gone. Its leadership had quietly left town. But I was still functioning, essentially as I had prior to meeting my overly-ambitious friends. We still had the resort cabins in Gatlinburg (with their negative cash flow). How I wished it were not the case, but we still had Dixie Development Center (with most of the space unoccupied and with a consistent negative cash flow of $3,000 monthly). We still had the shopping center land (which had never been developed). In fact, we still had virtually everything — except that three-fourths of the board of directors in the failed corporation had left town.

One thing we did not have was that uncontrollable team of extravagant spenders incessantly attacking the checkbook for another dollar. Another thing was missing — there was no money to keep the business operating. What we did have was an uninterrupted flow of envelopes with windows coming to us, courtesy of the U. S. Postal Service.

When I awoke from the nightmare, I became aware of the gravity of my situation. I could not quit. The utilities in the Dixie Development Center had to remain available to the few tenants we had in the building. Taxes had to be paid on the properties we owned. Insurance premiums on those properties continued to come due, and if not paid, they could create an even more extreme problem. Work had to continue on houses under construction. And not least in importance, payroll had to be met every Friday. Yes, Dixie Development Corporation had died, but Cleveland didn't know it yet. I had a responsibility to so many to keep the business operating and the bills paid.

In the years prior to Dixie Development, I had done quite well. I had a limited amount of cash reserve and a moderate amount of real property. I made a frantic effort to reorganize so my personal assets would not be indiscriminately eaten up to satisfy the daily demands from former activities of Dixie Development.

Conditions continued to deteriorate to the point that I began to realize there was a message for me in the last line of Humpty Dumpty. "All the kings men could not put Humpty Dumpty together again." It is possible to come to a point of no return and no way out. I was there!

I explored every possibility. I offered for sale every tangible asset the now-defunct corporation owned. Word had spread of our troubles, so most of the sales I made were at sacrifice prices. In some cases, I gave properties (or equities in properties) to creditors in lieu of cash payment to settle over-due accounts. I made no distinction between corporate properties and personal. If by selling, I could generate cash, I applied it to our debt. I tried, unsuccessfully, to sell Dixie Development for a tax loss. Regardless of how I tried, I could find no way to resolve the multiple crises that engulfed me.

For a time, I still believed I could survive. Possibly that was due to the fact that I was still being offered opportunities for investment or joint ventures by those who were not yet completely aware of the magnitude of the financial injury I had sustained.

A group of my acquaintances formed a corporation they named "Homes, Inc." In the name of the corporation, they purchased a 300 acre farm to be subdivided and sold for home sites. Their plan was for twenty investors to contribute $3,000 each to fund the down payment and start the work of surveying, road building and subdividing.

When I was approached as a potential investor, nineteen shares had been subscribed. I took the twentieth share.

In record time, the first section of the farm was sub-divided, streets paved and utilities installed. At a public auction, the 80 building lots sold well and brought a good price. Some of the investors decided this was a good time to take their profit, so a number of shares were offered for sale. I bought as many as I could get. At the end of one year, I owned 25% of the company's stock because I could see Homes, Inc. as a successful company and saw the subdivision as a very attractive location for some fine homes to be built.

At the first annual shareholders' meeting, the president resigned. It seems he saw he had lost control of the company he had formed. I was asked by some of the shareholders to take the position, to which I agreed. A vote was taken and I was elected as the second president of Homes, Inc. At that time, the outgoing president offered me his stock for the $3,000 he had originally paid for it. I bought it. That brought my ownership position to 30%.

Within days after the annual meeting, I received a call from the vice president of the bank that held the first mortgage on the land, which was the only tangible asset the corporation owned. It was time to renew the note for the money the company had borrowed to purchase the land and fund the development. It was then I first learned the bank had required personal guarantees from the officers to secure the corporation's note. The reason the retiring president offered me his stock at his original cost was becoming apparent to me. (Also a rumor was being circulated to the effect the corporation's president had collected a real estate commission on every lot that sold at the auction. When this information began to surface, some of the corporate members were more than a little disturbed at this alleged unscrupulous self-dealing. It seemed obvious to some that this may have been the primary reason the former president had resigned and offered his stock for sale.)

Double-digit inflation and record-high interest rates in recent months had slowed home building to the extent building lots were not selling. The officers of Homes, Inc. expressed fear that the potential risk connected to signing personal guarantee was too great. Some tried to sell their stock, but there were no buyers under current conditions. I tried to persuade the directors that we had a responsibility that should be honored, but they feared the risk and would not sign. As a result, the corporation defaulted and the bank foreclosed.

I had considered a number of the members of the corporation to be my friends, and also thought of them as men of integrity, but when it was a matter of standing up to their responsibility or protecting their personal assets, every one of them disappointed me. I signed the personal guarantee the bank had provided and hand-carried it to the other three officers for signature, but each one in turn declined to sign it. I did not sign that guarantee because I enjoyed the thrill of high risk. I agreed with the other officers that there was a strong likelihood the corporation was facing serious troubles. My only reason for signing was that I was cognizant of a moral responsibility which I believed transcended the possibility of personal gain or loss. Frankly, I was extremely disappointed with my friends who took the exact opposite position. As it ultimately turned out, they avoided a personal financial loss, but I believe their real loss was greater than mine.

When the notice of foreclosure was printed in the newspaper, I knew it was irreversible. At that time I spoke to the bank vice president to inquire about the sale. Believing we were responsible whether the situation was good or bad, it was my personal conviction that the corporation's officers should have signed the note to extend the loan. I offered to bid at the auction, if the bank would fund for me. The vice president assured me the bank would carry the entire bid price on my signature. I had intentionally waited this long before inquiring about buying the entire property in my name so no other corporation member could say I took an unfair advantage because of my position.

I went to the auction and submitted a bid for an amount equal to the balance due from Homes, Inc. It was the only bid offered. At that moment I owned the entire subdivision and also I owed the entire debt. The most significant disappointment was yet to come. When it became public knowledge that I had bought the remaining land at the foreclosure sale, three men whom I considered good personal friends and men of high moral convictions called me and threatened legal action. One man actually pursued his threat to the extent that I borrowed money and restored the amount of his investment to avoid a legal battle with a friend.

Over the next three years I put in water mains and streets in sections II, III and IV. In an effort to generate sales, I built a dozen homes scattered throughout the area to give the appearance of a developing community. A few lots were sold, but for all practical purposes, it is realistic to say sales in the subdivision had stagnated.

I had been building homes in Bradley County for about five years, but this was my first time to be involved in property development. It was definitely a different ball game. When I applied for final county acceptance of the streets in Sections II, III and IV, I met a new competitor in the form of the County Planning

Commission. I was told the development could not be approved because the street which was the only entrance to the subdivision restricted the flow of water and could cause flooding in properties just above ours. It was their position that the culverts under that street were inadequate to carry flood water in heavy rain.

When called by the county commission to defend my position that this requirement was not legitimate, I reasoned that the street in question had been constructed earlier to allow access to Section I, which had already been approved, subdivided and sold. The subsequent sections I had developed were directly behind Section I, and used the same street as their only access. Whether or not we developed additional lots would in no way affect how much water could pass under that existing street.

I was reprimanded for challenging the position of the planning commission and advised that if I wanted county acceptance of the remaining acreage, I would correct the purported water restriction at the entrance to the subdivision.

Word reached me, through a third party, that if I would give $5,000 in an unmarked envelope to a certain person, he in turn would deliver it to the person who could influence the vote and I could have the county acceptance finalized. I declined the offer. At a high cost, I engaged a heavy equipment contractor to break up the pavement and widen the deep ditch that drained the water along the county road at the front of our sub-division. He then installed side by side two 36" concrete culverts under the 40 foot right of way, filled in the excavated area and patched the pavement.

When I resubmitted an application for a permit, again it was refused. This time I was approached by a different individual and told that if I would go to a certain bank officer and arrange to use his bank to fund construction loans for residences in the subdivision, that banker could get the permit approved for me. In the same conversation, I was also advised that the banker wanted to be my silent partner in the building of those homes. He would have no known involvement in any of the work, but he would make the financing available and would expect to receive 50% of the net income from every home built. Again, I emphatically refused. I preferred to fail with integrity than to succeed by paying a bribe.

The situation worsened. Because I had not submitted diagrams and specifications prepared by a licensed engineer prior to installing the double culverts under the street, it would not be accepted by the county. They required that the culverts be removed and a steel reinforced concrete bridge be constructed. Further, to guarantee the county that the required bridge would meet minimum county approved standards, I was required to provide the planning commission a performance bond. It was money wasted, but having no alternative, I complied. I bought the bond, delivered it to the county commission and built the bridge.

With all of this wrangling, which became common knowledge in our small town, a stigma was developing and builders shied away from our building lots. Add to that the fact that high inflation would not go away and interest rates remained unattractive, making a difficult situation virtually impossible. In spite of all of my efforts I was not successful in my attempt to restore the credibility necessary to sell these very attractive wooded building lots, even at heavily discounted prices.

Finally, in despair, I went to the bank one day and offered to sign a quit-claim deed if the bank would cancel the debt with no contingent liability. I was one step nearer to total devastation.

(In this narrative of my saga toward ruin, I have intentionally omitted names or have used fictitious names so as not to imply blame or responsibility even to certain persons who contributed to my business collapse. However, I think it would be unkind and unfair not to mention the name of the bank officer who handled my business dealings with the Cleveland National Bank during those most traumatic times. I owe a great debt of gratitude to then Executive Vice President of Cleveland National Bank, William Ewing. Bill Ewing, behind his large mahogany desk, was all business. But when I was overwhelmed with insurmountable difficulties, I learned Bill Ewing was all heart. I am not sure how much confidence Bill had in my ability to perform under such pressures, but I do know he believed in me as an honest person and he put the resources of the bank at my disposal to the extent he may have jeopardized his own job security. Neither Bill nor I made any attempt at any questionable business transaction, but I did enjoy a favorable relationship with the Cleveland National Bank that most likely would not have existed had it not been for Bill Ewing. He was there for me when I desperately needed a genuine friend. In my lifetime, I have had few friends like Bill Ewing.)

Although I have been able to recount these details on a few pages, the collapse and demise of Dixie Development Corporation was not an overnight occurrence. The complete deterioration spanned well over two years. During those trying months, I grasped at many straws to survive. My association with Homes, Inc. was one such attempt at survival.

Within the same time frame, I met Al Taylor, who had recently moved his family to Cleveland to accept an assignment with the General Offices of the Church of God. Prior to this move, Al had been a very successful sales manager with a major firm which did business nationwide. Because of a personal concern and commitment to a ministry, he accepted the church appointment even with a significantly reduced income. To supplement his income from the church, Al gave a little of his time in the evenings to selling water distillers for home use.

One of Al Taylor's water distiller customers was Dr. Clifford Dennison, a chemistry professor at Lee College. Dr. Dennison is both a scholar and a pragmatist. Being aware, as a scientist, that water contamination poses a serious threat, he bought the distiller to provide pure water for drinking and cooking in his home. From a more practical perspective, he completely dismantled the unit to analyze the process of distillation utilized in this small unit. His conclusion was that he could make a fully automatic distiller which would be more efficient and produce water with a higher degree of purity than the portable unit he had purchased from Al. This ultimately resulted in the formulation of a new company to manufacture and market this newly invented machine.

A contract was made with a fabricating company to produce and market the Dennison Distiller. It seems the right company was selected as manufacturer of the all-stainless steel distillers, because they were equipped to produce a distiller that was completely efficient as well as esthetically acceptable for home installation. A problem developed in the matter of a manufacturing company also marketing its products. Manufacturing and marketing within the same office apparently generated some tensions which the manufacturing company was not willing to accept, so the relationship was terminated.

The manufacturer had expended a considerable sum in setting up special tools and dies as well as metal presses for the production of the distillers, so they were amenable to continuing as the supplier of the units if a suitable sales company would be the distributor. Al decided to try to form a new sales company. He brought in Sonny Pittman, a former manager of the firm whose distillers Al had previously marketed, to take responsibility for sales. Next he contacted me and offered a 25% ownership position if I would invest $50,000. I tried unsuccessfully for a month to gather the necessary funds. I had sufficient equity in one property to qualify to borrow $25,000, so Al and I agreed that I would invest the $25,000 for 12 1/2% of the stock and he would continue to look for one more investor for the other $25,000. Unfortunately, no other investor was ever located.

At that time, prudence should have dictated that the new company was woefully under-capitalized and because there was little likelihood additional investors would be located, we could not expect to survive. Sonny Pittman was willing to commit to the marketing challenge on the strength of only my $25,000 and hope to make it happen. He did his best, but we were trying to do the impossible. Before another investor could be located, our money was depleted — so we lost again.

Some people never learn. When the next opportunity was offered, again I reasoned, this may be what I have been looking for. Jerry Bowman called on me one evening to offer me some burial plots in a local perpetual care facility, which I hardly needed twenty years ago. I could not agree that this should be a priority, given my age and circumstance, but Jerry was a convincing salesman, and before he left our house, I owned four burial plots.

A few days later, Jerry visited my office to deliver the contract for my recent purchase. It seems now that neither of us were extremely interested in discussing burial plots that day, so our conversation took a different tangent.

Jerry mentioned to me that he had been considering the opening of a Buyers' Club in Cleveland. The intent was to create a membership basis for making purchases at wholesale cost, plus a small percentage markup. Members would select merchandise from catalogues and receive shipment directly to their homes. In this way, there would be virtually no overhead expense and the members would enjoy a meaningful discount on purchases. The club would primarily be offering household furnishings

Jerry told me that most furniture stores mark the retail price of their merchandise at double the wholesale cost. To make membership attractive to others who may not have a current interest in making a furniture purchase, we would add home appliances, televisions, radios, stereo components, C.B. radios, sporting goods, etc. (As it turned out, ultimately the club offered and furnished everything from golf balls to new cars.)

Membership in the proposed club would be offered for an initial cost of $449.00 with an annual renewal fee of $20. The projection was that half of the initial membership cost would be commission to the sales force and the remaining half would be retained by the company. Jerry's projection called for at least 1,000 members in Bradley County. After that, he proposed we expand the marketing into Chattanooga. His projections called for the first 1,000 members within a year. He further calculated the cost of a director at $50,000 for salary and expenses.

The expense related to registering the company, making contact with suppliers, printing sales manuals, contract forms, etc. should be completed for a cost not to exceed $20,000. Jerry had $5,000 and he had two potential investors in the Knoxville area who had each committed $5,000. He was hoping to locate a fourth investor with $5,000.

I quietly did a little quick math and came up with an impressive bottom line. Income from 1,000 memberships @ $449 would produce $449,000. From that, I subtracted 50% for sales commissions plus $50,000 for a manager's salary and expense. There was still a balance of $174,500. For an investment of $5,000, I would have 25% of that net figure by the end of the first year, which would be $43,625. Rather than planning for the maximum, I reasoned that by cutting the amount in half, it seemed realistic to expect my $5,000 could net me more than $20,000 the first year. I speculated further that if we could market 1,000 memberships in Cleveland and Bradley County the first year, surely by expanding into Chattanooga, with a population of 250,000, the second year should be better than the first.

I committed the $5,000 for a 25% ownership in the proposed venture.

At the organizational meeting of the corporation, we voted to operate a firm committed to providing wholesale buying power through membership in a Buyer's Club. We also voted that our memberships would be offered to the public at $449 for a one year membership, renewable for a fee of $20 in each successive year. The four investors agreed to serve as the corporation board without compensation. I was elected to serve as President and CEO Jerry Bowman was elected as General Manager.

A sales blitz was immediately launched to introduce our concept to Cleveland's populace. The idea was well received until the potential members learned that our address was a post office box number with no known physical location. Their skepticism was justified, and we faced the decision to secure an office as our permanent address or lose our sales force because they were experiencing difficulty in closing sales without an address where members could make selections and order merchandise. There went a significant portion of our first year's profit. The directors decided it was mandatory that we have a visible office and we authorized Jerry to find a suitable location.

Jerry did find a good location and signed a lease agreement in the name of the corporation for two years. But it was far more than an office. We were committed for 2,000 square feet in a large open warehouse. Jerry made a unilateral decision that we needed more than just an office. He contracted for enough space to put in a very impressive showroom where all sorts of merchandise

249

could be displayed. It was a first rate idea, but it did not fit into the scheme of our operations. With the 10% mark-up allowed by our plan, there was no money available to pay rent on a large show-room and no money to pay for display items of furniture, appliances, etc. We tried to invalidate the lease agreement, but could not. We were to learn that our manager was a compulsive spender, especially when it was not his own money he was spending.

To purchase enough samples to fill the showrooms, we had to spend about $50,000. There went the first year's net income. By listing these samples in the ledger as inventory, the financial condition of the company looked good, but we had no cash-flow. The Board of Directors met and reprimanded Jerry for making such a move without prior approval from the board. Next we voted to maintain a ceiling on the amount of inventory that could be carried in the showroom and required that Jerry operate strictly within these guidelines. I am not sure he heard us. If Jerry had a dollar, or the promise of a dollar, he ordered more merchandise.

Because of the attractive samples in the showroom, there was more credibility and membership sales increased. The only real problem is that we were not making any money.

By the end of the first year, two of our top salesmen saw the potential of our club concept and bought a franchise to open a similar operation in Chattanooga. They paid a franchise fee of $25,000 and agreed to remit to our office 2% of the 10% markup their club would charge its members. Our board was pleased with this expansion and the terms whereby we would have a small increase in revenues from the on-going franchise fees from the Chattanooga club. Without our knowledge, Jerry had agreed to furnish floor samples to the Chattanooga club until they could afford to purchase their own. The cost of the samples more than offset the $25,000 franchise fee we had taken in, so the initial net result of opening this second location was negative.

Next, Jerry was able to interest some investors in Knoxville to open a franchise operation there. Thankfully, no provision was made for our parent company to supply the sample merchandise for the Knoxville club, so the franchise fees received actually improved our financial situation somewhat.

When the board had placed a ceiling on the amount Jerry could spend for floor samples, he found a way to circumvent the limitation. He negotiated with the Cleveland National Bank to put kitchen appliances and stereo equipment in the showroom on a bank floor plan. That allowed Jerry to order merchandise without any cash outlay. As merchandise was delivered to our showroom, the bank paid the supplier. In essence, this became a secured loan because the bank held a chattel mortgage on that merchandise until it should be sold. When any item was sold, we were required to pay to the bank an amount equal to the wholesale price of the item sold, plus interest. Any money remaining was to be retained as our net income.

One Friday afternoon while in the bank, I was approached by Bill Ewing with an inquiry as to how he could contact Jerry. According to Bill's comment, Jerry had sold merchandise purchased on the floor plan without reducing our balance due at the bank. Bill told me it was a federal offense to be out of trust on this sort of borrowing, and that he had warned Jerry repeatedly about earlier violations. He said he would have two auditors at our showroom Monday morning and if he found any merchandise missing for which the bank had not been paid, he intended to go immediately to the Sheriff's office to swear out a warrant for Jerry's arrest.

As I walked out the back door of the bank, I met Jerry in the parking lot. When I told him of my conversation with Bill Ewing, Jerry immediately returned to his Cadillac and drove away. The following Monday morning, Jerry was in the parking lot at the club showroom well before the normal time for opening. He intended to check the inventory on the floor plan and issue payment to the Cleveland National Bank for any merchandise not accounted for, thereby clearing himself from any violation.

Upon approaching the front entrance, he noticed a bright yellow ribbon taped across the doors prohibiting entrance by order of the State of Tennessee Department of Revenue. The entire office and showroom was "off limits." Jerry had reported state sales tax for the prior two months, but the check he issued in payment was returned by the bank because there was not a sufficient amount on deposit to cover the check. Jerry issued a second check which also was returned "NSF." It was this second bad check which precipitated the action to lock the premises until the tax obligation should be satisfied. Seeing the yellow ribbons on the door, Jerry simply headed his Cadillac toward the Federal Courthouse in Chattanooga where he filed a petition for bankruptcy protection.

Having lived through so many disappointments, I had hoped this venture might somehow prove to be different. In the beginning I had thought of it as a possible escape from the ongoing nightmare I had experienced for so long. But, if anything, it was worse than my previous attempts to escape the shame and embarrassment of failure. I was to learn later how severely Jerry had betrayed all of us who had provided him employment with benefits plus a unique opportunity to own a significant part of a successful business. With a single stroke of a pen, Jerry committed our business venture to certain destruction without so much as a telephone call to inform the other three owners of what he intended to do. When Jerry filed the bankruptcy papers, he threw to the wind all the money, time and work we had invested.

Upon receipt of the petition for bankruptcy protection, the court appointed a trustee, an accountant and also an attorney to counsel the trustee and accountant. Jerry met with them and provided the information they required to settle the accounts of the creditors. There was an abundance of merchandise in the showrooms and an abundance of unpaid invoices in the files, but no cash to cover them. Jerry told the attorney that I was from a wealthy family in Texas with vast oil holdings, and that even though I did not personally have the money to pay the company's debts, under pressure, I could get the money.

When it seemed I had reached the bottom and things could not get worse, I walked into the office one Friday just as the postman arrived. He had a certified letter addressed to me. The return address on the large envelope made me aware it was from the U. S. District court in Chattanooga. When I opened it, what was left of my world collapsed.

A suit had been filed in the bankruptcy case of our Buyers' Club naming all of the members as the plaintiff and naming me as the defendant. The suit required that I return the fees of $449 to each of approximately 1,000 members who had purchased a membership from an under-funded company which could not provide to the members the services it proposed to give. Additionally the suit alleged, because there was an apparent conspiracy to defraud, the court assessed against me an additional $300,000 in punitive damages. Even though there were four owners of this business and each of us had an equal share of the corporation's stock, the fact that I was registered as the President made me vulnerable and totally responsible for the actions and omissions of all of the corporate officers.

I wanted to die!

It was not the monetary consequences of the suit that troubled me most. I had no ability to pay, so a $750,000 suit was no more disturbing to me than the smaller debts facing me. Because impossibility is impossibility, the amount made no difference. The only thing I had left was my integrity, and now that was being impugned.

In despair I took the letter to my attorney. Knowing he would quite likely not be compensated for his services, he went to work for me. My attorney advised the court's attorney it would be a waste of public funds to prosecute the case against me because I had no net worth, and the best the court could hope for was a judgment which could not yield any cash. Following the recommendation of my attorney, the court's attorney required that I provide him a list of all of my assets and liabilities. That list showed only one asset which was not encumbered. When I had sold one of the Dunkin' Donuts stores, the buyer had assumed my obligations, paid some cash down and gave me a note for $35,000 to be paid in installments. At that time there was a principal balance remaining due to me of approximately $30,000. Finding no other unencumbered assets, the court's attorney agreed to take that and dismiss the suit.

In my opinion, the court's attorney had no right to take this asset which was in no way related to the failed business, and I did not feel I was at all culpable as the suit alleged. But having no will to fight any more, I endorsed the note and gave it to him.

Finally, the long struggle was finished. Nothing remained but my obligations, still totaling roughly $250,000 because the periodic remittances I sent to the creditors was only enough to approximate the interest accumulating on the debts. The only satisfaction I had was that I had done my best. Even when I was offered an easy way out, I refused to compromise. There was nothing to do but start over, but I had no idea as to where I should start again. What was in my future was a complete mystery.

CHAPTER TWENTY-SIX

WHO IS TO BLAME?

Years ago I read about the world-renowned Christian missionary to Burma, Adoniram Judson. After having worked seven years in Burma without seeing one convert, he was questioned about the future. From then until now, his reply has continued to echo, "The future is as bright as the promises of God." When I first read that statement, I thrilled at the indomitable spirit which could so motivate a man to faith and faithfulness even while he was inundated with the humiliation of such obvious failure.

My thrill resulted from reading the report of another while he was being tried in the fire. When I was in the fire, it was something totally different. The facade of the romantic was replaced with the unpolished drab of reality. When the pressure was on me, I was not inclined to draw parallels between the bright, optimistic attitude of Adoniram Judson's missionary experiences and my present plight.

A quick glance at another missionary might be helpful. Few missionaries are more widely known than Hudson Taylor, who dedicated his life to God's service in China. His biography is divided into two volumes. The first was titled "The Growth Of A Soul." The title of the second book was "The Growth Of A Work." Without the former, the latter could not have been.

As I began to emerge from the midnight of my desolation, there was such comfort in the faintest glimpse of predawn light. It had been so long since I had experienced the pure exhilaration of watching a blazing sun force the darkest night to retreat in silent surrender. My new day was about to dawn. It would not be met as an ordinary second chance. Through much adversity, I had been conditioned to anticipate this new beginning appropriately.

It would have been completely wrong to accept the next phase of my life with an "it's about time" attitude. All I have written in the previous four chapters notwithstanding, what happened to me was essentially my own fault. It has taken years for me to acknowledge that and accept the full responsibility for everything that happened.

As you read the foregoing information about my multiple woes, you sympathized with me — and that is what I wanted you to do. You disliked the individuals I wrote about who mistreated and manipulated me. Why else do you think I wrote those things that would have been better forgotten? When my best efforts had been inadequate, and my loftiest ideals had been spurned, all I had struggled to achieve lay in ashes around me. In total disgrace and humiliation, I found a remote spot where I could cry and console myself with the undeniable fact that I had been the victim of a number of unscrupulous actions by my dishonest and unprincipled associates. I was convinced my innocence should have been obvious to the world.

As long as I permitted myself to wallow in that self-pity, the future was bleak. I was trying to garner satisfaction by placing the blame on anyone but myself. Of course, I was unaware of what was happening to me as a result of my placing the blame on others. The only thing I did was to reflect on what had happened and then draw the logically correct conclusion that all the negative things that occurred were the direct result of the miscalculations and faulty management decisions of my associates. If all of my ventures had been successful, I would have applauded myself for being such a genius and I would have claimed credit for every achievement. That had not been the case, but even so, I was still the leader and win or lose, any success or failure had to be ascribed to me.

It has been properly postulated that there are two things that try the character of a man: adversity and success. Many good men can point to former adversities as the foundation of current success. When they were surrounded by difficulties, they kept their integrity. Most of us understand that type of testing. It is the other test of character that is not so well known. Success can make us self-centered, bigoted, arrogant and unsympathetic. In essence, what first appears as success can become the precursor of the worst sort of failure.

If I had not experienced the horrifying losses enumerated in the prior chapters, I think there was a real possibility I would have reached the pinnacle of achievement usually considered to be success, but the final result would have been worse than any ordinary failure. Some valuable lessons were learned, not the least of which is that no measure of achievement or success brings satisfaction if one tries to enjoy the benefits alone.

As a young boy I had been endowed with one gift — a simple drinking cup. But in climbing the ladder to success, I had inadvertently laid it aside temporarily. In so doing, I had lost touch with the main purpose for my life. When I reached the top of the ladder to success, it became apparent that I had leaned my ladder against the wrong wall. If God can forgive the indiscretions and misdirected energies of some of the years I squandered, I am determined to make the latter years of my life conform more to His perfect plan rather than to my own flawed objectives.

The God of a second chance used my stumbling to teach me how to maintain my balance. I thought I had lost everything, but God showed me I had only lost what I did not need and had rediscovered the real values that had been lost. It was time to make a new start and I relished the opportunity.

CHAPTER TWENTY-SEVEN

IMPORTANT PEOPLE

In 1968, Robert F. Kennedy came to Logan, West Virginia where he delivered a campaign speech in an effort to generate support for his bid to become the next President of the United States. It was not my intention to vote a democratic ticket that year, and if I had voted for a democratic candidate, Mr. Kennedy would not have been my choice. However, being intrigued by the campaign, I attended the rally. I was near enough that the presidential candidate reached out and shook my hand.

On another occasion I attended a meeting where Senator Bob Dole was the speaker. After the session, I was introduced to the senator and we exchanged a few words. (Incidentally, when I was given an opportunity, I did vote for Senator Dole to be the next president, but in that election, the good guys lost.)

One of the favorite sons of Hawaii is the highly respected Senator Daniel Inouye, who became a legend during World War II. When Japan attacked his island home, he volunteered for service with the military forces of the United States, but because his ancestors were Japanese, there were some who feared he might defect to Japan under severe pressure, so he was assigned to serve in the European war. He returned minus one arm, but he had gained the respect of his country. I was honored to shake the hand of this patriot when I lived in Hawaii.

The United States President I most admire is the great communicator, Ronald Reagan. We met briefly at a political rally in Atlanta and Letha and I had the distinct pleasure of being photographed with the President of the United States. That portrait has occupied a distinguished place in our home for the past several years.

Those and a few other brief meetings with prominent personalities like Travelers CEO Sandy Weill, C.B.N. President Pat Robertson, General Colin Powell, Evangelist Billy Graham, movie and music star Pat Boone and West Virginia Governor Arch Moore were emotionally charged moments, but the thrill was only temporary.

On the lighter side, I recall the day I had an appointment to meet Jimmy Carter (not the Jimmy Carter whose address was 1700 Pennsylvania Avenue, Washington, D. C.). When I met Mr. Carter, he introduced me to his business associate, Ike. Believe it or not, when I returned home, on my desk was a telephone message which read, "Ron Reagan called this afternoon. He requested that you return his call as soon as possible." Such a coincidental meeting on the same day with three not-so-important people who had the names of three United States Presidents had to occur in actuality: it was too strange for believable fiction.

When I met the real celebrities, we shook hands or exchanged greetings, but there was nothing of lasting significance. My afternoon with the "same-name" people was interesting and a bit humorous. It was good for a smile, but there was nothing more of real value.

I was soon to meet a man who would effect a change in my life for good. There are always appealing public speakers and professional motivators conducting meetings in very convenient locations vying for the attention of just one more potential heavy-hitter. I had looked into a number of such companies with a desire to find the solution to my ever-present dilemma.

In 1975, I was introduced to Shaklee, which I feel is one of the better muti-level companies marketing health food supplements and environment-friendly household cleaning products. We decided to try it. Within one year, we had advanced to the senior supervisor level, our net income reached as high as $3,000 a month. Exactly one year after affiliating with Shaklee, we qualified to receive a bonus car. Ours was a sleek new Oldsmobile Cutlass Supreme.

Some of our acquaintances were logging large numbers of sales and earning attractive incomes with Sales Training Institute, an Atlanta-based company. Considering it to be an attractive venture with a potential for building a sales force in a number of large population centers throughout the state, a friend and I bought the exclusive franchise right for the entire State of South Carolina.

For a time, we developed a moderately successful business and the income was promising, but living about 100 miles from the nearest city in South Carolina, it was not as desirable as we first anticipated. It almost required moving to that State or reducing our sales activity there. Initially, when we were considering the purchase of the State-wide franchise, my partner had committed to devote his full time and effort to making the sales effort effective. Possibly, he should have conferred with his wife prior to expressing that decision, because when she tired of his being away from home so much, he opted out as director of sales. Actually, I had put up the front money to purchase the franchise, so when he resigned and sales slowed to a trickle, he had little to lose. Reflecting on that arrangement now, maybe I am the one who should have conferred with my wife prior to making the decision to fund another man's dream.

Too late, I learned one extremely valuable lesson: any partnership formed with my money and my partner's time cannot be in my best interest. At any time, the partner who commits only his time can decide to withdraw. At that time, he takes his time and goes on to something more attractive, but I can not take my money and leave. It has already been spent to fund a venture that will stand or fall completely at the whim of the partner who commits only his time.

I was still somewhat involved in residential building and a little remodeling. Having a strong interest in health foods and vita-mins, Letha took over the Shaklee business and she was able to realize a positive cash flow from the start, with a steadily grow-ing income. She was convinced there was a possibility we could build a Shaklee sales organization large enough to produce adequate income to maintain our family budget.

As building took less and less of my time and energy, and with Letha operating our Shaklee business without my help, I started to have a little free time occasionally. Restless as I was, I began seeking for additional earning potential through another part-time sales marketing plan. Ideal, Inc., a newly-emerging company developing in Atlanta attracted my attention. Ideal focused on health through foods grown naturally, with special emphasis on aloe vera juice. It seemed to me an ideal comple-ment to our Shaklee business.

Armed with my Ideal sales kit, I visited the Roberts Real Estate Office to try to interest Winston Collins in the valuable line of products I now had available just for buying a membership in Ideal. (Winston was vice president of the corporation we formed to buy the apartment properties in Florida a number of years ear-lier.) He was not even vaguely interested in what I had to offer. Good salesman that he was, true to form he offered me a conces-sion. If I would join his new company, he would join mine. I had no idea of what new company he referred to, but I agreed for the double transaction and we set a time when I would accompany him to a meeting sponsored by a company he called A. L. Williams.

Our wholesale buyers' club had been forced out of business by Jerry's irresponsible action of filing bankruptcy. I had to sell my stock in the apartment rental business in Florida due to the fact I could not carry my part of the operational over-runs. I found my expenses continued to mount, but my income steadily declined.

By 1979, I was devoting most of my daylight hours to building and remodeling. Evenings were spent in sales activity to market sales training institute's educational plan in South Carolina, con-ducting sales interviews or public recruiting meetings for Shaklee, or selling memberships in Ideal's wholesale buying plan.

It is understandable that when I told Letha I was going to accompany Winston to Chattanooga to look at a new business, she replied, "Promise me you won't go over there tonight and join another sales company. We are spread too thin already."

I promised her, and then Winston and I got in his car and drove to Chattanooga.

Letha was asleep when I returned home quite late. The next morning, I told her that I had not joined anything the evening before because I had given her my word I would not. But I told her I intended to go back the following week and join, which is precisely what I did.

That new business in Chattanooga, known simply as A. L. Williams, was directed by Ronnie Barnes, a former high school teacher. My meeting with Ronnie was hardly an auspicious event. In fact, he hardly recognized I was in the room, but the consequences of that introduction were significant to the extent they will be the subject of the remaining pages of this book!

CHAPTER TWENTY-EIGHT

A. L. WILLIAMS

When I walked into the office of Ronnie Barnes, I was taken completely off guard. Winston had told me that A. L. Williams was a revolutionary approach to insurance. Nothing more!

We entered a large room crowded with about 150 people seated on folding chairs. I had come expecting to learn about an exceptional business opportunity, but what I saw seemed more like a twenty-fifth-year high school reunion, with virtually everyone talking excitedly at the same time. I was not excited, but presuming they knew something I did not know, I waited quietly. (Actually, I think I was the only quiet person in the room.)

The meeting was called to order by a young man who suggested that all those in attendance for the first time identify themselves. Seventy-five percent of the group raised their hands. Then I was confused. If they were not a part of the insider group, why had they been so excited?

The preliminary speaker seemed to be a rabble-rouser intent on exposing banks, credit unions, savings & loan banks and insurance companies as the greatest enemies of the American people. His "great news" was that the consumer could cut his life insurance premium payment in half.

The second speaker explained how much money we could expect to earn just for telling our friends what the rabble-rouser had said. This seemed to be an obvious contradiction. First we were told we could help destroy the greed which caused life insurance companies to overcharge their clients. In the next breath, the speaker said we could become rich in the process. My big question was, "How is this group of enthusiasts any different from the greedy group they are castigating?" I was to learn that evening that the issue was not whether insurance companies should make a profit. The issue is that the profits are exorbitant and widows and orphans are the victims.

To conclude the session, the emcee introduced Ronnie Barnes, the high-school-teacher-turned-entrepreneur from Macon, Georgia. In down-to-earth terms, Ronnie explained how A. L. Williams as a company was started, and defined the crusade they espoused. His primary emphasis was that most families are under-insured simply because they cannot afford to insure themselves adequately. The premiums typically charged are too costly. It is as simple as that. A. L. Williams as a company proposed to right that wrong by making available inexpensive term insurance, with a premium cost of about one-half or one-third of the amount ordinarily charged. This meant the consumer would have more insurance without increased cost, or he could maintain the amount of protection currently in force, but dramatically reduce the premium cost.

The secret to making this new system work was as simple as reducing the profit margin in life insurance. Ronnie was calling for volunteers to help publicize this well guarded secret of the insurance companies. I came to understand completely the noisy enthusiasm that had filled the room before the seminar started. With that same infectious excitement, I volunteered.

I had come full-circle. Ronnie Barnes was inviting me to join him in a crusade to give a cup of cold water to the most needy sector of the nation's population. And in the process, I was to be well compensated for my time and effort. These were the two things I needed most: a crusade worthy of my effort and employment that could generate enough cash for our living expenses plus money to repay the staggering debt that had become my personal albatross.

The Bible message I had preached as a missionary and a pastor was returned to me by a new kind of insurance executive. The Biblical concept is presented in these words: "Pure religion and undefiled before God is this, to visit the fatherless and the widows in their affliction..." What a happy combination. I was to make available to my friends an insurance program they could work into their budget now, and when that tragic time comes that the bread-winner is taken from the family, the needs of his widow and his orphaned children will be properly met.

I was offered much more than employment. This was a mission! During my twelve years in Cleveland, I had worked hard to become successful, only to have all I had built crumble before me. I started in 1968 with nothing and functioned as a nonstop work-a-holic. I enjoyed a measure of success for a time, but at the end of a dozen years, I had no more than when I started. I could not know it then, but in the seventeen years ahead of me, I would experience far more satisfaction because my work was to be centered in others rather than self. As a bonus, I would also be compensated to a level that exceeded my wildest imagination.

Literally, my employment had come to be the culmination of my calling. Ronnie Barnes helped me to pick up the cup I had long since laid aside. He also taught me how to fill that cup with cool, refreshing water, ready to be given to the next thirsty person I might meet.

Thanks, Ronnie!

CHAPTER TWENTY-NINE

HAWAII

In the past three years, I had made numerous attempts at a new start, and as you have already read, each seemed to be a more disappointing fiasco than its predecessor. It came as no surprise, therefore, that Letha was not overly jubilant when I announced to her that I had applied for a contract to represent National Home Life Insurance Company as an affiliate in the A. L. Williams Agency. She was at a loss to understand why I was so gullible as to believe I could succeed selling life insurance. I had no background in this field; there were more insurance sales people already than necessary to harass the public; and it was a commission only contract. To be frank, there did not appear to be anything attractive about what I had just decided to do.

Letha reasoned that inasmuch as my building, real estate development, and other related businesses had failed so miserably, the ideal thing for me to do would be to make a clean break from all of that and let both of us give our full attention to our Shaklee business. Since we affiliated with Shaklee in September, 1975, our group development had been encouraging. We became supervisors within four months, and senior supervisors before the end of our first year. Our first bonus car was delivered in September, 1976, which was the earliest possible date to qualify for a bonus car. After using the Oldsmobile for two years at no cost to us, we had re-qualified and our new Mercury was delivered in 1978. These were lease cars, but so long as we maintained a certain level of production, Shaklee corporation paid the lease payments for us. We never missed a month.

A highlight in our Shaklee business was the annual convention. By meeting certain qualifications in sales volume and continuing development of new leaders, we were awarded these annual trips. They were conventions just to the extent the company could legitimately write off the cost as business expense, but to us they were vacations! At the end of our first, second and third years, we had traveled to San Francisco, Toronto and Washington, D. C. We just missed qualifying for the trip to London in 1979, but were on target to go to Hawaii in 1980.

Before the end of our second year, we had qualified as coordinators, which required that we have a minimum of four supervisors directly coded to us. We received the official promotion to coordinator with our diamond and ruby pins at the convention in Toronto. The next promotion, requiring nine direct supervisors, was key coordinator. With six direct supervisors in place, and a number of second level supervisors as well, we were beginning to think like key coordinators, knowing it was just a matter of time.

Shaklee was a recognized leader in the development and distribution of natural food supplements as well as a very acceptable line of biodegradable household cleaning products. We felt good about distributing these quality products. Coupled with their top quality merchandise, Shaklee had a marketing plan that allowed the diligent and dedicated to be appropriately compensated. We had met some master coordinators who were earning in excess of $100,000 a year and were driving new Lincolns or Cadillacs furnished by Shaklee. In our current circumstance, we could not relate to that, but we could dream, couldn't we?

By the time I brought home to Letha the exciting news that I planned to work the rest of my life in A. L. Williams, our Shaklee business was consistently providing us an income of about $4,000 a month, plus some benefits. Letha had added a very attractive Shaklee shop to our residence. This addition was twenty feet by twenty-four feet in size and attractively furnished with office furniture and shelving for displays. She had paid the entire cost within two years out of Shaklee sales. She had gradually developed a $10,000 inventory on hand, so she could immediately fill any orders as they were received. We had a beautiful red Mercury Cougar parked in front of the Shaklee shop, which was a utility for us and a motivational symbol for our down-line.

Looking back, I can agree, our Shaklee business was good to us. Maybe Letha should not be criticized too severely for being somewhat negative about my brash decision to waste my time with A. L. Williams when we were within sight of the top with Shaklee. But something in me insisted I had found the right thing, so I told Letha to handle the Shaklee and I would work the insurance. We could have the benefits of both. I believed I had found the answer to our prayers, and Letha knew she had the answer in Shaklee.

In the summer of 1978, Letha went to Hawaii for a week. The Crusader Choir of the North Cleveland Church of God had been invited to sing at the Annual State Convention of the Hawaii Church of God. When the Minister of Music announced to the choir that he had received the invitation, Letha was excited about the prospects of a week in Hawaii. I was not a choir member, but she suggested that I accompany her for the trip. It did not require an excessive amount of persuasion for me to agree to go, so she made the required deposit of $150 for each of us.

As the time for the trip approached, I felt it was not right that I take such an expensive vacation when my business was a shambles and my personal financial circumstance was no less chaotic. I had been treated so kindly by the creditors of Dixie Development when I announced to them that even though the corporation had failed, I intended to stand good for the corporate debts. Almost all of them agreed to my slow payment projection and some even called to tell me to put them last while I should pay those creditors first who may put me under pressure for payment. In light of their tolerance and kindness, I could not feel it would be acting in good faith toward my creditors to make the expensive trip. As a result, I told Letha to go alone. The deposit we had submitted was non-refundable because the travel package had been part of a group booking, but fortunately the tour coordinator permitted Letha to apply my deposit toward her trip.

My disappointment about Letha's travel to Hawaii alone is that she enjoyed the week there so much, I don't think she even missed me. When she returned, the first thing she said to me was, "We have to move to Hawaii!!!!" I responded, "Sure, we are $250,000 in debt, so it should be no problem to make the move." Ignoring my very obvious sarcasm she insisted, "Everywhere I looked in Honolulu, there were Japanese. We can not return to Japan because of my physical circumstance, but we can go to Hawaii and work with the Japanese people there. Our Shaklee business is doing well and we can open an extension office there in addition to the groups we already have in Tennessee, Georgia and South Carolina. I know we can make it work." She maintained a dream of moving to Hawaii and often made mention of the fact we could do it when our Shaklee business should become just a little stronger.

Immediately upon affiliating with Ronnie Barnes' hierarchy in A. L. Williams, I could see the potential for exponential growth. In my first eight months, I created an organization of approximately 100 agents, with a dozen of them already having junior management contracts. Within my first few months in Ronnie's office, I mentioned to him our interest in moving to Hawaii and I inquired as to whether A. L. Williams had any offices there. He replied in the negative, so I told him I would like to open the first A. L. Williams office in Hawaii.

My first license was dated February, 1980. The first week in July, Ronnie called me into his office for a brief conversation. He informed me he had been given approval to open an office in Hawaii and he wanted to know when I could be ready to go.

By that time, I had been promoted to the position of district manager — a misleading title, to say the least. I had earned nearly $25,000 commissions in my first six months and Ronnie had observed I was an intense person. He was ready to send me to a new area, but my earlier mention to him of Hawaii was not intended as an interest in going so soon. First, I needed to become familiar with what I was doing and what might be expected of me. It goes without saying, I did not have a clue as to what was involved in setting up a new insurance office in a state where the company was not even registered as a general agent.

I responded to Ronnie's suggestion about moving that I had in mind the possibility of relocating after a year or two with the company. He wanted me to be ready to go by the end of the month. I was too shocked to realize Ronnie was paying me such a high compliment even to think I could handle such an assignment — or did he just want to get me out of his office?

I had commitments through mid-August that could not be changed, but I agreed with Ronnie to make a trip to Hawaii the last week in August to assess the possibilities. Summoning the courage, and squelching the embarrassment, I mentioned further that I did not have the necessary funds to make the trip he had suggested. I quickly added there might be a way I could arrange it. Ronnie's office had sponsored a contest for the past two months. The top producers in each contract category were to be awarded a cruise to the Bahamas. I had qualified as the top producer in my category, so I was to go on that vacation trip. I told Ronnie I had already been to the Caribbean, so it would be no disappointment for me to forego the trip. If he were so disposed to allow me the cost of that trip in cash, I would apply it toward my expense to Hawaii.

He agreed and wrote me a check on the spot for $600. This covered most of my expense for that first trip.

Like a lamb to the slaughter, I boarded a Delta Jetliner August 31, 1980. If there had been any way for me to know what I would experience in the coming twelve months, someone else would have opened the first office in Hawaii and I would not likely be writing this book today.

CHAPTER THIRTY

STARTING OVER AT FIFTY-THREE

I arrived in paradise on a Saturday afternoon, along with a jetliner filled with excited vacationers. My trip was for a week, primarily because the lowest air fare required that I stay in Hawaii at least seven days. Prior to my going, I had made inquiry of the insurance department regarding testing requirements and dates. The brief response I received was that the test was given on the first Monday of every month at 9:00 a.m. and a minimum score of 70 was required as a condition for being licensed.

Two days after my arrival, I was in the office of the State Insurance Department when the doors opened. I was directed to the desk of the licensing deputy, a lady whose name was Grace Martin (not her real name). From the kind of treatment I received, I soon concluded that Grace was not an appropriate name for this lady, who quite obviously had been influenced to believe my company and I posed a serious threat to the entire insurance system in Hawaii. With the letter in hand that she had written me about testing on the first Monday of each month, I stated I was prepared to be tested. Her response was, "Have you submitted an application to test today?"

Of course, inasmuch as her letter to me about licensing requirements had not included any information about prior application to test (neither had her letter contained the necessary form to be submitted) how was I to know I should have made a prior application? Having been refused the right to be tested after traveling more than four thousand miles, I was told to submit a notarized application with a $10 money order, to be received in her office at least 10 days prior to the next test date. "When I receive your notarized application with the fee (all in good order), I will try to reserve a space for you in October. Of course, there is a limited space for testing and permission to test is assigned as applications are approved. You can understand I am unable to make any guarantees," she apologized with an affected attempt at a smile.

Mentioning that I had traveled from Chattanooga to Honolulu for no other purpose than to test for my license, I appealed for some leniency which would allow me to provide her the application and then test without the expensive delay. But there was no grace from Grace. Nor was there any graciousness in her rough response to my appeal.

Even though she had to know full well the time and expense involved, Grace would not permit any accommodation for me. Grace apologized that she was required to treat every applicant the same, and any favor she might grant me would be tantamount to discrimination against another applicant who may request an exception for any reason.

I returned home a week later, a little wiser but having accomplished nothing else. I worked long hours the next three weeks to generate enough commissions, above my basic needs, for the cost of another trip to Hawaii. The first Monday in October found me again in the waiting room outside Grace's office hoping to be admitted for testing. She welcomed me with a broad smile and invited me into the testing area.

Upon completing the test, I approached Grace again to inquire as to when I could expect my license to be issued. Completely aloof and acting as though she had no prior awareness of the urgency of my circumstance she replied casually that our office would be notified within two weeks whether I had passed the test. If I had made a passing score, the General Agent of our company would submit an appointment form and I could be licensed. Then she added, as a pre-requisite to being licensed in Hawaii, I would have to surrender my Tennessee license and provide her office with a certification of good standing in Tennessee as of the date I would surrender my license. This posed a real problem. From the time of surrendering my Tennessee license, I would no longer be legal to sell there, but until I should have my Hawaii license issued, I would be illegal there as well. This could create a very consequential delay of productivity.

I returned home to Tennessee to wait.

By mid-October I received word I had passed the test in Hawaii. Believing I would be licensed within a matter of days, we finalized plans to make our move to Hawaii. We packed a U-Haul trailer and I drove to Los Angeles, from where I shipped our car and the household goods I had transported in the trailer. From a purely practical concern, I kept my Tennessee license so I could legally make sales until the day of my departure. I drove through Nashville and hand carried the license to the State Insurance Commissioner to surrender it and requested a certificate of good standing which I could take to Hawaii and have my Hawaii license issued.

The clerk in Tennessee would not issue the certification I needed. She told me there would be an unspecified delay to allow any complaints to be filed prior to issuing a certificate of good standing. That certificate would then be mailed directly to the insurance commissioner in Hawaii. More bureaucratic delay!

Because I had the trailer load of boxes to be shipped and because I had already scheduled a shipping date for the car, I had no alternative but to proceed to Los Angeles as planned, but without any idea of when I could expect a license in Hawaii.

Two and a half months after passing the test, my license was issued on December 14, 1980. I wrote half a dozen sales as quickly as I could before returning to Tennessee to bring Letha to Hawaii. Letha had ordered another U-Haul trailer to move what furnishings and personal effects remained after we had sold nearly everything we owned so as to have a little cash for the expense of moving. She inquired as to the precise interior measurements of the trailer, then had our son, Ron, build the boxes to exact measurements so as to get maximum use of the space, but also to be sure the boxes would all fit in. We would pull the trailer to the west coast with our Shaklee car and return it to the lease company in Los Angeles. (Our third Shaklee car was to be delivered to our new address in Hawaii.)

Letha had failed to take into account the stabilizing steel ribs on the interior of the trailer so the boxes would not fit in. Having grown accustomed to improvising on short notice, we returned the trailer and rented a truck. We called Shaklee and arranged to return the car in Tennessee instead of California.

The day after Christmas, Letha and I, at age 53 stepped up into the truck cab and started toward California. Certainly many of our family and friends considered us insane, but with an unjustified confidence, we kept driving west toward our dream.

January 3, 1980, had been my first day with A. L. Williams. In the succeeding 361 days, we relentlessly pursued one goal. On the last day of 1980, we arrived in Honolulu, which was to be our home for the next twelve years.

CHAPTER THIRTY-ONE

RECRUIT, RECRUIT, RECRUIT

A long time ago someone made a very pessimistic statement to me which I believe he said was Murphy's Law. "Everything that can go wrong will go wrong."

I have never subscribed to that negative postulate. I agree that everyone does periodically face crises, but we are not required by some cruel, vague law to succumb to setbacks.

In this writing, I have enumerated so many negative experiences, it may appear I am searching for sympathy. Quite the contrary is the case. Rather, I have reluctantly recounted many things I would prefer to put out of my mind forever so as to establish that life does not get so difficult as to preclude a triumph over troubles. (When I use the word 'Triumph,' I sometimes think of the interesting definition of the word — 'Try umph!')

I firmly believe in the Biblical tenet that man was created in the image of God. I further believe in the Biblical doctrine that God is the Creator of all. Carried to a logical conclusion, these two principles strongly emphasize that we are capable of involvement in creation. Observe two well-known miracles credited to Christ in the Bible. The first is the incident recorded in the gospel according to John, chapter two, where there was a shortage of wine at a wedding reception. Jesus used clear water to make the needed wine. The second miracle, recorded by John in chapter six, is equally well-known. It involves 5,000 men (plus women and children) in a deserted place who were hungry. Jesus took five barley loaves and a few small fish to feed the vast group.

How did Jesus do those miracles? Indulge me please to offer a very unsophisticated explanation from the vantage point of three tradesmen. Any vineyard owner will tell you that if you put grape seeds in the earth and apply water in good soil in a well lighted garden, the ultimate result will be the delicious juice of the grapes.

Next, seek out a farmer and inquire of him as to what procedure he follows to put in his granary a bountiful harvest of barley. We all know what he will tell us. He puts a limited number of grains of barley into the ground. The normal process of nature will supply the required sunshine, moisture and temperature while the farmer waits patiently. After a few weeks, he reaps the harvest which is an expanded number of the same type grain he planted earlier. Assuming each grain will produce fifty, two seasons of planting and harvesting should be enough to cause one grain of barley to become 2,500. Using the same ratio of multiplication, five loaves multiplied by 2,500 will produce 12,500 loaves. If 5,000 men and their wives and children were given 12,500 loaves of bread, there must have been a very adequate amount. Now is it clear why Jesus told his disciples to gather the bread that remained?

Risking redundancy, let me suggest you seek out one more expert witness. Ask any fisherman about the source of his income. He will tell you he takes fish out of the water. Next ask him if he continues to move to new waters, or does he take more fish out of the same water where he fished before. Then ask of him how many times he can expect to take fish out of the same water. Unless he becomes impatient with this ridiculous line of inquiry, he will tell you there is no limit. Fish just continue to produce more fish.

Certainly I have made the point clear. Jesus, who established the laws of nature in the beginning, only collapsed time frames to make wine, barley and fish in a few minutes rather than waiting the normal two or three years.

Am I being unrealistic to apply precisely the same principles to my business activity as the Almighty illustrated to us in similar situations of practical need? I don't think so.

When Ronnie Barnes explained this business to me, he emphasized that I only had to do three things to be successful. They were recruit, recruit and recruit. I could have spent my time selling a very good product which was designed to meet the existing need of my friends. Alternatively, I could dedicate myself to learning how our product benefits the consumer and then teach that to a large number of people who were willing to work with me. In both situations, I have the potential for success. In the second scenario, the success can be realized much sooner because it utilizes the efforts of many instead of only one. Just like the miracles of the bread, fish and wine in the hand of the Divine, we can collapse time frames and thereby attain the desired success sooner.

Recruit one and you will have someone to assist you. Essentially, you have doubled your capability.

Recruit two or three (and teach each of them to recruit two or three) and you begin to understand the concept of exponential increase. When finally I obtained my Hawaii license, I found myself in a new environment with no acquaintances, so it was most important that I employ this principle of perpetual duplication. Let me illustrate for you what happened in the early weeks of my work in Hawaii.

I recruited Garry.

Garry recruited Joe. No other recruits.

Joe recruited Don. Next Joe recruited Paul. Then Joe recruited Tom.

Don recruited Gary, who recruited Rene and then quit. After that Don recruited Sam, Art, Maggie, Magdalena and many more.

Paul recruited Richard, John, Ray, Tim, and Vince plus many more.

Ray recruited Charles and then he quit.

Rene recruited Ron, Lydia, Victor, Ronald, Ben, Ed, and so many more.

Charles recruited Columbus, Iris, Ralph, Roosevelt, George and many, many more.

Charles has continued to develop Regional Vice Presidents and has taught them how to do the same thing, so that at the time of this writing, Charles has a team that extends from his home base in Albuquerque to St. Louis, Honolulu, San Jose, Chicago, Seattle, Cleveland, Houston, Kansas City, and growing.

Now let me try to diagram this development. My first recruit in Honolulu was Garry Johnson, who only found one recruit. Garry made three sales and then lost interest in our program and resigned without ever realizing what he had started. Within about five years it looked like the chart on the next page.

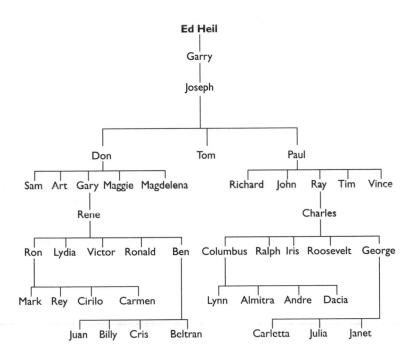

Every person named on the above chart, except my first recruit, Garry Johnson, and three others, developed a team of associate representatives and was promoted to the position of Regional Vice President or above. For various reasons some of them have chosen to disassociate themselves from our company, but because the system encourages continuing development of new leaders, even when one may leave, those he has trained will move up in the hierarchical tree that has blossomed and I have never experienced a reduction of production or income as a result of the leaving, even of influential leaders. This chart is not complete, but it does convey how this building concept operates to the advantage of the one who develops a team.

CHAPTER THIRTY-TWO

REGIONAL VICE PRESIDENT

In Hawaii, virtually no one had heard of A. L. Williams except the insurance industry. There is no question in my mind but that the hurdles placed in my way by the office of the insurance commissioner were directly orchestrated by lobbyists of that sector. All over America this upstart company, A. L. Williams, was viewed as an irritation and a menace to life insurance companies and their agents. If they could successfully obstruct the issuance of a license to the first sales agent in Hawaii, there would be no need to worry about a second.

It goes without saying that this was entirely a covert activity. It is equally safe to say I could not openly question any of the unreasonable demands placed on me, or I might have been restricted indefinitely from being licensed in Hawaii; and it would have all appeared very legitimate.

On the bright side, the general public had no awareness of the life and death struggle between our fledgling company and the established legendary giants. In my recruiting, I told the story about A. L. Williams exactly as I understood it. Since there was no obvious competitor in Hawaii to refute my statements, I was given credibility by default.

Thankfully, I survived the grueling process and was eventually licensed. I told everyone who would listen that I was planning to open a new business in Honolulu and was busy recruiting a team of the best salesmen I could find.

Because A. L. Williams as a company was not yet registered to transact business in Hawaii, we were told to introduce ourselves as representatives of Massachusetts Indemnity and Life Insurance Company. Once an agent in our office took an incoming telephone call, identifying to the caller that she had reached the office of A. L. Williams. The caller was Grace Martin in the Commissioner's Office. She instructed our agent to have me call her office immediately. When I called her, she was irate. Almost screaming into her telephone, she reminded me that A. L. Williams was not registered to sell life insurance in Hawaii and if she should be made aware of one more instance of using that name, she would have our authorization to market insurance suspended.

This government agency, created to control us and monitor our business, was requiring that we not identify ourselves as who we actually were. By complying with this unrealistic demand, we were essentially compelled to operate our business incognito. Virtually no one in Hawaii was aware that A. L. Williams was the marketing agent for Massachusetts Indemnity and Life Insurance Company. Therefore, trying to hinder our entry into Hawaii, our opposition had inadvertently built around us a wall of secrecy which became a terrific advantage to us. By the time most of the competitor companies knew about our existence in Hawaii, we already had a moderately strong sales team in intense training.

While we were under that duress and limitation, it was difficult to recruit associates into our business. One of the consequences was that we developed some exceptionally strong people. Among other things, this situation favorably impacted our incomes. My personal income in 1980 was $30,000. By 1983, it had increased to above $100,000. Because my income was directly tied to the production of the sales people in my team, that served as quite an accurate indicator of the success many of our representatives were experiencing.

Early in 1981, Ronnie Barnes encouraged me to try to qualify for promotion to the position of Regional Vice President, the company's highest contract. The promotion required that my office produce $40,000 annualized insurance premium in each of three consecutive months. That translated into roughly 70 new policy applications per month, which was a tough assignment for an office opened less than six months earlier and operating in a hostile environment. Our team made a concerted effort and we met the requirement in July and August. We started selling in September at fever pitch. At the end of the month, I checked our office sales log to find that we had submitted 170 new life insurance applications with $102,000 annualized premium. This translated to approximately $15,000,000 of protection for the new clients we added in September. That is a sales record that very few insurance offices with any company have ever attained.

Our first office in Hawaii opened for business February 1, 1981. By the end of September, I had qualified to be promoted to the position of Regional Vice President. That was the highest contract sales position in the company. My new contract called for a higher commission rate, plus over-ride commissions on the sales of my entire down-line sales team. Even though the policies we sold provided our clients substantially higher protection for less premium than they would usually pay for much smaller policies, we were able to earn exceptionally attractive incomes because of the over-ride commission system employed by A. L. Williams. My income grew dramatically, but I had the extreme gratification that every dollar of commission I received was the result of saving money for our clients.

At the convention in December, 1983, Art Williams created "The $100,00 Club" (later to become known as the Golden Eagles) and inducted into that prestigious group every representative whose earnings exceeded $100,000 in a year. In this company just six years old, more than 100 sales people were inducted as charter members in this top producing, top earning club. The ninety-second name called forward to receive the coveted $100,000 Club diamond ring was Ed Heil. I became a charter member.

CHAPTER THIRTY-THREE

EXPANSION

Ronnie Barnes traveled to Honolulu in October, 1981 to make the official announcement to my team that I had achieved the distinctive position of Regional Vice President in A. L. Williams. It was a great night for me. For years I had felt like a loser and I was embarrassed because of my failure. Ronnie spoke in complimentary terms of the accomplishment we had realized in Hawaii in just one year. A business failure of the magnitude I had experienced in Tennessee is not resolved easily, or forgotten quickly. To be recognized for some success and to be applauded as a winner again was exceptionally gratifying to me. Maybe there was still some hope.

Above all else that was said that evening, one comment Ronnie directed just to me was that from that day forward he was changing my job assignment. No longer should I think of myself as a salesman. From October, 1981 my first responsibility was to create Regional Vice Presidents. To me that seemed so unrealistic. How could one company have need for so many vice presidents?

To be quite frank, the title Regional Vice President may have been a little misleading. The function of a vice president in our company somehow resembles the designation of General Agent in the insurance world. A major difference is that typically a general agent receives a contract with an insurance company and then opens an office to service a defined community or locale. In A. L. Williams, we were encouraged to expand beyond local borders. Another very meaningful difference is in the perpetuation of the business one may develop. Once an agent is hired and trained, he will always be in the hierarchical organization of the Regional Vice President who hired him. This meant that whereas an average general agent may have three to ten agents working in his office, an RVP in the A. L. Williams system could conceivably have many hundreds of agents in his company-within-a-company.

At the time of my retiring from active involvement, my group numbered more than 1,500 associates in many states and territories. This phenomenal growth was made possible by maintaining computer records of every associate, including what office hired him and what level contract he may have at any given time.

The strength of the system developed by A. L. Williams was that as soon as a person may show himself capable of leadership and managerial responsibility, he would be promoted to a higher level, which included a larger percentage of the commission available on any sale he or one of his down-line associates may submit. At the top of that system was the position of Regional Vice President. I had reached that coveted position

That evening in October, 1981 I felt the elation of achievement for the first time in many years. How pleasant it would have been to relax and enjoy that comfortable circumstance for a while. But abruptly Ronnie brought me back from the idealism of easy success by telling me my new job description was to create and develop regional vice presidents. In the fifteen years to come, I would come to comprehend the potential dynamism of this system. When I retired, I sold a business which included the sales activity of 85 regional vice presidents and their sales teams.

The following day I adjusted my halo a little and returned to a routine of hard work. Within one year after my promotion, I was able to develop six Regional Vice Presidents. It was during that year a new position was created known as Senior Vice President. I was a regional vice president for thirteen months and then was elevated to Senior Vice President. To celebrate the occasion, we rented the ballroom of a Waikiki Beach Hotel in November, 1982. In one evening, I was promoted to the lofty position of Senior Vice President and also officiated in the promotion of three Regional Vice Presidents.

The honored guests arrived at the hotel in chauffeured stretch limousines. Everywhere friends were greeting each other with flower leis, and the celebrities of the evening had so many leis around their necks, they could barely see over the profusion of flowers. We were told not to drive to Waikiki for this celebration because some or our friends were to come to our condominium and would drive us to the hotel ballroom. What a pleasant shock when a Rolls Royce arrived at our residence on Hahaione Street to escort us to the celebration.

At that time my entire sales team included more than four hundred associates and my income for that year increased to more than $87,000. We were ready for liftoff into an exciting orbit.

CHAPTER THIRTY-FOUR

GUAM

The promotion of three new Regional Vice Presidents concurrent with my promotion to Senior Vice President was cause for a terrific celebration and our Hawaiian people did it up right. They are a fun-loving people, so they look for any reason to have a party or a celebration. They made it an unforgettable evening for Letha and me. I had come to like our crusade so much that even work days seemed more like celebrations than work. Maybe some of my usual tendencies toward being a work-a-holic were being affected by Hawaii's casual culture and attitude.

In my first year as a Regional Vice President I was able to promote six Regional Vice Presidents directly under my supervision, which formed a very strong foundation for a developing selling and recruiting business. The best part of our early growth was that the newly promoted RVPs were completely committed to winning and they were convinced they could do it. Our team today includes 85 RVPs, but those that were promoted in my first year are still among my strongest leaders.

One of those promoted to RVP when I became SVP was my brother Dan in Houston. I had recruited him the month after my promotion to RVP, and just eleven months later he was an RVP. It had taken me 22 months and Dan cut my record in half. He opened Texas for my hierarchy and shortly thereafter, he was also operating in Arkansas, Louisiana and Oklahoma. I was recognized and given awards at public gatherings for the expansion being achieved, but it was my super leaders like Dan who were largely responsible for my growth.

Promoted the same day as Dan was a young ex-Marine Seargent, Charles Whitener. Even though he was promoted to this top position of RVP at the young age of twenty four, he was quite aware of his objectives in life, and was destined to leave a mark on my entire organization. His first month in our business, he was paid $5,000 commissions. Within one year after his promotion to RVP, Charles had a record income of $16,000 in a single month. For that achievement, he was invited to Dallas for a special company function, and was recognized before about 200 of the top producers in A.L Williams. Charles is one of the most intense individuals I know.

Another RVP promoted that same evening was Rene Vargas. When he was promoted he had 102 associates in his organization. The company policy provided that when a division manager was elevated to the highest contract level (RVP), he left with his sponsoring RVP one leg of his hierarchy: i.e. one direct recruit and that recruits entire down-line team. Rene transferred to me one group of 35 associates, leaving him 67. Within one month, his entire group again numbered 100.

Rene was born in the Philippines. When he was still quite young his family moved to Guam and made that island territory their permanent home. Rene felt his promotion to RVP, along with the very handsome paychecks that accompanied the promotion, constituted a good reason to take his wife and three children to Guam for a vacation and to visit his parents.

Having just been named to the highest contract level available in our company, Rene was excited. His income in the past twelve months was considerably higher than he had ever received before. No one who was aware of Rene's success thought it strange that he could not conceal his enthusiasm. You're right, when he arrived in Guam, he continued to talk about A. L. Williams.

No one in Guam had heard of A. L. Williams before Rene's vacation there in January, 1983. His enthusiasm was highly contagious and before returning to Hawaii, some of those he contacted gave him their assurance they wanted to affiliate with A. L. Williams because they were in complete agreement with our business philosophy and the type of insurance we offered. Based on the response he saw, Rene was ready to start work immediately in Guam. Unfortunately, the wheels turn much slower at corporate headquarters than in the emotions of an excited salesman.

I shared Rene's enthusiasm about expanding our business to Guam and started dialoguing with the persons in the Home Office who could make the decisions for extending our efforts three thousand miles farther into the western Pacific. After two and a half years of corporate and legal red tape, we finally got approval to go to Guam and begin operations. Rene traveled to Guam a week ahead of me and was at the airport to meet me, along with about 20 local people who spent the entire day with us eager to learn about this phenomenal company that proposed to open for business in their island territory.

Actually, I was given authorization by our Home Office to open for business in Guam, but the real approval did not depend on Atlanta, Georgia. Rather it had to come through the office of the Governor of Guam and his Director of the office of Revenue and Taxation.

With the assistance of the man who would become our front leader in Guam, I was able to enter the offices of a number of Senators, the Governor's Chief of Staff, and finally we found ourselves in the office of the second ranking man on Guam — the Lieutenant Governor. He was exceptionally cordial and gave us a genuine welcome to do business in Guam. Then he telephoned the office of Revenue and Taxation and instructed the Director to give us priority handling so we could have the necessary approval in hand the following day.

Having been given assurance that issuance of the approval was just a formality, we made our plans for the remainder of the week. On the last Thursday of August, 1985 we received our authorization to conduct business on Guam. That same evening at 7:00 p m. approximately 100 interested persons crowded the restaurant facility we had secured for the meeting and I explained our company, our concept and our crusade. I invited all who had a definite interest, to speak to Rene, his wife, Carol, or me about completing and submitting an application for a contract.

Some applications came in Thursday evening. All day Friday we interviewed potential agents, accepted application forms and checked for accuracy and completeness.

Early Saturday, we resumed where we had stopped late Friday evening. When I boarded the airplane Saturday evening, in my briefcase, I had contract forms for 57 new agents. On Thursday at noon we had received from the government our authorization to do business on Guam. By Saturday evening of the same week our contracted sales force was more than twice as large as that of any other company doing business there.

I worked at record speed all day Saturday in Guam trying to get all of the necessary work completed prior to leaving for Honolulu. The airplane ride home required eight hours. Because of crossing the international date line, our jet departed Guam at 7:00 p.m. Saturday evening and touched down at the Honolulu airport at 6:00 a.m. Saturday morning. Based on information on the calendar and the clock, we arrived in Honolulu 13 hours before we left Guam. The rapid air travel was similar to the rapid work schedule I had followed for the most recent six days.

With the exceptionally busy week of non-stop activity, I was exhausted when I arrived at the office at 8:00 a.m. on the second Saturday morning of that week. Letha and I, with one secretary worked all day Saturday and all day Sunday to process contracts and issue license code numbers to those 57 eager new agents. The work had to be completed within that time frame because Letha and I were scheduled to depart for a ten day trip to England, Germany, Austria and Hungary on Monday morning. It was an all expense paid trip awarded us for qualifying among the company's top sales producers.

CHAPTER THIRTY-FIVE

THE COACH

In chapter twenty-seven, mention was made of A. L. Williams. At that time, it was only the name of a company that held out some hope to me that I could expect to have a second chance after a colossal business collapse. Since then, my repeated references to A. L. Williams seem to infer that my readers should know about this company and the cacophony of diverse people that were its nucleus. To understand the company which bears his name, it is essential that you meet the man.

About half a century ago, Art Williams was born into a rather typical small-town American family. His father was a high school football coach, and it seems Art developed an appreciation of his father which made him want to follow a similar career. As it happened, Art was not to experience the encouragement of a fond father as he began to chart a course for his life as a coach because of the untimely death of his father when Art was still a teenager. Being the oldest child in his family, Art learned the meaning of responsibility early in life as he assisted his widowed mother in the gargantuan task of caring for all of the physical, emotional and material needs of the family without the presence of a father.

As I heard it from Angela, his grammar school sweetheart who later became Mrs. Williams, Art excelled in sports in high school. Angela remembers that in high school Art lettered in football, baseball and basketball. Possibly this was indicative of the versatility and dynamism this young man was to display when he emerged on the American business scene.

After completing his education at Mississippi State University where he played college football, and having wed Angela, his childhood sweetheart, Art returned to South Georgia where he joined the coaching staff of the local high school. Early in his coaching career, he was offered the position of Head Coach at the Appling County High School, in Baxley, Georgia. Baxley had the dubious distinction of being a consistent loser, so it was no coveted prize that was held out to the young aspiring coach, but Art had learned early to disregard difficulty and to pay the heavy price that winning always exacts from those who would excel.

Under Art's capable coaching, and motivated by his indomitable spirit, the Baxley football team won seven games that year, beating the "top" AA team in the state. Art went on to be chosen coach of the year twice, taking a brand new AAA Columbus, Georgia team to State finals. This was the first and only time this has happened in the State of Georgia.

At a family gathering, Art had what may have seemed a chance conversation with a cousin who was an accountant by profession. In that discussion the subject came up about life insurance; its costs and benefits. Being fully cognizant of the hardship his family had faced at the time of his own father's death, Art showed more than a casual interest in the subject. After a few visits to the local library, he was to learn that there are basically two kinds of life insurance — expensive and inexpensive. Art was appalled to reminisce on the fact that his father had left the family woefully underinsured because someone had sold him the wrong kind of insurance. Art found that for the amount of premium his father paid for a $15,000 policy, he could have secured $100,000 of protection.

Art was livid to learn of the injustice this imposed on his mother! He diligently pursued his study of insurance and finance, with the end result being that he took part-time employment selling the right kind of life insurance. Soon he combined his insurance selling with offering his clients an opportunity to invest in mutual funds. The two concepts in tandem formed an ideal program to provide maximum financial benefits whether his clients should live or die.

After a relatively short part-time career in financial services, Art left the classroom for a full-time career with a major company and very soon became a top producing Regional Vice President with that firm.

Art was impatient to realize wide acceptance of his crusade. He also had an intense desire to provide maximum benefits to the corps of committed sales people who shared his convictions. Art found himself extremely frustrated that he could not promote his most capable people beyond a certain level. The company simply had no openings for top-level management and it was not amenable to creating any more positions at the top. Art ultimately found it necessary to form his own company. That new entity, chartered as A. L. Williams and Associates, emerged quietly on the American business scene February 10, 1977.

Although the organizational meeting was conducted in a small, unpretentious office without the slightest hint of sophistication, it was to impact the American insurance and investment industry like an atomic bomb. Within its first two decades of existence, this new company was to become the number one marketer of individual life insurance in the nation no less than eight times with annual sales approaching $100 billion at its zenith.

There is no intention to present the complete story of the accomplishments of A. L. Williams and its successor, Primerica Financial Services, in this book. Rather, it was necessary to include at least this minimal information about "The Coach" to put into perspective how it became possible for me to be lifted out of my morass of misery and also to provide at least some sketchy information about the crusade that has become a driving force in my life for seventeen years.

When my outlook was so bleak, A. L. Williams as a company and Art Williams as a person, reached toward me with a helping hand. In the years of our business relationship, Letha and I became personally acquainted with Art and his charming wife, Angela. In sharp contrast to what seems to be the norm in business, where the owners and top management people remain somewhat separated from the sales force, they have proved so many times on a purely personal level to be such special friends. We are extremely grateful to these two wonderful people.

CHAPTER THIRTY-SIX

BALANCE

From February 10, 1977 through mid 1990, Art Williams was at the helm of A. L. Williams. My affiliation with his company started before the company passed its third anniversary, so in a way, I grew up with the company.

When I met Art, I saw him as a leader completely in control. He was extremely passionate about many things, but especially, there were two things which were not negotiable with Art. He was in a perpetual battle to provide the consumer a better product for a lower price. Secondly, he wanted us (his sales force) to receive the maximum income for our efforts — consistent with fairness to the consumer. Art was an exceptional leader, and few people approach his capabilities as a motivator.

More than once, I heard Art say "What we need as a leader is a benevolent dictator." He was precisely that. Because he was in control as the owner of the company, he dictated policy. Because he wanted the best for us, he worked incessantly to improve our compensation and our economic future. In the process, Art Williams became one of America's wealthiest men. But that is as it should be. Few men can equal his record for creating wealth and spreading it out to a larger number of his associates than Art did. I came to Art's company with nothing but a record of failure and a frustrated attitude. He helped me solve those two problems and today I am retired with an exceptionally comfortable income.

There are many approaches to success and many men can teach others how to earn money — even large incomes. What was unique about Art Williams is that he guided us wisely regarding all aspects of succeeding. To become successful is not just developing a large income or accumulating a huge sum in reserve. Many of my acquaintances have exceptional incomes, but they live on the brink of bankruptcy. Art Williams' wife, Angela, often insisted before large convention crowds, "It isn't good enough to live within your means. You must live below your means." Possibly that is one of the most powerful statements in this book!

In 1980 our taxable income was $30,000. The next year it increased to $63,000. In 1982 the company sent to me, with a copy to the IRS 1099 forms indicating our income had reached $87,000. In our fourth year with A. L. Williams our gross income exceeded $102,000. I was told that put us in the top 3% of the population of the U. S.

I was in new territory. Never had I expected to have income of these proportions. Without some wise counsel, there was a possibility I could have developed an extravagance and dissipated even this large income.

My readers may recall that when my previous business failed, I assumed responsibility to all of the creditors. Seven years had passed since I volunteered to pay those debts and if I had defaulted, by that time it would have been difficult for my creditors to enforce payment. Further, living thousands of miles away, it would have been possible to forget those old debts and rationalize I had done my best, and besides it was not my responsibility only to pay those old corporation obligations as I was just one of the four corporate officers in Dixie Development. However, a glance at my check register would have indicated to anyone who cared to look numerous checks every month in the amount of $100. Every creditor received a payment of at least $100 each month until his account had been settled. When an account was completely paid, I made adjustments upward to the extent of my ability so that as the number of checks became fewer, the amount of each check increased.

I worked with A. L. Williams, and its successor, Primerica Financial Services for seventeen years. In my thirteenth year I was able to settle the last of those old accounts. Initially, my debts totaled $250,000, but with the inclusion of interest, I am not sure how much I paid. My vocabulary is inadequate to express the satisfaction in my conscience that I did what I felt should be done. Had I taken an easier course, there is a real likelihood I could have made some profitable investments instead of paying for a dead horse all those years. But looking back and looking forward, I prefer to have the peace rather than the profit.

Taking seriously the wise advice of Angela Williams that we live below our means, when our income soared above $100,000, we continued to live in a rented apartment and in the parking building behind the condominium complex, was my Mark VI, which I purchased at a substantial discount when it was a two year old model.

After occupying a rented apartment for nearly three years in Hawaii, we did purchase a condominium when we found one offered at an attractive price. With a six-figure income, many people are inclined to find a house with a price tag approximating three or four times their annual income and with monthly mortgage payments large enough to consume about 25% to 35% of their after-tax income. Thanks to the good advice of our "benevolent dictator," we bought a condo in Hawaii with monthly payments equaling approximately 12% of our income.

In an all-out effort to economize, we continued to buy slightly used cars until our annual income exceeded $400,000. We developed a pattern of living that did not allow for much extravagance. I can tell you now, it may have been difficult to say no when we could have arranged to spend more personally, but waiting has its rewards. Three years ago, we moved into our retirement home. It has a value of more than $250,000 and when the last paint touch-up was finished and the last piece of new furniture was set in place, we had a beautiful home without a mortgage.

CHAPTER THIRTY-SEVEN

THE LOFTIEST LESSON

Winston Churchill is credited with having said, *"The only thing we learn from history is that we don't."*

Repeatedly all of us have known of wealthy people who lived miserably because they put too much emphasis on the retention of their monetary and material holdings. Conversely, there are the saintly souls who do not have very much of this world's wealth, but in giving what little they possess they generate happiness wherever they go. It is they who possess real wealth.

We understand those lofty principles, but far too often are not willing to apply them personally. Somehow, each of us believes we are the exception and we try to rewrite the laws of God and of his universe to accommodate our personal circumstances. Just like Mr. Churchill said, we are not willing to learn from the mistakes of others. We want to make our own mistakes.

As a very young person I set the course for my life. In response to a spiritual atmosphere that had been created around me, before I reached the age of ten I made a conscious commitment to believe on Jesus Christ as God's son. Since that time I have determined to make Him the Lord of my life. There have been times that my personal weakness has been more predominant than my spiritual convictions, but my resolve has never changed.

My life has been an interesting series of experiences and I have enjoyed living it. As my readers are now fully aware, not everything I did has been right. Nor has every decision been wise. Many times my stupidity has been projected on a brightly illuminated screen and caused me to look like an experienced fool.

One thing cannot be altered: what I do, how I think and how I react to any circumstance is directly related to the person I have become as a consequence of everything in my past. Some of the mistakes and bad decisions I made in my past were the raw materials needed to make me what I am today.

I have come to believe that success, just for the sake of succeeding, is hollow. Similarly defeat and failure, seen in proper perspective, are only temporary obstructions we must overcome if we are to realize our ultimate legitimate objective.

A number of decades ago, I determined that I would much prefer to be overlooked and unnoticed as a dispenser of cups of cold water in service to God and my fellowman than to manipulate myself into a more prominent role in life, only to become a first-class failure. I have failed a number of times, but I am not a failure. Each time I stumbled in an attempt at what was important to me at the time, I stood up, assessed my damages, bandaged my wounds and started again.

As of today I have achieved what many consider success. The business I started to develop seventeen years ago has flourished to the extent that the team of Primerica Financial Services associates who report to me number more than one-thousand-five-hundred agents, most of them working under the supervision of intermediary managers. Eighty-five of those intermediary managers in my hierarchy have the designation of Regional Vice President, Senior Vice President or National Sales Director.

In my career with Primerica Financial Services, I have enlisted, trained and coached more than twenty executive level leaders whose incomes have exceeded $100,000. Annual income for some of them has reached as high as $200,000, $300,000 and even $400,000. For the past number of years, my personal gross annual income has exceeded $500,000. Most people consider income at that level to be an indication of success.

If all of these advantages and benefits are retained just for me and mine, I have achieved no success! It is not my intention to impose on my readers any of my convictions, but I find purpose in life and gratification in following the wise words of King Solomon preserved for us in the Bible. For example, the following words have become the fundamental tenets of my philosophy for living.

"There is that maketh himself rich, yet hath nothing: there is that maketh himself poor, yet hath great riches." Proverbs 13:7 King James Bible

"O God, I beg two favors from you before I die: first help me never to tell a lie. Second, give me neither poverty nor riches! Give me just enough to satisfy my needs! For if I grow rich, I may become content without God. And if I am too poor, I may steal, and thus insult God's holy name." Proverbs 30:7-9 Living Bible.

Ecclesiastes 5:12 reads as follows: "The man who works hard sleeps well whether he eats little or much, but the rich must worry and suffer insomnia." Living Bible

Dr. E. V. Hill is a prominent pastor, whose services as a speaker are widely in demand. Yet he devotes a major portion of his time and efforts to an enterprise known as God's Kitchen. The only reason for the existence of God's Kitchen in Los Angeles is to provide a hot meal and a cup of cold water to some of the needy in that vast city.

Whether you see Dr. Hill in action or hear him preach, the same message comes through crystal clear. This benevolent man of God cares. It is His philosophy and theology that God calls all of us to bless others. He further emphasizes that we serve Him best when He can use us to channel His blessings to others near us. Very succinctly he states it, "Sometimes when God blesses you,

He doesn't even have you in mind." I can relate to that because I believe there have been times when God allowed me to be a conduit through which His blessing is conveyed to others.

Why God chooses to make us His helpers in dispensing His grace to the needy, I do not understand, but it seems so very obvious in Scripture that God does endow some with a gift of helps and then uses them to reflect His divinity as they go about doing good. This could well be what Jesus meant when He stated, "Don't hide your light! Let it shine for all: let your good deeds glow for all to see, so that they will praise your Heavenly Father" Matthew 5:16. Living Bible.

If by providing a cup of cold water to a suffering individual, I can help him take his thoughts away from his misfortune long enough to get a glimpse of God through the small kindness I bring him, he and I will both have been helped greatly.

CHAPTER THIRTY-EIGHT

RETIRED

In 1993, Primerica Financial Services announced a sensational program which they called the "Own Your Code Number" plan. This highly innovative program provided that after a Regional Vice President should have reproduced himself with at least five direct Regional Vice Presidents, reached a certain volume of business with continuous growth for at least five subsequent years, and maintained certain company mandated minimum on-going production, he could own his code number in perpetuity.

The company distributes all commissions for every sort of sale to a computer code number. The computer tracks the hierarchy lineage to six generations, and every time a sale is submitted, the friendly computer produces for everyone in the up-line hierarchy a check for the proper amount of override commission. From this perspective, it becomes immediately apparent that this code ownership can have great value for many years to come.

The perpetual ownership of the code includes rights of inhcritance. The plan provides that when I die, full right of ownership will pass to my wife. Then at the time of her death, ownership is to pass to our children. If the recipient of the business is qualified and properly licensed he/she may operate the business. If he is not licensed, he may either employ a knowledgeable person as a manager or he may sell to any person who qualifies, subject to approval of the company.

Simply stated this is a wonderful provision for anyone who will build a strong business on a good foundation.

One item incidental to this ownership and transfer to our children was of great concern to me. When they inherit it, what will be the tax implications of receiving this ownership? For a number of years I have wanted to know how my children could inherit this asset without being unfairly subjected to an unrealistically high inheritance tax.

Federal law has established the estate tax at 55%. I was advised by a representative of a very responsible consulting firm that the estimated value of my business, based on the formula used by the IRS, is $3.2 million. That is the amount (adjusted for lapses and attrition) the IRS considers my business should produce within the next 15 years. Using that as a base, 55% calculates to be $1,760,000, which is the amount my two children should expect to be assessed by the IRS. This is based on the amount of income they may expect to receive in the coming 15 years. That is a lot of tax responsibility to be based on an anticipation of income.

I was advised to offer my code for sale as a capital asset, because it is an agency which I had built over a period of years. I sold the capital asset, which was the sales force and its activity, rather than an income stream. In this way, it qualifies as a capital gain and is subject to a different tax rate. Further my consultant recommended that I sell on an installment contract which will spread the income over a number of years and will accomplish two things.

1. It will provide me a continuing income stream, rather than bring in a large sum in one year and with it negative tax implications.

2. Because income from an installment sale becomes taxable as it is received, it will alleviate the undue stress of inheritance tax on my children at the time of my demise.

Following that advice, I offered my code number for sale and was able to find a buyer with whom a satisfactory sale contract has been consummated effective January 1, 1997.

Having taken my first job at age twelve, I have worked continuously for 58 years. In the earlier years, some of my jobs were part-time in conjunction with my schooling. Most of my life I have been self-employed, so when I completed one job, I created another. I have never been without a job, so I am completely unaware of the frustration that must surely come as a result of being unemployed.

As an employee, I have paid Social Security Tax. As a self-employed person, I have paid in the larger counterpart of Social Security Tax. As an employer, I have paid matching Social Security Tax as well as Federal Unemployment Tax, Workmen's Compensation, liability insurance premiums, builders risk insurance premiums, E and O insurance premiums — and possibly some others which I cannot now recall. Essentially, all of the above-named taxes and premium payments were necessary and/or required to try to guarantee my continuing income in case some tragedy should strike. As of this date, I have yet to file a claim or receive a benefit from any of these various plans. I was officially retired as of January 1, 1997, so in February I will receive my first social security check. I have paid in for 52 years; now if I live to be eighty-five, I will collect benefits for 16 years. That is almost a one for three return. But that is the best part. If I should not live to be eighty-five, , the rate of return will be even lower. Then, the ultimate negative — I hear opinions of knowledgeable people that the Social Security program is in trouble. Thankfully, my future is not tied exclusively to Social Security.

It hardly seems like 58 years have slipped away since I was hired to sell ice cream from a bicycle.

From age twelve to twenty-five I had a random selection of jobs, but I had no definite goal in view. I simply worked to survive, like everyone else did.

At age twenty-five, with my wife as a full partner, I embarked on what was intended to be a lifetime career as a foreign missionary. That was abruptly terminated when she was injured in an automobile accident, forcing us to return home after only four-teen years. So much for missionary life.

For twelve years I was an amateur entrepreneur in Cleveland, Tennessee, wearing at least five different hats during those few years. You have already read the details of those activities, so I will not repeat it here.

The final phase of my work history includes the years after I reached age fifty-two and continued until age seventy. These have been very rewarding years. Looking back, I can now realize the purpose for some of the earlier difficulties. This final phase has been rewarding with relatively few problems, making this an enjoyable time for me. This has been a gratifying employment with virtually none of the problems normally expected to accompany a job with heavy responsibility and above-average income.

A few days ago I joined the ranks of the retired. Retirement should be a pleasant situation and I expect to make it just that. Some retirees tell me they are frustrated; others even bored. I did not apply for membership with that group!

Because officially, Letha and I are now retired, we may have more time to do things together. In the 52 years our two lives have melded into one, we have not tired of being together. Now that we are not rigidly controlled by schedules, we anticipate catching up.

We are retired, but not unemployed! More than a year ago, Letha started making definite plans for a service we can provide for some of earth's finest citizens. Her plan in action is described in the final chapter of this book in some detail. Quite simply stated, we have dedicated two rooms of our home to a facility that functions like a "Bed and Breakfast Inn." In some specific ways, it is different.

1. Our services are offered to missionaries, pastors and evangelists. These people usually appear as being upbeat and positive. But we know from personal experience, they get tired, too.

2. Our plan is intended to provide a relaxed atmosphere for a

brief respite: not long-term care. Visits here are limited to a five day maximum.

3. Two meals a day are available with no precise schedule.

4. In the Heil Haven we have no accounting department, so no invoice is presented when our guests depart. To offer our facility and our service to some of God's choice children is our "job in retirement," and it is our delight to do it without any cost to our guests!

Technically speaking, our working years are finished. Ordinarily, that would suggest that our income also has been reduced. Thanks to Primerica Financial Services' unique code number ownership plan, that is not our situation. At this point I should mention that two fine friends, Ronnie Barnes and Charles Whitener (who are still affiliated with Primerica) bought my code number on terms very attractive to me. So essentially they are partners with us in the Heil Haven because the monthly installments they pay according to the code purchase contract make it possible.

The bed and breakfast operation is primarily Letha's department. I am in charge of the heavy work. I write the checks.

If our income continues, our giving also can continue. Take a look at what one retired couple can do. Without including the dollars allocated to each item, let me list the projects and people to whom we presently send support on a monthly schedule.

* Tithe to our local church
* Contribution to two television and three radio ministries
* Contribution to two orphanages
* Contribution to fifteen pastors
* A memorial fund to provide furnishings in the missions classroom in a graduate school
* Partial support for thirteen students in foreign Bible Institute training
* Partial support for three college students
* Partial support for one seminary student
* Partial support for seven overseas missionaries

* A twenty year endowment fund for our local church
* A twenty year endowment fund for overseas missions
* A twenty year endowment fund for retired ministers
* A perpetual scholarship endowment fund for seminary students

This information is presented only to emphasize how it is possible for us to continue ministering to the needy by proxy, even though personal activity may be restricted. We simply have made the dollar our servant, rather than allow it to be our master. I sincerely trust that nothing reported here will be interpreted as self-aggrandizement.

The intent is not for us to grandstand, but rather to give testimony to the inexhaustible bounty of God's provision. We are indeed honored that we have been invited to share in His concern for humanity.

The title of this book is taken from a statement of our Lord that even a small gift like a cup of cold water will not go unnoticed. Throughout, I have used this metaphor in a general way so as to apply it to any small gift or service. However, to a certain extent, I have also equated the giving of money or material equivalent with this concept, because this is the means we have used to provide some help to the needy.

I should add that there are many ways to provide assistance that are not dependent on money. I know a lady who spends much of her time sending out greeting cards to shut-ins, to people who are sick and to people who are bereaved. How can anyone calculate the comfort and happiness generated by those small cards. They are her "cup of cold water."

A friend who is a retired missionary has served with the Minneapolis City Police Force for the past seventeen years as a volunteer chaplain. Every person he meets is someone with a major problem. He is not remunerated in cash for the service he provides. Maybe he is not paid because the police department cannot afford to pay what his services are worth. This volunteer service is his "cup of cold water." This missionary is now seventy-five years old, but even at that age, he is one of the most vibrant individuals I know. His wife is deceased, so he lives alone. Rather than relax in idleness, or wither away in loneliness, he chooses to help people in crisis. How can you calculate the size of his cup, or the gratitude of those who drink the refreshment he brings with him?

Each Sunday a floral arrangement is placed on the communion table in the church we attend. Left until the next service, the flowers would wilt and die. Letha takes the flowers home and divides them into a number of small vases to be delivered to shut-ins in our town. This is her "cup of cold water," and you can depend on it, a warm light of kindness flows into the room of each one who receives the flowers.

A question: could it be that the multiple reverses we experienced in Cleveland, Tennessee, were tests to determine whether God could trust us to handle a small portion of His wealth, which he wants distributed to some of the world's needy? From our current vantage point, we can look back at those reverses and thank God that even when things were at their worst, quitting was not an option.

Even though we are theoretically retired, we have not quit! I did lay aside my briefcase and now, once again, I have in my hand a canteen of fresh, cool water. To my amazement, no matter how often I give a thirsty soul a drink, the canteen is always full when I need it.

Chapter Thirty-Nine

Giving Is Living

Approximately a year has gone into the preparation of the forty chapters of this biographical report, which basically has been my personal reflection on the events of the past seventy years. Although I strongly resisted writing my own biography, it has become one of the most pleasant things I have ever attempted.

I was able to recapture many events that were positive, and in the process experience again the thrill of personal accomplishments, the achievement of projects, the celebration of commendations, the joy of friendships, etc. When such events were first experienced in real life, some of them were understandably mingled with adversities. However, when those events were recalled by my biased memory, I could relish all of the joy, but re-live none of the pain. Similarly, when dwelling on some of the more severe problems that have been a definite part of my past, I was able to evaluate realistically what I could not comprehend the first time around. In the process of putting it all on display, I have come to understand that nothing is so negative as to be all bad.

The lessons I have learned when confronted with the most severe circumstances have actually served me well in the ultimate forming and testing of my character. Recollection of those times of testing has been of inestimable value to me. By looking over my shoulder, you have had a glimpse into the recesses of my private struggles in past years. I trust this has motivated you to take another glance back through some of your own difficulties and find they contained much good for you. Also, I trust you lived with me the sheer joy of recounting some of the simple but satisfying scenarios of a young boy who grew up in the endemic poverty of the great depression, then emerged from a bashful background to live a most gratifying life.

After having written thirty-eight chapters of background material, now it is time to tell the story many friends have requested. I must inform you about the money we give, and how this giving has impacted our lives. This is something that is ordinarily considered to be private, but in the process of developing a complete biographical work, this somewhat personal information demands also to be included.

As a child I experienced some privation, so I understood the joy of receiving. Conversely, at an early age, I was taught to share regardless of how little I possessed. Later I was to read the words of Jesus recorded in the Bible, "It is more blessed to give than to receive" Acts 20:35. It may be correct to conclude that my background coupled with early instruction has taught me to appreciate both giving and receiving.

Giving is not a "trait" I acquired at some specific point in time. It was a part of the teaching I received when I was quite young and a process that has been cultivated through the years.

I face a certain dilemma as I start to reveal this information. Jesus instructed His followers, "Take care! Don't do your good deeds publicly, to be admired..." Matthew 6:1. Living Bible. On the other hand, if by reading of my experiences, you can be motivated to be more caring and more generous, then a good purpose has been served. Within these parameters, I will proceed.

The most significant giving I have ever done was placing in Pastor Smith's hand a few coins every day when I was a twelve year old boy earning my first income (chapter five). It was significant because it started the development of a pattern. Possibly the giving which I view as among the most important was when my business in Cleveland capsized and almost over-night I plummeted from being financially comfortable to near destitution. During that strenuous period, we continued to give through our church as we did prior to the collapse. It was a difficult decision to keep giving when we were so deeply in debt. We determined to continue giving as we had done, while at the same time reducing the old debts as rapidly as possible.

My personal conviction is that anyone can do more with 90% under God's blessing than he can do with 100%, not having God's blessing. Before I proceed further, allow me to register one more personal belief. Within the framework of the Christian community, much has been said in recent years to emphasize certain advantages available to the giver. Some who lecture frequently on the subject of finance from a Biblical perspective insist that we can have a guaranteed return by giving to Godly causes, thereby making God responsible to return to us what we gave, plus an increase.

I do not challenge the fact that a number of scripture passages deal with God's bountiful blessing on those whose giving is truly altruistic. My contention is that many teachers severely modify one very major precept, thereby invalidating what appears to be a proper logical conclusion.

All of the Bible verses used in support of this system are specific references to "giving." Anything that is given is no longer controlled by the giver. Giving is totally relinquishing one's claim to ownership. The lecturers I often hear by way of radio and television use the word "give," but there is no relinquishment. Instead, the listener is taught that what he gives is the equivalent of planting a seed, and as a consequence, God is responsible to return a harvest of bountiful dimensions.

In this context permit me one additional observation, please. When you plant a seed, the harvest is rightly yours. However, if you give away the seed, you cannot plant it with expectation of harvesting the increase. What you transfer away is either a seed or a gift. If you plant a seed, you retain ownership. A gift is con-

319

veyed to another and you relinquish ownership. You cannot use the same dollar as both a gift and a seed. Planting it with the expectation of reaping a harvest in return obviates the giving.

Planting seed is both good and wise. When you plant seed, it is completely proper to expect you will reap a harvest, which is a multiplication of what you planted. Giving also is good. The giver is gratified and the recipient has a need supplied. A problem develops when a theory is presented to equate planting with giving. They are not the same.

I cannot subscribe to such a flawed theory, nor sanction its promised benefits. This is not giving! It is bartering! My view is that attempting to barter with God with an intent to utilize a spiritual principle as a means to obtain material gain borders on blasphemy. My testimony in this book cannot be linked to that type of materialistic spirituality!

Allow me the liberty of borrowing from Rudyard Kipling a well-known line — and then permit me to substitute two key words. It now reads, "Giving is giving and bartering is bartering and never the twain shall meet."

When we moved to Hawaii, we wanted to locate a church where we could worship and find fellowship with other believers. In the process, we visited a number of churches and then made a decision. The church we decided to attend was smaller than most. We made our decision primarily based on one fact. Having a small membership of lower income people, the church we chose was experiencing serious financial difficulty. We wanted to be of help, so we became members of that church.

In the formative months of our business relocating to Hawaii, income was almost non-existent, so during our first few months there, our limited giving to that church did little to alleviate its financial pressures. As our income increased, we could make a larger contribution. We attended that church for twelve years. In our eleventh year, the pastor showed me the record of the previous year's total income. He pointed out to me that what Letha and I had contributed that year was 50% of the total tithe received from all members. The conclusion generated by that conversation was not that we were the most generous members of the church, or that our generosity had favorably impressed the pastor, or that we rightly deserved special recognition. The real thrill was that God had provided for the need of our church and pastor. We were only incidental to the entire matter.

The building where we worshiped was quite old and in serious need of extensive renovation. Termite infestation was so severe that it was unwise to delay the repairs, but the financial situation of that small church was such that they could not qualify for a loan. It was my happy privilege to guarantee the loan, thus making three year financing possible and the building was renovated. At that time my financial situation had not improved to the point I could make a large gift, but what they needed was not the total amount in cash. My guarantee served to help them secure their loan. To that group of sincere, but needy believers, I was able to offer a "cup of cold water."

Some time later a friend went to the little island of Molokai where he bought an old abandoned church building and started ministering to the community. He agreed to make annual payments toward the purchase. It came to my attention at the end of the third year that he did not have funds to make his payment. Looking into my bank book, I found I had enough to be of assistance. I had other obligations that needed attention, but I saw the pastor facing a difficulty he could not handle. Putting him in my place, I stood in his place and asked myself what I would like that pastor to do for me if we had actually changed roles. Then the decision was easy: I wrote a check for the amount due. He accepted it as a "refreshing cup of cold water."

As our income increased, our ability to give increased proportionately. With our background in missions, we always feel a keen concern for that part of the outreach of the Christian church. As we were made aware of needy missionaries and deserving projects, we accepted a responsibility to become involved with the missionaries in some of those ministries through our giving.

Once we committed a certain amount of money to a deserving cause, we no longer considered that to be our money, so we modified our personal budget to live without it. When that specific need had been totally satisfied, we simply looked for another place to contribute that dedicated money.

As our business grew, increased income followed. With more money coming in, we had some options. The options were:

1. Raise our standard of living to the level of available resources
2. Put the money back for our retirement
3. Invest in eternal values: i.e. give it to needy causes
4. A combination of all of the above

We elected option 4. Admittedly we enjoyed a better standard of living when our income increased. We achieved that better standard not so much by spending more money, but by eliminating all debt and buying only on a cash basis. This allowed us a better lifestyle without retaining personally a part of the money which more appropriately can be utilized to assist with "cups of cold water" for the thirsty who live among us.

During our first decade with A. L. Williams/Primerica Financial Services, I diverted a major part of my income above our living expense to paying off old corporate debts. Consequently we had virtually nothing set aside to supplement my woefully inadequate social security. When we finally began to accumulate a modest nest egg, I was approaching my sixtieth birthday, so prudence demanded that I make provision for retirement without further delay.

In my first months with Primerica Financial Services, I worked very hard to earn enough to exist. After that, I continued to work diligently so I could become free of debt. When I started to enjoy an above-average income, I continued to be a work-a-holic so I could develop a reserve for emergencies and retirement. Even when I was no longer under pressure to provide for these basic essentials, simply because I followed the work ethic I had learned in my youth, I was not inclined to relax. As a result, our income kept growing and we now have more to give.

Ten years ago I noticed a tremor in my right hand and a tendency toward weakness in my right leg. The doctor diagnosed it as Parkinson's Disease. Thankfully, with medication and good professional treatment, it has not become a serious restriction to me. The rigidity that accompanies this malady has made travel uncomfortable, and since travel from Hawaii to any destination is a long airplane ride, I found it advisable a few years ago either to relocate to the U. S. Mainland, which would require less travel, or retire. We chose to move.

When we located in the Mobile, Alabama area in 1992, we were essentially isolated from all of our business operations. Normally, that would suggest a decline in income because we did not have a hands-on relationship with our key leaders. Amazingly, our income remained essentially unchanged.

When we were preparing our records for the accountant to file our income tax returns for 1992, I noticed that our giving for the year had slightly exceeded $50,000. That year our gross income had been $315,000 before operating expenses of approximately $50,000 and taxes of $60,000. I was pleased that we had been able to give $50,000 to various church programs and charities, while also living comfortably and putting back a reasonable sum for retirement. I mentioned to Letha that I would like for us to try to increase our giving to $60,000 the following year. We agreed to make that our goal in 1993.

Anytime a need was presented to us, we considered it on its merits and arrived at a decision as to whether or not to make a contribution. At the end of the year we sent our records to the accountant for tax calculation and were pleasantly surprised to learn our contributions for the year totaled not $60,000, but $72,000. Even more shocking was the fact that our gross income was $410,000. This was an increase of $95,000 gross income over the previous year.

At this point I should reiterate my firm belief that we do not obligate God to give us more by increasing our giving. Nor was I playing that game to try to increase our income. We gave out of concern without consideration of advantage to us. It became our conviction to relinquish the money without stipulations.

Did God return to us a profit on our giving? The undeniable fact is we did have more money. However, our giving must be without conditions. If we give without ulterior motives, God does reward us in His own amazing way. In 1993, we increased our giving by $22,000 but our gross income increased by $95,000. After having given $72,000 in 1993, we were gratified that we had enjoyed the privilege of making life a little better for others through our gifts. We did not make any specific projections at that time to increase in the coming year, but our tax-exempt contributions for 1994 exceeded $84,000. Interestingly, our gross income was near $500,000.

Most of our giving is systematic and we intended in the coming year to continue our support of the projects we had been funding. We did add some others as needs came to our attention. That year, our giving was $103,000. You guessed it: 1995 gross income topped at $510,000.

Our income increased again in 1996 to more than $550,000. From that gross figure, we deducted a healthy amount for business expense and taxes. Then using only about half of the remainder, we lived comfortably besides investing as much as we were allowed into our retirement program. The other 50% we gave where we found needs. Our tax accountant surprised us again early in 1997 with a federal income tax return which reported our tax-deductible giving for 1996 as $172,000.

I am at a total loss to try to explain our success and our above average income, except to repeat we worked diligently, we represented a good company that offered a properly priced, client oriented product, and the good Lord has been gracious to us.

When we sold our business on an installment payment basis, it established a continuing income for years to come. Following the advice of our accountant, we set aside a certain portion of that projected income to be paid directly into a church managed trust account, utilizing an "Irrevocable Assignment." By the use of this instrument, the amount of each monthly installment we are to receive will be reduced so a significant part of our giving is assured for the next twenty years.

This dedicated money does not come to us, but it is being paid directly to the trustee of the fund for distribution. Twenty five percent of the fund is designated to support Gospel missions in Japan from which we were separated a number of years ago. An equal part is creating a scholarship to assist ministerial students in seminary. Twenty-five percent is being sent to retired ministers whose income in retirement is inadequate. The remaining 25% is forwarded by the trustee to our local church to be utilized for special projects not in the regular budget.

The Ultimate Financial Miracle!

By means of this assignment, we are able to channel even more money into the Lord's work after retirement than we have been giving while employed. We retired January 1, 1997, and our income is continuing precisely as predicted. Actually, according to the terms of our installment sale contract, our net income after taxes is expected to remain approximately as it has been in recent years. This is possible, partly because we now have no business-related expense, and partly because we will be taxed at a lower rate now that we are no longer considered to be actively involved in business.

Also of importance to us is the fact that if Letha and I should not live another twenty years, our giving will continue even after our death.

According to responsible professional calculations, the amount assigned to the trust is projected to approximate $40,000 per year for twenty years, making the total gift eight hundred thousand dollars.

As a young person, I learned to set aside my tithe and offerings for the Lord's work first. The amount was usually very small, but I did exactly as I was taught and that was sufficient. When my income increased, the amount I gave increased proportionately. Now, because of the amazing business ownership plan Primerica Financial Services has created, we have an enviable continuing income even in retirement. This allows us to continue giving just as though we had not retired.

When I was first made aware of my moral and spiritual obligation to give a cup of cold water to the thirsty, that was about all

I was capable of giving. I had just a cupful, so I could give only a cupful.

My circumstance has dramatically changed. I now have a reservoir of refreshing water. It is no longer acceptable that I give a cup of cold water. My capability has been expanded, so my responsibility has increased proportionately. Not only has the responsibility increased, the sheer pleasure of involvement in something of intrinsic and eternal value has increased even more. Daily, Letha and I are learning the exciting fact that uninhibited giving generates uncontrollable satisfaction and indescribable joy! Short of eternity, this is life at its best.

Based on the commitments we have already made, plus the money deposited each month into the trust through the absolute assignment agreement, in our retirement, we believe we can give approximately half of our income and we are confident there will be adequate resources to provide for us a comfortable standard of living. What more could anyone desire?

"The only wealth you keep permanently is what you give away." According to that maxim, we are becoming wealthier every year, and enjoying the benefits of this real wealth!

CHAPTER FORTY

A LENGTHENING SHADOW

When a short man casts a long shadow, it suggests that sundown is near.

A person who has had a long life, enriched by numerous friends and blessed by God's grace, can anticipate the sundown pleasantly and without apprehension. Before this book goes to press, both Letha and I will have already celebrated our birthdays for the seventieth time, so we are aware that the shadow is lengthening. That is not to suggest that this chapter will concern itself with withering away and dying. Quite the contrary!

The Bible records in Acts 5:15-16 that many sick were brought to the place where the Apostle Peter was ministering, that at least his shadow might pass over them. Everyone was healed! Read the earlier chapters of Peter's life and it will become painfully apparent that Peter certainly had his Achilles heel. It almost seems that more of his blunders than his successes found their way into Holywrit. Yet, when he was transformed by God's power, his nation's leaders were amazed. It hardly seems that the shadow of Peter on the sidewalk had power to heal the sick. It is significant that those who were touched by his shadow, of necessity were very near him. They were near enough to come under the influence of this dynamic spiritual leader. Similarly, as we approach the sundown, we want our final years to be the most influential for good and for God. We desire to cast our shadow over some who may be benefitted by our association.

Like many others before us, we have a dream. This is not a fantasy for the future: it is a wonderful reality here and now. Frankly, the dream originated with Letha. When our house was nearing completion and she observed how spacious it is and how attractive the environs have become, she immediately wanted to share it with others. We have traveled extensively in ministry all over the nation as well as numerous foreign countries. She realizes firsthand how weary one can get from constant moving and continuously being surrounded by people. On the brighter side, she is aware also of how refreshing it is to have a few days away in a totally relaxed atmosphere.

We have vacationed in some of the world's premier resorts, and have spent many relaxing days in some of the world's finest hotels. For the past seventeen years we have been affiliated with Primerica Financial Services, a terrific company. As the guests of Primerica, we have been accommodated in deluxe hotel rooms and sometimes in luxurious suites. We have eaten gourmet cuisine, cruised on ocean liners and once in the owner's suite of a private yacht. To put it mildly we have been pampered like royalty, and frankly we enjoyed it!

A plan formulated in Letha's mind that would make available to tired ministers some of the good things we have enjoyed. The more she talked about this dream, the more I decided I also would enjoy it. Since our youth, giving has been an important part of our lives. With the fulfillment of this dream, giving can become a more major emphasis for us. If giving in the past has brought such satisfaction, the full implementation of this dream should bring us uninterrupted pleasure.

The transaction to sell our business has been completed and we are now comfortably retired in the quiet little town of Loxley, Alabama. Nearly three years ago we moved into our retirement home. We built this house with the intention that it will be our "last house." Actually, it is our fourth "last house." We built the first "last house" in 1971 in Cleveland, Tennessee. When we moved to Hawaii, we found a fabulous condominium facing the blue Pacific waters, so we bought our second "last house." Twelve years later, we located a very attractive penthouse condominium overlooking Mobile Bay in Daphne, Alabama, which we bought. Living in that penthouse, I was sure we had made our last move, but the penthouse became the third in a series of "last houses." Hopefully, there will not be a fifth.

Living in such a comfortable home helps make our latter years so pleasant. Not only is it both functional and commodious, it is unusually special to us because just a few short years ago, there was a real question as to whether we would have any sort of home after completing our working years. Thanks to the exceptional business opportunity afforded us by Primerica Financial Services, we built our house at a cost of $250,000 and the day we moved in, we owned it and everything in it without a mortgage!

This home is an integral part of our dream. Having enough funds to build it without having to cut corners, we went a little beyond bare necessity. Even though Letha's dream did not have any influence on our planning, there are two spacious rooms ideally suited to a "shadow ministry" for some of God's choice children, who will visit in our home as honored guests. These rooms are quite a distance removed from the space we occupy at the opposite end of the house, so it provides privacy for us and our guests. It is our pleasure to make available a quiet place where overworked ministers can find a few days of respite and relaxation. If in this way we can take the heat off by making available a shadow where their weary spirits and tired bodies can be refreshed and healed, our retirement years can be the most gratifying of our lives.

Having been associated with clergymen for half a century as we have moved throughout the world, we are cognizant of the tensions and stresses under which many of them work. Occasionally, they need to take two or three days away from their responsibilities and relax totally. We feel we have an accommodation suitable for ministers needing to find a hideaway. There are times when pastors experience temporary burnout. It could be they are too close to so many problem situations and need to put a little distance between themselves and their work. It very well may be that a short rest can keep temporary burnout from becoming permanent. Some evangelists travel continuously for many weeks and we want them to find a comfortable room in the Heil Haven where they can relax and be refreshed for four or five days.

The rooms are tastefully decorated and fully furnished with new furniture. In each room is a color television with a video player and an assortment of video tapes of worshipful music and attractive natural scenery. We have no schedule. For early risers, there is a small refrigerator on the sun porch stocked with sodas and fruit drinks. In season, there is usually always a chilled watermelon or other fresh fruit. Guests are welcome to join us for regular meals (at irregular times).

Nothing is scheduled or structured. Everything is conducive to resting and relaxing. In the fenced back yard surrounded by more than one hundred flowering bushes and trees is a large gazebo ideal as a place to eat, rest, meditate, or do nothing at all. Nearby is a shuffle board court and a place to play croquet on a manicured half acre lawn. Our residence is on a loop with very little traffic, so it is ideal for walking or bicycling for carefree relaxation. In an effort to have a room available at any time we may be called, advance reservation is a must. We have set a maximum stay of five days for any guest, but in this limited period of time, we do everything we can to make a short stay at the Heil Haven a complete spiritual, emotional and physical therapy.

With the sale of our business on an installment payment basis, we have enough income to maintain a comfortable life style plus create this atmosphere of comfort for weary travelers. This is not limited to our friends and acquaintances only. Any pastor, evangelist or missionary, properly referred, is welcome into our little country castle. There are no fees or charges for this facility, including meals, if our guests can be satisfied with the simple fare we usually eat.

It is interesting that after our having spent fourteen years in Japan as the first missionaries from our church denomination, when we made these rooms available for this special ministry, within one week after completion, the rooms were occupied by two of our pastors from Tokyo as the first guests.

As long as Letha is in charge, our guests find one final touch that says "welcome" in their room. She loves to grow all sorts of flowers, and especially roses. The last thing before visitors arrive, Letha enjoys placing a beautiful bouquet of fresh cut roses in the room as her personal signature that the room has passed inspection.

When a visiting couple enters the room they will occupy, they may expect to find on the table a bowl of fruit, tea cakes, hot coffee and tea. When none of these man-made refreshments seems to satisfy, it is always our delight to serve them "a cup of cold water."

EPILOGUE

Life has been interesting. As a Bible lecturer, a businessman and a sales executive, I have learned a few things. One of the most important lessons I have learned is that one does not need to know all of the answers.

Now that this acquired knowledge and experience has made me better qualified to compete in the game of life, possibly I could be more productive in any of the various roles I have tried to play — and maybe more successful. On occasions the thought has occured to me that I could possibly even pastor a church now if I had the opportunity afforded me.

Yes, I could do many things — now that I am too old to fit into the scheme of things. So I have learned to be quiet and tolerant while well-meaning younger persons are unknowingly and unintentionally pushing me aside so they can get at their important business at hand.

Thankfully, not many are clamoring to take away my current job. To pass a cup of cold water to a hurting stranger, who may not even say 'thank you' is not a position often sought after. So I will keep my water cup clean and readily available. Just maybe, I will meet a thirsty stranger today to whom I can offer a cup of cold water.